A Thinker's
Damn

A Thinker's Damn

Audie Murphy, Vietnam, and the
Making of The Quiet American

Best, 😊

William Russo

WILLIAM RUSSO

Library of Congress Number:		2001116310
ISBN #:	Hardcover	0-7388-6465-X
	Softcover	0-7388-6466-8

This book was printed in the United States of America.

To order additional copies of this book, contact:
Xlibris Corporation
1-888-7-XLIBRIS
www.Xlibris.com
Orders@Xlibris.com

Contents

For Jan Merlin

1

"MONTY AND LARRY? Together? What a boffo pairing!"

So cried the publicists and shills of Hollywood in 1956. How they wanted a chance to savor this potent combination of Method acting and classic form; of prestige thespian performance and crazed teenage fandom. Montgomery Clift and Laurence Olivier, at their zenith, jointly on screen, were to play protagonists of dissimilar age and rank caught in a story of inter-generation antagonism—fighting over an Asian girl. Clift and Olivier, technical wizards, had elevated acting in the movies to a new sphere. They could frame every moment of a film into an Instant Classic. Such a team offered the possibility of a firestorm for Hollywood hoopla. Their co-starring movie would test the hyperbole of the most outrageous publicity hounds. With his clout as a multiple Academy Award winner and most literate director in Hollywood in 1956, Joseph L. Mankiewicz effortlessly assembled the best cast for his pictures. Actors and movie stars jumped at the chance to work with him. Two of the most celebrated and famous stars, critically acclaimed, with enormous box office appeal and industry respect, were Olivier and Clift. The idea to co-feature them excited producers, critics, and fans. No one in Hollywood contemplated a better duo for making a blockbuster movie.

When the casting of *The Quiet American* reached the stage of offering scripts from Figaro, Incorporated, the two film stars had seven Academy Award nominations and one Oscar between them. Clift had been nominated for The Search, his first picture; for *A Place in the Sun,* and for *From Here to Eternity*. Olivier had garnered nominations for

Wuthering Heights, Rebecca, Hamlet (his Oscar winner), that year for *Richard III.*

Joe Mankiewicz could easily match his actors, respect for respect: his own winners and nominees for the Academy Award included *A Letter for Three Wives*, two Oscars for writing and directing, *No Way Out*, a nomination for directing, and *Five Fingers* (nomination, directing), and *The Barefoot Contessa* (Oscar for writing). Seldom had such immense talent come together at the zenith of their careers when their vigor and power could overwhelm an audience. If Joe Mankiewicz sent a script to an actor, it received the closest of attention; some might accept a role in the picture without even reading the screen treatment or scenario. Joe Mankiewicz, and no one else, found the initial inspiration to team Laurence Olivier and Montgomery Clift for his movie version of the Graham Greene novel, *The Quiet American.*

Doubtless, too, he'd be able to persuade them to travel to the ends of the earth for an assignment with him. He proposed such a movie–to be filmed on the actual locations in Vietnam. These two stars, at the top of their game in reputation and talent, consistently ignited the screen with their separate presence; together, they ensured a sure-fire box-office bonanza.

Whatever such a film's critical judgment or reaction, a movie with Olivier and Clift would be destined for greatness and regular exhibition on the classic movie circuit and, later, on television movie networks. With impressive casting, devoutly wished and ready for assembly, this production had the potential to quicken the pulse of movie-goers, then and now.

The dream became a nightmare as Mankiewicz negotiated for the rights to the novel, *The Quiet American*. He had given over the duties of lining up the cast to Michele Waszynski, a producer with the usual implied heritage as Polish royalty and whose persuasive talents were legendary. His first task, to sign Clift, hit a wall with the impact of a speeding car. To Misha's dismay, the troubled star didn't often behave with the wisest of judgment in his personal life. Many industry people feared that Monty would come to sure self-destruction, as did his adoring clone, James Dean.

The prediction fell shy of realization, but just barely. While in the middle of the production of *Raintree County,* Montgomery Clift suffered severe injuries in a car crash in May of 1956, after attending a party one late night. Requiring extensive surgery which included having his jaw wired and being fitted with false teeth, he was barely able to recover enough to finish the production six months later.

Monty's problems on the set related to his use of pain-killers and alcohol to numb himself from the accident's discomforting and lingering effects. So exhausted and depressed was he over the accident and what it had done to his looks, he informed his agents, MCA, not to send him any scripts for the remainder of the year. Misha needed to break through this order and convince Clift that the best tonic for him was a trip to Vietnam with Joe Mankiewicz.

Because Monty declined to look at new film offerings, some biographers had doubted that he ever saw *The Quiet American* script from Mankiewicz. Waszynski could not be easily derailed from this keystone of the casting, especially with pressure mounting from the director. Misha used his regal tenacity to insure the script reached its target. Whatever the after-effects of the accident, the injuries never dissuaded Mankiewicz from pursuit of Clift. Even a battered and bruised Monty would be preferable in the role of *The Quiet American.* The public craved to see him, morbidly intrigued by the idea to gaze upon a once-beautiful man who had been disfigured by fate.

Mankiewicz ally and executive Robert Lantz served as Clift's agent in subsequent years, after the movie producer part of his career ended. He unequivocally stated he saw to it that Clift received one of the early drafts of the screenplay. As Monty himself complained in a television interview given in 1962, "It's one thing to get a good contract. It's another to get a good picture." Waszynski could put the script in Monty's hands, but after that he was at the mercy of Clift's zeal for working with Mankiewicz and his ability to see the script gave only a vague hint of how he could dominate a film.

Joe Mankiewicz was a glib writer who could dash off quality scripts in a few days; he could also create shoddy work with just as much of this casual attitude. With the help of Elaine Schreyeck, his customary

II

assistant in the creative process, who transcribed his words in short-hand, he penned a highly complex version of *The Quiet American*. According to Schreyeck, the director was a man who "always liked to be well-prepared." He had to work fast in order to be ready to go to Vietnam for Tet, the Chinese New Year in late January, which served as a pivotal backdrop to the story. In his haste adapting the novel, the script reached convoluted heights and depths.

It may well have been David Lean, director of *Bridge over the River Kwai* and *Lawrence of Arabia*, told a film executive who toiled on *The Quiet American* that a good director must keep his concept in mind at all times, despite the daily complexity and diversions. Layer after layer, whether it interfered or enhanced the story, required the director's sense of purpose. When a good director maintained his equilibrium through the daily hazards of production, the film could still go askew if the concept itself was flawed.

The process of film-making, explained former Figaro Vice President Mike Mindlin who worked with all the great directors of the 1950s, encouraged complete trust in the director throughout the production; only when the finished product was screened could the participants know whether it offered them a chance to celebrate—or to cry out in horror.

To be in Saigon when Mankiewicz needed him, Clift must begin inoculations by late November to allow for any delay caused by sundry distresses associated with inoculations for travel. As Mankiewicz's right hand man, Robby Lantz, clearly recalled Clift expressed great unhappiness with the script he saw. It was well-known that Clift never accepted a script in which he didn't believe. His New York apartment was filled with scripts, which languished often unread and unacceptable to him. The obverse of the coin: Mankiewicz never changed a script to justify hiring an actor. Their cross-purposes, together with Clift's dubious health, contributed to a stalemate over a redacted storyline.

For Bill Hornbeck, one of the finest film editors in the business, Clift was an ideal choice for the picture; after all, they were friends. Hornbeck's Oscar was for his work on the masterpiece called *A Place in the Sun*, which starred Clift with his lifelong confidante and foremost co-star Elizabeth Taylor. Hornbeck's name surely could inveigle Clift to consider the role, or so thought Joe Mankiewicz and his casting director. It was the first chess move in the casting stratagem to capture a star.

Still in pursuit of the script's title actor, Waszynski believed in his winning trumps to play: He assured Clift he'd be surrounded by his favored professional associates if he agreed to *The Quiet American*. Yet, even the award-winning respectability of Bill Hornbeck and the association with Robby Lantz, old friends of Clift, didn't entice Monty to appear in what looked like a bad role on paper. The word broke through the barriers Clift had set up; he would consider the Mankiewicz film if the script were re-written.

One may well ask why Joe Mankiewicz wanted Montgomery Clift to play the lead role–after all, Clift had deep personal problems and a history of drinking and drug abuse. Though this was not known to the public, Clift hardly represented traditional American family values. The character in the book was a conservative symbol. Monty's promiscuous homosexual lifestyle, never hidden by the Method actor, and vehemently concealed by the industry's nervous public relations machine of 1956, had not yet reached widespread audiences.

Hornbeck himself probably felt some disappointment Monty balked at doing the film, but professional that he was, Hornbeck expressed willingness to accept any other choice made by Mankiewicz. Lantz too wished Mankiewicz would simply revise the adaptation he had dashed off so precipitously, though his loyalty to Joe transcended the issue.

Having a vision, Joe charged ahead. The scripts may have gone out prematurely to the major stars. As good as Joe was, Monty Clift wavered. If the script could be refined, his attitude might change. For the first time in his career, Mankiewicz was thunderstruck. Never before had the Oscar winning *auteur* been prepared to eat crow–or worse, rewrite his dramatic adaptation. Yet, now the idea of signing Clift caused him, at least, to think about it.

What didn't occur to him was the presence of a formidable rival. Clift had a lifelong dream of making a movie with Marlon Brando, and it was about to reach fruition. A long-standing hope on both their sides, having been acquainted for many years, they were eager and ready to act together in a movie. When it came between Brando and a doubtful script, Clift had a cleareye. He sat home and gathered his strength for a different prospect. When filming of *The Quiet American* began in late January of 1957, Clift was home in New York, studying the recently scripted version of Irwin Shaw's *The Young Lions*, for Edward Dmytryk. He'd wait a year for another script from Joe Mankiewicz if that was necessary.

The recuperating actor didn't begin principal photography for the World War II film with Brando until mid-May when *The Quiet American* finished up in Rome. Between his heavy drinking of alcohol and fragile health, it was unlikely Clift could have done three pictures in a row without rest, or hospitalization, even though Monty always claimed the damage to his face was all below the surface. His jaw, his gums, his teeth, and nerves in his face, suffered the damage and caused his face to age prematurely. And, his nose had to be set after the accident.

What Monty wanted, above the prestige of a Mankiewicz film, was to go head-to-head against Marlon Brando on screen. *The Young Lions* offered him that chance, at long last. He would be able to establish himself as the premiere young actor in movies. He was amazed Brando had accepted so many roles Clift rejected, and still won critical praise for them, be it Desiree or *On the Waterfront.* No matter the films he chose instead, Monty still felt he came off second-best. Rejection of the Mankiewicz project had to do with the strange competition between Brando and Clift more than any other factor. "We're both originals," he often stated, but he was "touchy" about comparisons. Clift finally turned down *The Quiet American* with a curt, "No." Asked to take a medical risk for a picture he could not fully believe in, for a script for which he had little enthusiasm, Monty summarily rejected Joe's offer.

Clift's precarious health would have made his trip to Saigon unworkable. Despite the downplaying of his ills (disinformation designed to counter not being insured for pictures), the likelihood he could have done the Mankiewicz film, even if he wanted, was slight. Whatever shock this rebuff caused, the great director rose above it. Sam Spiegel, a producer on another picture with Joe, said: "Mankiewicz is an excellent director but devoid of a great many human considerations when it comes to weaker beings than himself." Joe lost no sleep over Clift. He moved on to the next target.

In essence, the inability or reluctance of Monty Clift to accept the role of *The Quiet American* became the first crack in the foundation of the project the director envisioned. Like Samson, Clift pulled the picture down around Mankiewicz by not being able or willing to aspire to the project. The less kind have hinted Clift was like Delilah, clipping the locks of the director and sapping the production of its strength. As a result, Clift was the first domino to fall, thus preventing the "dream" casting by Mankiewicz.

Art be damned, casting director Waszynski went to the next level of box-office power. The name of the year, the political symbol of a generation, now toiled in B-pictures as a cowboy star. He had played himself figuratively in every picture; in his greatest success, he literally played himself in *To Hell and Back*. Misha tendered the Mankiewicz script to the Universal-International contract star's agent, Paul Kohner.

One of the old-time agents, Kohner had a de rigeur accent right out of central casting as a lovable, old, show-business type. Genial and personal, he maintained his small Los Angeles office for nearly half a century, with a list of impressive clients including William Wyler. Misha Waszynski sent the script, neither unchanged, nor revised, to his second choice for the title role. After all, Audie Murphy didn't have a reputation for discriminating taste in scripts, nor a well-developed sense of literary properties.

As a cowboy star who had done second-string efforts, Audie Murphy didn't usually concern himself with scripts. With a few friends whose education and insight he respected, Audie simply farmed out scripts to trusted aides who then advised him. These were, first, David McClure, an alcoholic intellectual who had worked as Hedda Hopper's leg-man for many years, and Willard Willingham, a stunt-double stand-in who had an erudite air and literary knowledge.

As separate entities, rarely acknowledging the other, these two men assumed for themselves the role of care-takers for a national mythic figure. Each served Audie Murphy, first, as acolyte, and later as high priest. If Audie gave either a script to doctor, they might alter dialogue to suit the star's ability and style. They made him comfortable and earned his trust. Associates having formal education he lacked, they believed Audie relied on their grasp of literature and ideas and that he put his movie fate in their hands.

In 1948 Audie had begun the process of educating himself. During that time he read voraciously, or so the press releases stated. He told one interviewer his favorite novel was *Look Homeward, Angel*, the epic story by Thomas Wolfe of a rural boy making his way in the world, but it sounded like David McClure's favorite novel, rather than Audie's. His other new friend, Willard Willingham, had ties to the Great Books Movement and its founder, Mortimer Adler, who had caused upheaval in American education's philosophical circles in 1950. As a result, Audie's new-found advisors' opinions held sway with the heroic Texan. Despite Audie's docile acceptance of whatever Universal-International tossed his way, Murphy occasionally exhibited a streak of stubbornness when his advisors chose to rattle his cage.

Willard Willingham, in his first statements for the public, nearly fifty years after meeting Audie, reported he served as "a mentor" when it came to the reading of screenplays. Audie never personally checked over the script, unless absolutely essential. "He would not make a picture until we had discussed it." Willingham said Audie's agent, Paul Kohner, recognized the importance of a Mankiewicz film treatment and sent it over to Audie who, in turn, gave it to Willingham who knew the novel by Graham Greene and its prestigious reputation. Willingham also realized the impact a picture produced and directed by Joseph L. Mankiewicz could have on Audie's career, but doubted Audie even recognized the name of the Oscar-winning director. "He wasn't much concerned with that sort of thing," he shrugged.

Upon receipt of the script, Willingham read it immediately–and gave it to his wife, Mary, who held a Master's degree from UCLA and had training in the classics, to study. Neither liked the script and couldn't understand the convolutions and philosophizing which Mankiewicz interjected, especially at the climax when a quick denouement provided the audience with its expected catharsis. It was Willard's contention that, usually, Audie would make a picture only if he and Mary "would be able to re-write it." Willard felt that the great Mankiewicz, like the Great Wizard of Oz, the little man behind the curtain, had tried to pass off a weak screenplay with an illusion of quality.

At this point Audie Murphy, the essence of a quiet, heroic, Western film cowboy, started to feel his oats at Universal-International. Approached by the Figaro company, he was tempted to tackle an unpopular and uncharacteristic role, a literate British political drama. Having faced death squarely in war, he was never rattled by the silliness of movie-making. Besides, Murphy had been hoping for something to expand his range. He had been unfavorably compared to John Wayne. Now, he might overcome that with a script likely to enhance his reputation and take him out of the Western genre.

Informed of the plot, its convolutions appealed to him, yet he was apprehensive. The more complex and adult, the more it stretched away from his usual film product. If his erudite alter ego, David McClure, known as Spec, said to do the picture, Audie would do it. He was under the spell of a high-brow Ivy Leaguer, the man who had ghost-written his successful biography *To Hell and Back*. When McClure realized how much Mankiewicz wanted the war hero for the role, Spec knew what to advise Audie. McClure responded by telling Murphy to do the role.

The Universal-International Studio westerns bored Murphy, and he yearned to leap up a notch into a big picture, far from the ranch. Foremost in his reasoning, he had tired of co-starring with horses. In 1956 Audie Murphy was the hottest property around and exerted appeal and power. When McClure encouraged him to stretch, Audie conferred with Willard. Willingham, reluctant about the property, also told Audie to accept the script, but "only after he had met with Joe Mankiewicz and discussed making a few changes."

At the end of November in 1956, Audie finished another big budget picture, yet again a western, this time with James Stewart called *Night Passage*. He played the Utica Kid. On location in the Rocky Mountains, the film completed its principal photography after Thanksgiving Day, 1956. To accept an offer from Mankiewicz meant he would leave home after the holidays for extended location work; some predicted they would be in Vietnam for three months. Short notice for any film project was never an impediment to Audie Murphy, yet he balked at doing it.

Also on the western movie in a minor part was Willard, who played a dozen roles in Audie's life and, this time, had been cast as a supporting actor, thanks to Murphy's recommendation. Willingham frequently worked at his friend's pleasure. During the making of the James Stewart picture, Willard—who always enjoyed location shoots—observed it might be interesting to visit Vietnam, but Audie still expressed reservations about the project.

Willard belonged to the star's eclectic coterie, a bizarre and wide-ranging group of associates Audie assembled after his arrival in Hollywood. Murphy agreed with the idea he'd feel somewhat inclined to do the script if Willard joined him on the grueling trip. They were hunting buddies and shared other diversions, like gambling, a pastime at which Audie was inept and often failed to follow any advice from Willard regarding it. The nature of trust between the two weighted the scales in favor of signing onto *The Quiet American.*

Under the guise of Audie's "script doctor," Willard served as Audie's consultant on the quality of any screenplay, was his faithful companion on the set, and performed as his teacher and acting coach off the screen. For him, a Mankiewicz script on a Graham Greene work could boost anyone's film career, and he told Audie this. Then, he pointedly announced he was willing to provide companionship to Audie if the star wanted to travel 14,000 miles to the political hot-spot of Vietnam.

At his two advisors' encouragement, Audie decided to make an appointment with Mankiewicz. Willard maintained Audie "didn't know Mankiewicz at all." It fell to Willingham to convince Audie about the merits of the project while giving him a quick synopsis on the career of Mankiewicz. "What an opportunity!" Willard assured the star repeatedly. "My goading probably made him accept the script. You know, he had no real interest in it. He was not at all anxious to make this picture."

Audie shared the concerns of nearly each person who saw the early draft: Willingham and Audie conferred several times, in preparation, before the visit to Mankiewicz. "The script had a great, great deal of talk. Far too much of it. We could see all the problems of making it into a film."

Through agent Paul Kohner, Audie set up a meeting with Joe Mankiewicz whose time constraints demanded he set the cast; deadlines pressed him from all sides. A few members of his Figaro production crew had already gone to Vietnam to prepare the way for the filming, and he needed a big star on the scene for the Tet celebration which served as the pivotal opening sequence of the picture.

Audie went to the meeting, having been briefed by Willingham as to what revisions were needed. During his negotiations with Mankiewicz, Audie expressed his basic reluctance to do a picture so far afield from his unsophisticated oaters. Long, complicated dialogue scenes were not his forte, and though flattered to be a replacement for Clift, he was uneasy about his own competence. More determined than ever to sign him, Mankiewicz had to promise whatever it took to cause Audie to join the film troupe.

Whether the director thought Audie's coyness was genuine or not, Joe countered, assuring the star, begging for trust: "The script's just a rough draft. I expect it will be completely rewritten by the time we reach Vietnam." Indeed, according to Audie, Mankiewicz made a verbal pledge "that he'd change the script." Willingham had no reason to doubt it. "I thought Joe Mankiewicz, if anybody, could turn the script into something really good. It was worth taking a chance."

The timing of the Chinese New Year and the shooting schedule arranged by Mankiewicz gave Audie his window of opportunity to make *The Quiet American*. A workaholic thriving on being busy, Audie didn't need lengthy vacation periods between films; neither his acting style, nor the simplicity of his roles, ever wore him down. His availability, his box-office appeal, and his political correctness were the sum of assets he'd bring to the role. Mankiewicz likely dangled the name of Olivier: shared billing with the foremost actor of the time, certain it would snare him at once.

Whatever motives gripped Joe Mankiewicz and his Figaro company's obsession with this movie, most leading men in pictures would respond with a knee-jerk to two compelling reasons for taking such a role: Laurence Olivier and Graham Greene, two Britons with towering intellectual reputations. In an industry overwhelmed by Anglophilia and pretense, Olivier and Greene symbolized all that Hollywood considered respectable artistic status. Nearly every actor wanted the respectability of a top-drawer project, but Willard Willingham thought Audie neither knew, nor cared, that Laurence Olivier was a potential cast mate. "I never heard his name associated with the project," Willard said flatly.

Though critics argued Audie was not right or trained for an important role like this, he prepared to accept the hard work. Willingham indicated that Audie never shirked from any challenge. When he put his mind to it, Audie tended to overachieve. In this way Audie believed himself to be a consummate professional. He answered carpers by observing, "I couldn't act worth a zinc cent when I got into this work. I'm not much better now." Audie stated he didn't read his reviews, but said in 1957 how much he resented those in the industry who "relegated me to the role of a specialist in westerns."

Robby Lantz had to marvel at the contrast between Clift and Murphy, and Mankiewicz's idea that either could play *The Quiet American* character. As actors and as men, there were no two in Hollywood's pantheon who stood quite so opposite and juxtaposed, personally and professionally. In the view of many industry insiders, the selection of Murphy to replace Clift was calculated and insensitive, not so much offering Murphy a chance to grow as an actor, as to throw an untrained box-office draw into the breach.

That he was even under consideration for the title role in *The Quiet American* surprised many fans of Audie—and all the fans of Graham Greene. The part of Fowler, *The Quiet American's* foil, was an acting role of great challenge—and translated into a formidable task for co-stars. The original script by Mankiewicz provided a character with complex facets for the likes of Laurence Olivier, the purported greatest actor of stage and screen. If Audie were to match himself against Olivier, the consensus in Hollywood held that the general public would go into shock, mortifying Audie, at the quality of his inadequate performance. Speculators proffered the theory that his casting in such a role was a publicity stunt, illogical and mad.

The simple fact was that Murphy's autobiographic war picture, *To Hell and Back*, made him "a star of the first magnitude. His fan mail jumped to the top ranks," noted Spec McClure. "Producers who previously could not see him for sour apples" sent him dozens of scripts, including *The Quiet American*. Some literary periodicals and critical circles spoke of typical commercial cynicism and Murphy's desperate and calculated bid for credibility. Audie confounded them all by saying in one press release: "It is my belief it has always been the American way for one to try and better oneself. This is exactly what I am trying to do."

What Audie Murphy didn't know was that he was in the hands of a director who frequently stared at artistic failure in the face. Proud and difficult, Mankiewicz believed his films deserved their artistic reputation, as did he. He pampered his films from script to premiere. A man always ready for adversity and opposition, he clearly remained resolute in his roguish Figaro troupe. He was prepared "to do a little bit of everything" in order to make the films he wanted.

First choice among the Figaro executives for the central role of the British reporter continued to be Laurence Olivier. The idea of Audie Murphy and Laurence Olivier on screen together was nearly as intriguing as the happenstance of Olivier and Marilyn Monroe performing together. Throughout 1956, Sir Laurence Olivier had buried himself in a film project marred by a miasma of trouble. Larry's Waterloo was titled *The Prince and The Showgirl,* which developed into a nightmare. Olivier's directorial disaster evinced itself in a piece of fluff, a version of a child's fairy tale for adults. He cast himself as a generic Slavic prince and Marilyn Monroe as her traditionally stereotyped blonde showgirl—and Olivier expected them to lampoon their own film personalities.

The lightweight confection, a movie change-of-pace for Larry Olivier, turned into an epical struggle and a masochistic exercise. Olivier could hardly afford any delays resulting from inoculations for a long trip to the Far East. The over-extended shooting schedule with Marilyn brought him to the brink of exhaustion and depression. For a definitive exploration of the movie set problems at Pinewood, the book by film assistant Colin Clarke described the daily crises. Though Olivier's *The Prince and the Showgirl,* with Marilyn Monroe was a disappointment in many ways, and though the film developed into a box-office failure, the picture exploited a fascinating meeting of legendary performers. Unfortunately, audiences shunned it.

The shooting at Pinewood Studios in England ran weeks over schedule for Olivier, much longer than expected. Marilyn Monroe's notorious delays, insecurities, and emotional detachments, all grated on Olivier's nerves. He became irascible and short-tempered. The cast had begun work before summer and finished near the end of November, 1956. Olivier still faced the task of overseeing the movie's editing. It appeared likely Olivier had his fill of working with American "movie stars" who had no formal acting training or discipline when Misha Wasynski reached him with the ponderous Mankiewicz script, richly layered in convoluted philosophizing.

Olivier admitted to friends he had reached a defining moment in his life. "I was getting profoundly sick–not just tired–sick . . . The rhythm of my work had become a bit deadly: a classical or semi-classical film, a play or two at Stratford, or a nine-month run at the West End . . . I was going mad, desperately searching for something suddenly fresh and thrillingly exciting. What I felt to be my image was boring me to death." As a result of this crisis in his professional life, Olivier probably judged *The Quiet American* to be another "classical" film, though a trip to Vietnam surely would have given him the thrill and excitement he wanted. The script did not impress him, but he left the door open for a revised version. If Mankiewicz capitulated, Olivier would consent.

The official story about Olivier's state of mind claimed scripts hadn't been forthcoming in a timely fashion from Mankiewicz. For that reason, the British star was unable to judge the validity of the project, hence choosing to do other work on the London stage, rather than take a chance with an unknown quantity, even if it came from a highly respected director. Some film insiders speculated Olivier wanted to work with Montgomery Clift–and no one else.

Mankiewicz played a sleight of hand through Waszynski: hinting to Olivier that Clift might do it, and the same to Clift about Olivier. Others confided that, upon learning whom Mankiewicz finally lined up for the role, Olivier hesitated. Audie Murphy's personality and demeanor dismayed Olivier. Colin Clarke reported in his memoir Olivier was much disappointed with Monroe because he thought "all the top stars should be able to act anything."

Learning otherwise became an unpleasant lesson. In addition, Graham Greene's complaints about the proposed movie had reached Olivier, who had worked on another Greene project some years earlier. He expected to feel the writer's tart criticisms if he made a film version of a script of which Greene publicly disapproved.

The Mankiewicz film required Olivier be ready by the first of the year to go to Vietnam. The idea of traveling half-way around the world to work with another "American movie star" (Audie) might just put him off. Another key Figaro executive with ties to Olivier, Robert Lantz remained convinced Larry wanted to work with the celebrated American film-maker, but simply didn't want to make the dangerous and uncomfortable trip to the dangerous Far East.

Assuming that Olivier–acting with supreme ego–imperiously made Audie Murphy's dismissal *sine qua non* of his participation in the role, a dream match of these two actors from entirely different spheres could never have been remotely possible. As an intimate of the great British actor, Robert Lantz simply dismissed the idea that Olivier based his decision on the personality of his co-star.

"Larry Olivier was so talented, such an amazing man. If he put his mind to it, he would even be a better shot than Audie." To Lantz's way of thinking, Audie's participation in the film had no bearing on Larry's rejection of the role. Olivier simply had another commitment. Nearly fifteen years later, Mankiewicz and Olivier did team up for a picture called *Sleuth*.

In order to be ready for the trip to Vietnam, Audie Murphy had to ink his contract no later than early November. His signing became public knowledge immediately. Once Audie was definitely in the cast, Olivier definitely was not. Laurence Olivier knew of Audie from film gossip of his on-set practical jokes, his gun-carrying ways, and other anecdotes, which may have made his decision easier. It may be too that Olivier was professionally uneasy about those who could upstage him; there would be nothing more embarrassing the world's greatest actor than to be matched, and perhaps, outmatched, by the likes of Audie Murphy. "Not Olivier!" rebutted one waggish veteran actor. "It was more likely that he was not attracted enough to Murphy to be inclined to give him a leg up, so to speak."

In London, Laurence Olivier committed himself to the interests of a new play, written by one of the new generation of realists who presented English working-class life in all its pathos. He preferred a John Osborne script called *The Entertainer*. In it Olivier sang and danced as a second-rate vaudeville star. This was also the occasion during which he met his future wife, Joan Plowright who had a co-starring role. With Clift's inclusion in the proposed film cast utterly impossible, and with Audie's casting prominent in the trade papers, Olivier's interest dissolved entirely. He would not suffer any ordeal which necessitated his going to Vietnam. So, the titan of all actors embarked upon his graceful pirouette out of *The Quiet American*, and he never looked back.

Not quite an epical struggle brought *The Quiet American* to the end of its pre-production phase of casting the major roles. In its initial stages, casting might be a problem in light of Greene's public reactions to an American production. The author issued torrents of disapproval. He preferred his works to maintain their British character and personality, never truly approving of an American production of any of his stories. So, it is with dismay that film historians read about the British star's departure from the production.

To appear in a Joe Mankiewicz movie signified, in a nutshell, prestige for an ordinary actor. For Audie this kind of film role was to be an earnest attempt at serious art, putting his acting peers on notice that he joined their ranks. Of course, the Hollywood establishment and the media never accepted him as anything other than an amateur actor doing B-level westerns. Noted film producer and, in 1956, United Artists executive, Eric Pleskow dismissed Audie's casting as having two mercenary motives: "First, he was probably the only person available. Second, he was a war hero who brought something to the topic of the picture."

Many disparaging comments emanated, of course, from those who had never seen an Audie Murphy movie, nor planned to ever do so. Most of those who disparaged Audie offered mean-spirited commentaries. Among Audie's supporters, the role was dubious, representing the worst of America in an obviously anti-American novel, to be filmed in Vietnam in the midst of Communist revolt. In today's argot Audie was portraying a patriot and a Cold Warrior, and now had fallen prey to be a Communist dupe.

From all sides, the selection of Audie caused puzzlement. Greene certainly believed that with a British director and a script by an Anglophile could circumvent all this controversy: but Mankiewicz–like Audie– was a true democrat of his nation and a self-made man with a sense of pride in his American heritage. Neither man wanted to act as another fool in the Greene landscape.

Nonetheless, to studio people at Universal, Audie's newfound fervor to do *The Quiet American*, a talky Mankiewicz picture, seemed to be a joke, a scheme for achieving respectable failure. If Audie made fools of his following, and a fool of the director, he might end up a bigger fool himself. Of course, during his preparatory year before entering movies, he had shed much of his Texas drawl and learned to speak a middle American English. He had the will to recreate himself. Seduced by what he might gain by doing a Mankiewicz film, Audie believed the promise the script made. This movie would be bigger and better able to express an intelligent statement than any film he had previously done.

According to industry sages, Laurence Olivier would have blown him off the screen. That didn't matter. All of Hollywood appeared a grandiose sham to Audie, and he shunned it. "He was protective of himself. As an actor, he could not open the gates. As a result, he never achieved what he wanted," commented one fellow movie actor. "I'm not an actor," Audie told television fans later in another interview. "I

25

have nothing in common with them. They're dedicated souls with just one driving goal in life, and I'm not. I don't malign them. I just don't spend any time with them."

Mankiewicz informed Audie that, with Olivier out, Michael Redgrave expressed interest in the part of the cynical British journalist called Fowler. Redgrave's name was one from a list of great British film actors–like Alec Guiness, Jack Hawkins, Leo Genn, Ralph Richardson, or Peter Cushing. Misha Waszynski had proposed for the foil role opposite the character of *The Quiet American* after Olivier bailed out.

Michael Redgrave joined the cast as a replacement for Laurence Olivier when the latter refused to work with Audie Murphy. Seen here on his fiftieth birthday, on the set of The Quiet American, Redgrave was suffering from the early effects of Altzheimer's Disease during the filming.. Photo courtesy of Vinh Noan.

Indeed, the constant refrain of mature British stars dominated every publicity campaign coming from Figaro. It seemed the company believed that for American audiences, British status rendered each actor just as capable as another of their rank, constantly referring to Redgrave's selection from a group of British "prestige'" actors.

Audie never gave an opinion about Redgrave's entry into the picture. At least one friend of Audie believed his knowledge of the theatrical world was so slight he probably had no idea who Olivier's replacement was. In fact, Murphy's rare non-reference to Olivier arose slyly on a panel show in the late 1950s. The evening's celebrities named their ideals in the acting profession. When several stars mentioned Olivier, Audie followed quickly by naming his role models: "Gene Autry and Harpo Marx."

Sir Laurence Olivier's putative nemesis appeared to be his possible replacement. Olivier sensed a so-called "friendly" rivalry from Michael Redgrave (e.g., both ended up knighted). Many years earlier they had appeared on stage in *Hamlet*; Olivier in the lead, and Redgrave as Laertes. During the fencing scenes, night after night, the vehemence of the dueling resulted in a need for cotton swabs and antiseptic after each performance.

The two great British actors were actually at crossed swords for the rest of their careers. Over many years, Redgrave consistently performed the roles Olivier dismissed; this may have been one part smugly turned over to Michael. Daughter Lynn Redgrave related in a *Genre* magazine interview a saying that her father often told her: "An actor makes his own luck," which tended to offer evidence that the elder Redgrave deliberately and actively courted the roles Olivier refused. As to Michael Redgrave's opinion of Olivier's acting, he stated in 1958: " . . . Olivier, though frequently physically unrecognisable for several minutes, remains Olivier."

Corin Redgrave, son of Michael, admitted he hated Olivier for many years, that he reacted to rumors he heard about Olivier's cruelty to other actors who threatened his pre-eminent role in any production. Corin, also an actor, held some other simmering resentments for the great Olivier, having concluded his father envied Olivier's "showmanship" and gladly took those parts the most famous British actor tossed aside, like crumbs off his dinner table.

In one infamous incident, Olivier cruelly dismissed Redgrave from the British National Theater for not being up to par to handle key roles in a play. Olivier then played the characterizations himself, to glowing reviews. Olivier's action was the *coup d'grace* to Redgrave's psyche. It was not a conduct of compassion toward Sir Michael who had been ill with Parkinson's Disease, though most contemporary observers believed the worst rumors about Redgrave's behavior.

As a human being with goodwill, Olivier left much in his personal life to be reserved strictly for the stage. "Acting's a beastly profession," Olivier later said. "I don't mean the competitiveness, the out-of-work risks, the cruel bad luck and the intoxicating good luck (which is worse), the jealousies, the tensions, the wear and tear–not that. All that's an occupational hazard in many other walks of life. But in theatre, it is exceptionally hard to keep friendships."

In New York City, Sir Michael Redgrave's agent informed him *The Quiet American* featured "just about the best part this year–" and the stage star eagerly snapped it up. He was aware Olivier was first choice and had declined the role at the last minute. This compelled director Mankiewicz to put full energy and warmth into wooing Redgrave, stroking his ego and smothering him with compliments. Since the thespian had a television commitment, Mankiewicz graciously agreed Redgrave could arrive later than the other members of the cast and film crew. The British stage and screen star would not embark for the Orient until the beginning of February.

So, with permission to join the crew much later than the rest of the production company, Redgrave basked in Mankiewicz's attentive courtship. Cables were sent to New York where the actor did a TV show, addressed "Dearest Michael–" and citing humorous clichés, like "chin up," *etc.* Mankiewicz signed one telegram: "The Quiet and the Disquieted." Unlike others in the crew, he didn't realize Mankiewicz's purpose was to allay fears about filming in a dangerous and unstable country.

The eminent Mr. Redgrave, a tall and imperious man, enunciated slowly, was extremely deliberate in his diction, and did not speak out so much as suck in his words. A stage performer, discovered and promoted by John Gielgud years earlier, he believed acting was a great art acquired only through the achievement of portraying all the great Shakespearean roles on stage. George Cukor once gave Redgrave the advice: "Don't go into films, kid, until they go on their knees to you." In fact, Redgrave reported firmly that he "refused film tests–which only intrigued the producers more and caused my agent some embarrassment."

Though some trained actors didn't hold such extreme beliefs, most career-minded and experienced performers resented the intrusion into their profession of pop singers, athletes, and other celebrities, whose lack of formal training made them problematic cast members. This was not the case with Redgrave. He welcomed newcomers to the theatrical whirl with open arms, requiring only that they be suitably youthful, attractive, and accommodating.

Contingent upon Mankiewicz's hiring of Michael Redgrave for *The Quiet American* was the inclusion of Fred Sadoff in the cast. Misha Waszynski knew a happy cast meant fewer headaches on the set; if Redgrave wished to play paladin for a younger actor, then the casting request would be granted. With an apparent willingness to mix business and pleasure, Freddie Sadoff quickly found himself the recipient of plum roles.

Sadoff, a swarthy and attractive young man, had launched his acting career at the famous Neighborhood Playhouse in New York, studying under Sanford Meisner. As a student, in the spring of 1947, Fred was cast as Orestes in a production of *The Eumenides.* The redoubtable Martha Graham was called in to create the costumes for the play. She made her usual exotic and revealing dramatic robes. When Sadoff was modelling his relative nakedness for her, he looked distinctly uncomfortable–and Martha said, "When you're on stage, you'll have the protection of your role." Unfortunately, the role Freddie chose to play in later life failed to protect him at all.

When one cynical peer made disparaging remarks to others about Sadoff's sexual ties to Meisner, the indiscreet student found himself temporarily dismissed from the Playhouse while Fred's sexual contacts insured that he succeeded. "Freddie was quite social in New York," said one who knew him, "He devoted his life to being a protege in order to avoid ever having to wait on tables to get by. He developed the roundest heels in town: every man with position or contacts was a target." A long-ago friend of the actor speculated he actively sought out Redgrave for his advantage.

While in New York in 1956, acting in Giraudoux's *Tiger at the Gates*, Michael Redgrave received an introduction to Sadoff, a devotee of the Method and the Lee Strasberg version of it. Redgrave felt infatuation with Sadoff and took him to London. This was when Redgrave's son Corin first realized that, "My father was gay."

Sadoff lived in one of Redgrave's London townhouses, but owing to Redgrave's constant financial and tax troubles, soon had to find his own flat in London. He had come to England to work in the Arts Theatre where he had a "modest" success, according to Corin. However, as an American resident alien in the United Kingdom, he encountered a restriction on his right to perform regularly on London stages. This may have contributed to the sudden decision of Redgrave to return with him to New York in late 1956 to work on television (a video version of *Ruggles of Red Gap*). During that engagement, the young companion of the star learned he'd been cast in the pivotal role of Dominguez, the fellow who misleads Fowler into the murderous plot to kill *The Quiet American*.

Corin was impressed by Freddie because he claimed association with the Brando and Clift crowd from the "Method" school of acting. Sadoff and the elder Redgrave maintained their relationship until the 1970s. Corin Redgrave, the actor's thespian son, recalled Sadoff as "cheerful, funny, and loyal after a fashion." Vanessa too became friendly with her father's "chum" in Rome where she often inquired for advice about acting from him, as she too respected his connections to the New York school of acting under the Method—and partly too because he knew so many of the notable graduates.

Sadoff proceeded to Saigon and, of course, prepared the adjoining accommodations in the Hotel Majestic for Redgrave. He waited for the British star's commitment to American television to conclude so he might reunite with his new "lover"—a term used by Michael Redgrave's wife (Rachel Kempson) in her correspondence to her husband. An extrovert by nature, Sadoff pursued an active social life during the weeks in Saigon while he awaited Redgrave.

A disquieting fact, unknown to Audie, was that Redgrave's *grande passion* in life had been a former American G.I., a war hero named Bob Michell, whose appearance was definitely a cross between Montgomery Clift and Audie Murphy–a point observed in the 1950s by Redgrave's teenage son, Corin. Michell and Redgrave had parted after many years together–a few months before the filming for *The Quiet American* commenced.

Redgrave's attraction to soft-spoken American military men with heroic comportment might have been an intriguing motive for him, at first, to accept the role in Mankiewicz's movie. When he learned he would work opposite Audie, his initial reactions positively gushed with anticipation; however, their growing antipathy in Vietnam indicated a personal relationship with Audie did not develop the way the British actor may have wished.

Yet, both actors now trod the same path, thrown together by chance. Their road led them firmly into the world called Greene-Land by the intelligentsia of the reading public, a term coined by the aficionados of Graham Greene's peculiar and idiosyncratic literary world–a place familiar to Redgrave, but far from the plains of the American West, where Audie flourished. They were the replacement cast–and both were determined their performances would fulfill the potential of what Joseph L. Mankiewicz's vision originally expected from Olivier and Clift.

2

BORN IN 1909 in Wilkes-Barre, Pennsylvania, Mankiewicz had come to Hollywood following in the footsteps of his older brother, Herman, who co-authored *Citizen Kane*. Joe also started as a writer and producer, often in prestige pictures like *Keys of the Kingdom* or *Philadelphia Story*. Mankiewicz found the post-war years in Hollywood required a new generation of directors as well as actors. The actors from silent days on had mainly been drawn from the theater. It was sound which changed their style of acting, eliminating those without suitable voices or diction. The style of film acting ceased to be exaggerated mime and became more understated.

Matching the mentality of theatrical actors, Joe's work was smart, sophisticated, intelligent, and well-suited to the new breed of stage actors who converged on Hollywood during the post-World War II years and changed the style of acting and, consequently, the style of moviemaking. His greatest success depicted the New York off-stage world in *All About Eve.*

If one could describe Mankiewicz aptly by metaphor, he looked like Babe Ruth in his prime; the comparison was not merely physical. Both were larger than life figures with big egos and bigger talents. If Ruth was the Sultan of Swat, Mankiewicz was the Sultan of Cinema. He was the *auteur* Welles never could become. Studios, predicated on profit, actually produced his ideas into film. By the mid-1950s, he had outgrown the studio system that had created him. He founded his production company in order finance his ever more personal interests in subject and style of films.

One of Hollywood's first auteurs, Joseph L. Mankiewicz had made a deal to suit his puffed sense of self, and the contract provided the new route he wanted to take his gift for film-making. A man with Faustian powers, Mankiewicz wore three hats—writer, director, and producer. Needing money to finance his variety of projects, Mankiewicz became NBC's consultant. He sold half-interest to NBC which had in mind that the most prestigious and intellectual director reigning in Hollywood would condescend to do some television productions.

Though this was an age when great movie stars did occasionally appear in great dramas on many of the Golden Age anthologies, television was not for Mankiewicz himself, but merely for his director proteges in Figaro, Incorporated.

Having NBC invest in his production company allowed Mankiewicz to explore deeply the theatrical film projects worthy of his name and talent. Because of his Hollywood success, Mankiewicz was driven to pursue a better and important reputation. He won back-to-back Oscars in 1949 and 1950. His *All About Eve* was the biggest Oscar winner of all-time for several generations. Its script with its literacy was beyond anything the Hollywood moguls had known.

Soon, Mankiewicz, in not unprecedented fashion, searched for properties "worthy" of his intellect, however unpopular they might be with the general public. If he wanted to do films about famous painters or versions of relatively unknown Shakespearean plays, he now had the seed money from NBC.

Stars gravitated to him, especially those seeking to become more than the stereotype of their success and who believed public entertainment under-utilized their abilities. Mankiewicz had complete autonomy from the non-creative executives of the 1950s' motion picture studios.

With script control and final cut, Mankiewicz was on a level that few directors had achieved. Joe's reputation caused both of Audie's advisors to insist that Murphy could put his trust in him; the redoubtable John Huston had his labor of love, *Red Badge of Courage*, hacked to pieces and was powerless to prevent it. The same year Orson Welles lost the right to determine the future of *Touch of Evil*, another masterpiece not to be restored for forty years. Thus, Mankiewicz's allure to actors desiring to tie their star to integrity could prove a heady tonic.

Audie Murphy was ripe for the intoxicating feel of a major picture; Joe Mankiewicz was the man to give it to him.

After his successes with *All About Eve* and *The Barefoot Contessa*, some might say Joe harbored delusions of grandeur. He tackled projects like *Guys and Dolls,* though musicals were not his forte, and he was no Busby Berkley, but wanted to try to do one. Bert Allenberg was Mankiewicz's agent before *Guys and Dolls,* and he also represented Frank Sinatra. Allenberg's legendary efforts included the heavy work to win Sinatra the role he most coveted in his life, Maggio in *From Here to Eternity.*

Now, Allenberg brought together his two great clients for a mutual project, however ill-fated the teaming. With *Guys and Dolls,* despite the musical's legendary run on Broadway, Joe seemed out of his element. A musical with Marlon Brando and Frank Sinatra, each miscast, each famous for temperament, was the start of Joe's new habit: biting on the stem of a pipe too big for his mouth.

In fact, the Goldwyn people expressed dismay at how much he tended to overwrite a script. He had revised the Broadway musical scenario, turning it into a songless four hour epic in one of his rejected, unused drafts. Sam Goldwyn, in his legendary fractured English, told him: "You write with great warmth and charmth."

Finishing a traditional and studio-bound musical, he looked for new horizons. What he hadn't attempted was a picture in a place that imposed its own obstacles to filming. No Hollywood director had gone to Southeast Asia. Therefore, Mankiewicz marveled at the possibilities of ambiance and flavor. At this fateful time Joe Mankiewicz discovered the controversial novel by Graham Greene, called *The Quiet American.*

Robert Lantz recalled years later: "Joe really liked the book. He wanted very much to make the movie." Not one member on the supervisory Board of Figaro could say "no" to Joe. The worst that could befall him did: the production company gave him *carte blanche*, a dangerous freedom, which often leads to serious ramifications for those among the Hollywood elite who succumbed to unlimited power.

Thus, he decided to film a Graham Greene novel about Vietnam, a place barely known to the average American in 1957, a full decade before the war shredded the United States to pieces in generation protest. Associates attribute to Mankiewicz the idea to show, in the most dramatic of terms on film, how "emotions can very often dictate political beliefs." If he needed a controversial novel about a hot political situation, the answer rested in the furor Graham Greene's latest novel created in 1956.

Of course, it was anti-American—one of the fashions of the times. Greene was glib in his dryness, arch in his wit—yet, more people were indignant that Greene's latest novel condoned and trivialized the murder of an American abroad.

Mankiewicz found the thesis disturbing that the American's death found facile explanation with "a noble, political sacrifice," by a dissipated British writer (whether he meant Fowler, the character, or Greene, the author, is unclear). Mankiewicz thought Greene had duped, not only the other characters in his novel, but more frighteningly the vast readership who accepted the narrator's pretentious explanation of his vicious action.

Like Greene, Mankiewicz was highly intelligent, thoroughly able to manipulate words and audiences, and he entered into a chess match with the British author. The American director expressed his deep and abiding admiration of Graham Greene publicly. "I love the way he divides his work into 'entertainments' and serious work," stated Mankiewicz who held the same opinion of his production. To top it off, the director hinted, "I've always wanted to do a picture about one of those ice-blooded intellectuals whose intellectualism is just a mask for completely irrational passion."

Around that time Robby Lantz, Joe's partner, and Bert Allenberg, Joe's agent, had a meeting about the scripts Mankiewicz wrote from other sources. Lantz expressed legitimate concerns that screenplays should suit the story and the actor, as well as the original source, but Allenberg told him, "Oh, I never read the scripts. That's an artistic kind of decision, and I never get involved in that side of things." His colleague did read scripts, and Lantz was increasingly disturbed at what might devolve from the novel. Joe Mankiewicz would hardly be sympathetic to his judgment under question by one on the business side of the ledger.

Lantz repeated what he felt for many, many years. "I do remember I was very troubled, very troubled, by the script." Robby, with his producer and agent's eye, found problems in the translation of the novel into screenplay. "First problem was that he changed the story."

As reasonably could be expected, Lantz worried that Mankiewicz had stirred a hornet's nest by tampering with the writer's novel. Another Figaro staff member who saw an early version of the screenplay was Mike Mindlin. Based on his earlier film work (*Trapeze* with Carol Reed and *Summertime* with David Lean), Joe and Robby Lantz hired Mike to be their publicity and advertising man at Figaro. They did not know him beyond that.

Yet, much to Mike's surprise, his first job was to read the script Mankiewicz had just completed of *The Quiet American*, "even though they barely knew me." Robby told him that Joe wanted a thorough analysis, "in writing." Years later Mindlin said how: "I just couldn't believe that my comments would have any importance to a man as famous and respected as Joe Mankiewicz."

The reason was simple. With the script rejected by his primary choice for the leads and with demands from Larry and Monty to revise the draft, Joe Mankiewicz was, for the first time in his life, over a barrel. Hence, Mindlin drew the editorial job, as well as his daily production logistics. He grew to win the trust and loyalty of Mankiewicz who continued to regard him as a friend and respected advisor. Having worked with David Lean and Carol Reed, Mike had reputable credentials. One of the few men whom Mankiewicz found palmary with script decisions, Mindlin learned, later, his insights into the revising of copy only took hold at the editing phase.

Eager to read the screenplay, Mindlin quickly became shocked by what he saw in the adaptation of Greene's work. The word he used to describe the script was "overwritten." To be completely honest and forthright, Mike decided to state what he perceived as obvious problems. "The man was addicted to flashbacks. I pulled the thing apart piece by piece. I also objected to the ending. I thought it was a total corruption of the Greene novel."

What the young executive did next could have cost him his job, but he gave an unflinching appraisal. "I wrote a long memo." He labeled the scenario he saw, and the same one sent out to people like Olivier and Clift, as "incredibly complicated" owing to its use of flashbacks (a Mankiewicz specialty). In this picture, however, Mankiewicz went off the deep end in his use of the flashback. He put dream sequences within various flashbacks, weaving layer upon layer of dense and complex narrative. The director refused to underestimate the intelligence of his movie audience.

Much to Mike's surprise, Joe Mankiewicz quite easily accepted his criticism. He was absolutely forthright in his appreciation of Mike's comments. To this day, however, Mindlin cannot fathom why Joe wanted to make that particular story into a movie. "Perhaps he just wanted to get away from home problems, but Vietnam is a long way to go just to do that." Mike later learned how reluctant to change scripts Mankiewicz could be, and the director's willingness to listen indicated how much he must have trusted the young executive. "Joe always re-sisted change suggested by the powers that be. He simply did not like the United Artists powers. I guess you could call him an elitist."

As a measure of his respect for Mike, Joe Mankiewicz gave assur-ances he would trim the script as recommended. He would change, tighten, and eliminate scenes and overdone elements—at least that's what he promised. Mindlin modestly professed not to understand why the director listened. "Of course, it became a running joke between us." Mindlin explained one day at a major staff meeting prior to leaving for Vietnam, Joe Mankiewicz solicited opinions from his production staff—but stopped short suddenly—to say: "Let's not ask Mike what he thinks. He doesn't like anything about this picture we're making," to the be-mused group.

To illustrate Joe's stubbornness and resistance to ideas not his own, a few years later Mindlin told Joe to see *West Side Story* on Broadway. "I told him how terrific it was, that it would make a terrific movie," that Joe should be the one do the film version. According to Mindlin,

Mankiewicz and his agent Bert Allenberg went to the Leonard Bernstein musical, and promptly left at intermission, not liking it at all, though years later Joe expressed his regret to Mindlin for not listening to his advisor.

Like other Figaro production team players, Robby Lantz "really trusted Joe. I loved Joe, and I was really crazy about Joe's work, his brilliance." So, those raising objections to the earliest scenario drafts simply deferred to the man they considered a master wit and the leading literary person in the business.

However fascinating the subject might be on academic levels, one must seriously question Mankiewicz's judgment about *The Quiet American* material for its public appeal. After all, movies in the 1950s were entertainment for most, with only a small number recognizing the artistic element of the medium.

Mankiewicz acknowledged the success of another Graham Greene story, entitled *The Third Man,* less than a decade before. As if to give insurance to his own production, he brought aboard the Figaro team two of the most successful behind-the-scenes people from that movie: Robert Krasker, cinematographer, and George Frost who did the make-up. Since they had helped make one Greene story transfer to the screen artistically, he expected they could repeat the job for him.

Joe Mankiewicz stood at the opposite end of the scale from Audie Murphy's B-western movie world. A man at the height of his power and talent, if he'd been an actor, he would out-do Barrymore; if he'd been a despot (and he certainly played perfectionist), he would out-do Napoleon. The leading lady of *The Quiet American*, Giorgia Moll, had a first impression that coincided with this: "He was so exacting and very precise. He knew what he wanted." He had a scathing wit and shrewdly observed all that occurred around him. Joe Mankiewicz's great-est films were literate, talky, and sarcastic: what passed for mature film-making in this town. He enjoyed doing complex narrative and subtle human motivation.

The making of any motion picture goes beyond the work of stars and director: the day-to-day work grinds away at a supporting crew who often go swiftly named and billed on the credits, if at all. Nearly sixty people went to Vietnam with the stars to make this film, including spouses and traveling companions. Only a handful of them received credit in the roll of names after the title sequence, and none received recognition in the movie's pressbook.

One man, in particular, proved to be the most dedicated of all the behind the scenes' people: film editor William Hornbeck. Working with the Figaro production company on all its key 1950s' movies, Hornbeck served as Mankiewicz's lieutenant and chief advisor, and to this unassuming man fell the onus of all the significant production work. His daily diaries of the events in Vietnam, never before consulted or read since his death in 1983, reveal much of the activity involved in the making of *The Quiet American.*

Hornbeck signed on with Mankiewicz for a second time without reservation. William Hornbeck matched Mankiewicz respect for respect, award for award. They had found in each other compatible workmates after *The Barefoot Contessa.* In addition, Hornbeck's work on *A Place in the Sun* for George Stevens won him Hollywood immortality (assisting Montgomery Clift and Elizabeth Taylor to achieve their zeniths of beauty and effectiveness on screen).

A true Hollywood pioneer, born in 1901, his career started with extra work and behind-the-scenes activities with the likes of silent film-making legend, Mack Sennett. Hornbeck's loyalty, discretion, and talent, won him a place in the sun with many great directors who chose to use him regularly on their films. As one movie veteran said: "Hornbeck was very well admired for his work in Hollywood and envied for his film credits."

One of Hornbeck's primary associations had been with Alexander Korda, doing most of the prestige films of England during the 1930s (*Elephant Boy, Jungle Book, Thief of Baghdad*). He later formed a partnership with Frank Capra (doing *Magic Town* and *It's a Wonderful Life*). He also worked with George Stevens on *Giant* featuring James Dean in 1955. Another of his favorite film directors was Joe Mankiewicz. Their partnership on *The Barefoot Contessa* had been so pleasant that, when approached about a trip as far from a studio as possible, Hornbeck didn't hesitate to accept. He was one of the first to sign on for the trip to Vietnam for *The Quiet American*.

Down to earth, reasonable, and with few pretensions, Hornbeck proved to be the true chronicler of the days of filming *The Quiet American*. Once the project was confirmed, the dedicated film editor kept a diary of his experiences in Vietnam and wrote detailed letters to his wife back in America about the shenanigans as well as professionalism that surrounded the making of the picture.

Mankiewicz had implicit trust in his judgment and advice, frequently consulting him on all issues. Hornbeck is seldom remembered nowadays (Robert Lantz said: "I know the name, but I cannot put a face to it.") However, Mike Mindlin eulogized his former associate as "just the most lovely man."

In early October of 1956, Bill Hornbeck completed a grueling schedule of editing the George Stevens epic, *Giant*. The work had been long and arduous, culminating with the tragic problem of the death of star James Dean. Hornbeck was supposed to do loops with Dean in early October, 1955, for his final speech in the epical movie, but lost the legendary star to a fatal car accident on September 30th. It fell to Hornbeck to find a replacement. He mentioned in his film diaries that he found "a suitable young actor," but never stated who it was.

Of course, when he signed with Figaro, Incorporated, shortly thereafter, he immediately arranged to have a two week vacation before his next project. Not only did he know the arduous work ethic of Mankiewicz, the added problems with a location shoot in the faraway and unknown conditions of Vietnam presented constant headaches. His vacation would, in essence, be his only time free of *The Quiet American* project from October of 1956 until early 1958 when the picture premiered.

A junket to Vietnam to make a movie teetered on the rim of a perilous adventure in 1956 and 1957; political troubles erupted on a daily basis, but for most Americans it was a far off and needless worry. Any Americans who wished to travel to the newly partitioned country of South Vietnam discovered a labyrinth of red tape impeding the way. To receive the proper assistance and clearance from the United States government for its citizens to spend time in the Asian hotbed, the would-be traveler required "special permissions."

The government of the United States considered Vietnam a menacing location and discouraged citizens from visiting there. For the task of cutting the bureaucracy and obtaining all permissions, Figaro Inc., designated its vice president Robert Lantz to go to Washington, D.C., where he visited the Central Intelligence Agency headquarters to meet with Allen Dulles, then its head, and brother of the Secretary of State under President Eisenhower, John Foster Dulles.

These two brothers in government service wielded a power and control of American foreign policy; the installed president of Vietnam who was the first of a line of dubious American-backed appointments had connections to the Dulles brothers, considered by some to be a protege of the Secretary of State. Of course, this meant Allen Dulles could clear the path of all obstacles for the Mankiewicz film troupe to go to Saigon. Robby Lantz revealed Dulles cut the political red-tape to make it possible, if not "easy," to produce a picture with on-location work in Vietnam.

The complicated arrangements were only possible through the cooperation of the highest levels of the United States government. Multiple Oscar-winning film producer, and founder of Orion Pictures, Eric Pleskow worked for United Artists in those days on all "overseas" pictures, though he said he had no connection to *The Quiet American*, which happened to be United Artist's biggest overseas project that year. He was adamant in his comments, however, when asked about the State Department's interest in the film, that his studio would "never, ever, ever" allow a government agency have control over a film script. He insisted strongly that United Artists were "not subject to such influences." Mr. Pleskow also added that, of course, as Americans, they were not making pictures "harmful to the United States." Of course, Mr. Pleskow was less than disingenuous; he explained government officials certainly could offer their opinion of the film after it was produced.

To some extent Pleskow was absolutely correct. Though the United States Department of Defense offered military and technical assistance to hundreds of movies between 1948 and 1968, *The Quiet American* was absent from the list. During 1957 the DoD offered help to movies like *Enemy Below, Battle Hymn, Heaven Knows Mr. Allison,* and Audie's other quasi-military picture, *Joe Butterfly.* At this point in history, the United States military sent no advisors to Vietnam–for movies.

Though he was scheduled to leave for Vietnam with Joe Mankiewicz's entourage, Mike Mindlin went to Joe and Robby Lantz with a proposal. He suggested he ought to depart early for Vietnam to settle all the issues related to media relations. "I told them I had to go ahead and establish press relations in Tokyo and Hong Kong before we ever set foot in Saigon. Of course," Mindlin laughed, "it was all bullshit. I wanted to see the Orient. Never having been to Asia, I figured this was a good way to get a free trip, first class, to all the places I always wanted to see."

At the end of Mike's presentation, Mankiewicz and Lantz, knowing what he was up to, gave their permission for Mindlin to leave when he could arrange it. Mike's assistant on publicity Alfred Katz, a chubby man, would come in on January 15th, leaving a day before Fred Sadoff, but arriving about the same time, one on Air France, the other on Pan American Airlines.

Another immediate concern to Bill Hornbeck, or anyone else who made the journey to a Third World nation with its rampant disease and poverty, was his inoculation schedule. Though he initiated his vaccinations in early November, he had shots in mid-November, and still found himself receiving additional inoculations against the plethora of widespread tropical diseases. He did it all in one week, before he undertook the long journey to Vietnam, in late December. The studio doctor at Paramount commenced the series of shots.

The troupe faced medical worries which included yellow fever, smallpox, dysentery, cholera. Doctors always recommended salt tablets for frequent use. Paludrin was suggested for protection against malaria (tablets taken daily). There were no shots for malaria. Production Assistant Rosemary Matthews accompanied Hornbeck on these trips, apparently for moral support, and to prepare herself for the inevitable trip. His other early task was the reading of the Graham Greene novel, annotating the text in preparation for his many roles in the production of the movie. Unfortunately, with the harried rush of dozens of important chores he had to perform for the production, he forgot to pack the text and had to have it sent along to Saigon in late January, reminding his wife to send the book shortly thereafter.

To meet the tight shooting schedule, actors and crew had to commit themselves in time for their arrival in Saigon to coincide with the Chinese New Year, called Tet. Mankiewicz had a critical four day window at the end of January to film the festivities. These moments needed the reality that could not come from a recreation either in Vietnam or later in Italy. Anyone from the cast who was to appear in this sequence at the opening of the movie must have had his inoculations and able to do perform.

With the number of shots required to travel to this exotic and tropical location, depending on medical history with update of vaccinations, the latest time-frame in which actors must end their series of injections to protect against Yellow Fever, tetanus, and the like, would be the first week of January. Injections also required a time to take effect. Certainly with the possibility of becoming ill from them, and tight and prolonged travel, the earlier shots could be arranged, the better.

Other key production people involved in the early process were Forrest 'Johnny' Johnston, a regular Mankiewicz member of the crew, who served as Production Manager and needed to be the first on location in Saigon, arranging the accommodations and other necessary logistics to making a movie. He arrived on December 4th with Rosemary Matthews, Joe's greatest supporter and ardent defender for the rest of their lives. During the production of The Quiet American, Rosemary had an official position as Johnny Johnston's Production Assistant, but she was the person closest to Mankiewicz.

Giorgia Moll remembered her fondly, "Always on the set and a fantastic person." All these hard-working and dedicated professionals served a role in an extended Mankiewicz creative family; Rosemary Matthews accompanied Hornbeck to procure his visa before leaving the country in late October. Other early arrivals included the assistant director, Piero Mussetta. Gloria Piconi disembarked two weeks later, to serve as the Wardrobe specialist. Babe Hornbeck, Bill's wife, joined the troupe in mid-February. Johnston's wife Ethel also worked on the picture.

Another regular with Mankiewicz was one of the most respected Continuity Editors in the history of the business: E.C. Schreyeck. In the 1950s she was often called a Script Girl. "Irrespective of age," she laughs. Her job was to make a record of everything that happens during a shoot. In her field she transcended routine; Mankiewicz relied on her frequently as a script consultant, being with him at the development of each script. Her career comprised everything from *Cleopatra* to *Sleuth* with Mankiewicz. And, she would be among the first ready to go to Vietnam, if that was what the director asked. Hornbeck was in constant communication, too, with Roscoe 'Rocky' Cline, the Special Effects man on the project. Joe Mankiewicz had called from New York and expressed interest in building their projection machine in Vietnam (at a cost of $4500).

In fact, negative film went by airplane at regular intervals to Rome, to be processed, and "rushes" were flown back to Vietnam. Sometimes called dailies, these pieces of film are the results of each day's shoot. Mankiewicz and his crew viewed them days later, making judgements on whatever had to be redone. One of the first hires in Vietnam to work as a liaison with the film industry in the new nation of South Vietnam was Vinh Noan.

His official title was Associate Producer, though the manifest in Rome listed him as the Technical Advisor. Mankiewicz knew of him from an award-winning film which had impressed everyone at the Asian Film Festival in 1955. Having made that picture along the new partition in Vietnam called *We Want to Live,* Vinh Noan incurred the wrath of the Hanoi Communists in his frank depiction of their cruelty to the two million peasants who tried to flee life in North Vietnam during that year. Not yet organized to the degree they would exhibit during the war with America, the Communists made life filming along the Ho Chi Minh trail a perilous undertaking. Vinh's movie was the all-time popularhome-produced picture of his generation, playing endlessly in Saigon cinemas.

Joseph L. Mankiewicz and his Associate Producer Vinh Noan.
Photo courtesy of Vinh Noan.

Vinh Noan later commented about the dangers he encountered: "When I made my film, I have many threats from the communists, but they were not so sophisticated back then." The interns working on the film fell under his aegis. "These were really government observers," he explained ambiguously in an interview. Their ties to the Diem regime may have transcended their ties to the movie business. Vinh had strong support from the government and seemed to maintain his powerful reputation through a variety of regimes.

Johnny Johnston hired Vinh as his first duty, and then turned over all hiring prerogatives in his own country to Noan since he knew everyone in the fledgling Vietnam film industry–and those in the government. A regally handsome young man of twenty-nine, he persuaded

45

reluctant bureaucrats to cooperate with the Figaro troupe and through his charm and diplomacy could always assure the production of top-notch security. Graham Greene could write about the elusive General The in *The Quiet American,* but Vinh Noan was his personal friend– and a dedicated anti-Communist. That was also his strongest motive in joining the Figaro crew to make an American movie in his homeland.

In many ways he was able to provide Mankiewicz with a director's perspective in a foreign culture. If he felt frustration about anything, it was serving as a producer, rather than a director. Though he held Mankiewicz in the highest esteem, like many others in the picture business, he believed Joe Mankiewicz was a better writer than director. The American auteur admitted to Noan that action pictures were not his forte, and he preferred the stage-set dialogue scenes to action moments.

As an elemental contributor to the picture, his duties transcended production and ran the gamut of activities associated with film-making. Speaking French from his studies in Paris, and having mastered English, he also communicated in his native Vietnamese. For logistics, he was second to none. And, as a film director in his own right, Mankiewicz needed someone familiar with the art of the cinema and with the technical work required in motion pictures. He lucked out with Noan who provided his cultural expertise, and far more importantly, gave Audie Murphy the anchor of stability and friendship that helped his withstand the stress of the location work. Without Noan, the Vietnamese side of the story would have gone forever untold.

Now called Frank Vinh, he adopted the first name with kudos to Frank Sinatra. One of Vinh's photos showed Mankiewicz and his associate, beaming happy, their arms around one another's shoulder. When he settled in the United States later, he brought many souvenirs, including his scrapbook of mementos featuring many prized photos of him with Audie Murphy. As they became fast friends during the filming, Audie often took photos of Vinh Noan. If Don Quixote needed a Sancho Panza, the American hero had found his devotee, ally, and foil, in the person of the smart, young, Vietnamese with movie star looks.

December's pre-production phase of the movie continued to generate havoc with some whose duty it was to see all ran smoothly for the arrival of the picture's stars and support staff in Saigon. Delays occurred as expected, and though Hornbeck sent Johnny Johnston and his wife Ethel ahead to Saigon in mid-November to expedite the readiness for the director, events–including the death of his wife's mother–simply caused more postponements for the film editor.

Executives at Figaro, Incorporated, finalized Hornbeck's departure as December 27th for Vietnam, giving him time to spend with his wife over the Christmas holiday. Special Effects man Rocky Cline wouldn't be so lucky; his departure for the Southeast Asia fell on Christmas Eve. He arrived in Vietnam with his assistant for special effects, George Schlicker, on December 27th, just a day ahead of Mike Mindlin and cinematographer Robert Krasker.

Logistics between the Figaro, Incorporated, main offices in New York and the home base of the professionals in Los Angeles continued to cause consternation for those whose job it was to make the movie. Projectors, splicing machines, multitudes of various lenses, spare parts and other supplies, fell under the aegis of Hornbeck who organized, prepared, tested and re-tested every piece of equipment and then double-checked each item. Once in Vietnam, broken or inoperable equipment could ruin Mankiewicz's restrictive timetable. The movie was at the mercy of the calendar. Tet, the Chinese New Year, was the pivotal backdrop to the entire picture's plot.

Some equipment was simply not ready. Other essentials needed tinkering, which created stress on Hornbeck. As some repairs required at least a week, he now had to arrange to take, as part of his personal luggage, key movie equipment. On top of this, he nearly forgot his Yellow Fever inoculation. He received it at the Los Angeles Federal Building on December 19th. The day after Christmas, Hornbeck took the projection screen to the shipment cache scheduled to depart on Dec. 29th. The inventory of supplies and equipment was entirely his responsibility.

Figaro executives: Production Manager on The Quiet American Forrest 'Johnny' Johnston and Oscar-winning Film Editor William Hornbeck. Photo courtesy of Vinh Noan.

A comedy of errors ensued. Hornbeck, as point man for Mankiewicz, linchpin of the production, realized on December 27th no one had sent him a plane ticket. A flurry of phone calls to the Figaro executive in New York, Sigmund Muskat, assured Hornbeck that his ticket would be available through the local Los Angeles Pan-Am office. Not until late the following evening did the ticket arrive. His departure from Los Angeles was abrupt, within the next two hours. The visa for Japan and Hong Kong was already in order. In short time, he wended his way on the adventure of a lifetime. First stop would be a delightful lay-over in Honolulu. Unfortunately, it lasted less than twenty-four hours.

On Sunday morning, early, Hornbeck left for Japan with one stop at Wake Island. He expected to arrive in Tokyo on New Year's Day and stay at the elegant Imperial Hotel. To his bad luck again, the holiday prevented him from procuring his visa for South Vietnam; instead, he celebrated the holiday with a dinner for various United Artists officials, though his concern for his wife and her bereavement still bothered him. The next day he arranged for a visa with the British Consul and boarded for Hong Kong on a red-eye midnight flight. Eight hours later he was at the Miramar Hotel.

The final leg of the journey entailed another flight the next day: a short three hour hop brought him into Saigon. The shock of the heat and unpleasant smells horrified him instantly. Like all travelers to the country, he found rubbish burning in streets, creating smoky haze, as well as the use of human excrement as fertilizer, throughout the area. So pervasive was that odor, it eventually ceased to be offensive among so many other stenches. Waiting patiently for him at the gate were Johnny Johnston and Ethel.

The ordeal began in earnest.

3

COMING BETWEEN JOHN
Wayne's *The Quiet Man,* released in 1952, and Marlon Brando's *The Ugly American,* released in 1962, both more commercially successful and famous than their middle sibling, *The Quiet American* suffered from its chronological placement. Released in 1958, it's a movie everybody thinks they have seen—but probably have not.

The film is confused with the other two constantly and is not helped by the fact that *The Ugly American* also details America's pre-war involvement in southeast Asia. Yet, of the three, *The Quiet American* provides a fascinating array of behind-the-scenes activities which parallel the disasters of American involvement in Vietnam. *The Quiet Man,* set and filmed in Ireland, featured John Wayne in one of his most beloved serio-comic roles. A few years ago, a biography of John Wayne entitled *The Quiet American* contributed further to the confusion over the titles.

If anyone was entitled to copyright the name of *The Quiet American,* it was Audie Murphy. Always known as a quiet and polite young man, Audie impressed everyone who met him. Being a mythic figure, he inspired awe, but he knew he had more to give the world, but needed to grow as a creative individual in his chosen field of motion pictures. He fell short within his Western genre in Hollywood.

Old-timers like Randolph Scott dominated movie oaters, and crooning cowpokes like Roy Rogers had television conquered. Those who knew him will be the first to advise that Audie became a movie actor because of his wartime fame, not his own desire. A man misled into show business, he might have found happiness in a dozen other places.

Once set on the path, he made it his duty to give all he had. Yet, he viewed his movie career a mediocre failure after twenty photo-copy westerns.

As a man whose exploits shook life to the core, whether it was rising in the ranks of the military, single-handedly winning battles, or proving lack of formal education was no handicap, he expected more than he received. Spec McClure revealed: "His only formal training as an actor was acquired by attending a drama school for a few months." Audie later explained his view that acting "is day-dreaming. And I have day-dreamed all of my life. It was the only way I could escape my environment."

In Hollywood "artistes" made a respected name by doing prestigious, but unpopular work. Audie often mentioned the name of John Huston in this regard and expressed amazement at the frequency of his failures. The opinion among some Hollywood insiders on Huston was that people in the movie capital dropped money into him all the time as they would a slot-machine—and received big lemons.

Audie ached to achieve a respectful eminence in Hollywood, even if it was a town he detested as much as any Nazi enemy on the battlefield. If he could devastate the enemy in a war, he could surely impress the heavy-weights in the world of silver-screen fantasies. If it took failure to create respect, he felt as able as Huston. "I'm just a mediocre failure; so everybody notices it. John is such a colossal failure that nobody can possibly believe it." Audie was innocently dedicated, and shrewd, but came to this town only to watch his war heroics parlayed into an uneasy celebrity after seven years in western B-movies.

Audie's career had ridden hard for seven years into the banality of light-weight popularity in programmer westerns. The public, the fan magazines, and the children who went to Saturday afternoon matinees, made Audie a folk hero, which tended to make his life off screen hazardous. He mentioned to Ben Cooper that "he didn't go out to places much because someone would always pick a fight with him."

Jack Elam recalled that, in a bar, Audie ordered "a coke chaser," but only drank the coke, giving the Cutty Sark to Elam. As they stood there, one patron began harassing them. Murphy silently reacted: "Audie

51

spun around and hit him and never said a friggin' word. Just hit him. And he went flat." Elam concluded, "He had that attitude about him of Don't Tread on Me."

Audie wanted, in his inimitable style of over-reach, to be known as a real actor working with literate scripts, anything that differed from the assembly-line western movies in which he was headlined. He wished to illustrate to all that he was serious, perhaps a contender for the industry's high honors. Spec McClure admitted in his memoirs, "Audie was not always an easy person to be around." To break one film contract the previous year, he demanded from Universal-International Pictures two impossible and non-commercial film treatments (*The Idiot* and *Peer Gynt*).

The wise producers refused to accept these projects and stated: "Mr. Murphy has deliberately chosen projects that are unsuited to his limited talents." Audie expressed his disgust when he commented: "Some people might say I'd be perfect as *The Idiot,*" to an actor. One of the producers claimed to Spec McClure that Audie didn't make the offer in "good faith." McClure's response was: "Do you want to bet? Have the producer ready scripts. Audie will make the picture."

Audie's response, known to a close friend like Spec, was not a bluff. "Before I let anybody call my hand, I'll do *Peer Gynt* or *The Idiot* in grand opera even if it ruins both me and the producer." As McClure confirmed, "When Murphy had his ire up, nobody called his hand."

At the peak of his movie stardom, Audie's book about his wartime experiences came to the screen. McClure, who co-wrote the book unbilled as the ghost, said he believed "the movie failed completely in catching the spirit of the Audie Murphy I knew." The star of the picture refused to see the film, but finally relented in New York City at the premiere. He immediately called Spec to tell him, "I was right, that the movie had missed the target by a mile." Both agreed the picture did not prove Audie's range as an actor and "helped his screen career very little."

Incredibly, Audie Murphy was asked by a legendary director to take on a political drama about an ethical crisis. The unexpected choice validated his feelings of self-worth in many ways. To be selected as replacement for Montgomery Clift was a singular sort of honor, one Audie was more than flattered at the offer. *The Quiet American* centered upon a vapid, Ivy League American patriot, dupe of his government, in Vietnam before the French evacuation of 1954. Audie was to play a character who suffers murder for the most tawdry of reasons. In this movie his fans would find no cowboy hats, no horses, no Western panoramas, no Technicolor, and no chance the story could be anything remotely viable in a commercial sense.

The consensus of friends and associates concluded Audie wanted to work in prestige films. The strongest recommendation to do "literary properties" as his film subjects came from his well-educated friend, David McClure. It had been Spec who gave him *Red Badge of Courage* to read and argued he must do the film version. McClure later berated himself for so often giving Murphy bad advice. He believed of himself, "I had not only a gift, but a positive talent in giving Audie the wrong advice." Despite this, Audie continued to heed McClure's opinion. Their closeness combined with their extreme opposite characteristics often amazed by-standers.

Yet, after signing with *The Quiet American,* Murphy went to Saigon with Willard Willingham, whom one witness described as "the kind of guy you often see in Hollywood who does everything for the star—from getting him coffee to making sure he has a chair to sit on. It wasn't enough to be a double or stand-in under the lighting set-ups for him; Willingham was like wallpaper around Audie." McClure remained home in Los Angeles, but was never far from influencing Audie when they were apart.

When one hears about Audie's "inadequacies" in the role, logic begs whether the viewers have seen the movie. The bizarre elements of the story are hints the fictional character had ties with Central Intelligence Agency and its subterfuge. According to Graham Greene, the young American of the story was powerless to prevent his own murder.

In a traditional western role, Audie automatically knew his enemies stalked him. He always escaped the attack in the final reel. Like his previous dozen movie roles, Audie could see the Greene/Mankiewicz script provided no impediments to his particular natural style of acting.

He played it exactly as written, having no trouble with the verbose dialog, and gave a heroic flash to his stock character (who was NOT the hero). Since the nameless American was a variation of every role Murphy played in Westerns (stalwart, wholesome, idealistic, moral, kind-hearted, and with a sense of direction), it was not beyond Audie's ability to play the role well.

More than anything else, Audie expected to achieve, with his role in *The Quiet American*, a kind of prominence he had not yet remotely enjoyed. He wanted acceptance by his peers in a profession into which he had been thrust. When he arrived in Hollywood nearly a decade before his role in the Mankiewicz picture, he advanced as an international celebrity–but also as an innocent. He wasn't prepared to be an actor, one whose primary business is to make believe. Actors usually dislike reality and love the dream; they live to command an audience. Audie was somewhat bewildered by the phantom world of movies. He epitomized the survivalist who could withstand vicious warfare. He may not, at first, have understood the convoluted battle zones of Hollywood, but survivors learn fast.

Audie could play nothing but himself. No script, no co-star's emoting, could shake that. Actors and directors had to face the bald reality he represented; he played no games with them. He went to Hollywood as naively as he had gone into military service, and in the movie world he encountered just as intricate and deadly campaigning as he had previously endured.

The most decorated soldier of World War II, Audie Murphy received 24 medals from the American government, three from the French, and one from the Belgians. He reportedly killed many German soldiers in a skirmish on January 26, 1945: another Sergeant York and Davy Crocket rolled into one. Estimates of the number whom he killed have stretched from 210 to 270 enemy.

Audie Murphy remained in appearance, a slight all-American boy, presenting the gaze of a guileless child. After viewing his photo in *Life* magazine, James Cagney said: "I saw that Audie could be photographed well from any angle, and I figured that a guy with drive enough to take him that far in the war had drive enough to become a star." Cagney telegrammed Murphy about coming out to Hollywood, which Audie simply ignored. A contrasting figure to some observers, he often appeared to be a demon-driven man with conflicts and resentments in every phase of his life.

Yet, when Cagney did finally meet Audie, he exclaimed: "Dignity from within! Not the kind imposed upon you from without. Spiritual overtones. He looks like Huckleberry Finn grown up. No, not really grown-up. There's something in those eyes that is as old as death and yet as young as springtime."

Born on June 20, 1925, on a Texas farm, he was the oldest boy of nine children. Most earlier accounts listed his birth year as 1924, all predicated on the false birth certificate Audie used to enter the U.S.Army. He was actually born a year later than the date he gave to enlist. According to family sources, his sister Corinne assisted him in falsifying the data. When his army tour of duty was over, he was nineteen–not twenty years old.

As for his childhood, the family's life was poor. They lived in a shack, and a local East Texan said: "Who would have expected Shorty to be anything more than another kid from Texas?" In his pre-Hollywood days, Audie even signed letters himself with the nickname, "Shorty."

Audie's father deserted, leaving the boy to fend for the entire family. The desertion by his father proved a factor that motivated as well as frustrated him. Growing up between two small Texas towns, McKinney and Greenville, under the cloud of family trouble, made Audie feel like a pariah. After he became a war hero, Audie later told Willingham, "When I was a kid, neither town wanted me. Now they both claim me." Indeed, in those early days after the war, Audie "was a god in Texas," informed Willard. But, it hadn't been that way in the beginning.

As a boy, Audie was a mere five feet five inches in his teens. He weighed a slight 112 pounds when he tried to enter the military. Of course, he did grow some, but as one co-star recalled about his height: "We were the same size and we worked well together. Well, actually he was shorter than myself . . . but with his heeled boots, not too much shorter . . . and I was not that much taller. I stand five feet and ten inches." Portraying Jesse James in *Kansas Raiders* in 1950, Audie was pleased to tell people, "James was exactly my size and weight . . . even wore a size nine shoe and size seven hat . . . which is me from head to foot."

Quitting school in the fifth grade, Audie sold newspapers and worked in a gas station, to bring home a meager salary. His mother sickened and died in May of 1941 of heart disease, complicated by pneumonia. Unable to care for his younger siblings, they had to be sent to various orphanages. Audie managed to bury this disturbing image for seventeen years, but it scarred him badly.

In July of 1942, when newly enlisted Private Audie Murphy was at Camp Wolters for training, he enjoyed bayonet practice and making friends with other Texas boys who sought glory. By July 1945 his boyish, handsome face was on the cover of *Life* magazine. Spiffy in his beribboned uniform, he seemed plucked out of central casting. The magazine proclaimed his feat. A second lieutenant, he suffered wounds three times, yet (while outnumbered) engaged his platoon with the Nazi enemy in eastern France. It was during that battle he personally routed the Germans, counterattacked, and secured a victory.

The genuine article in a land starved for heroes, his memoirs described the journey *To Hell and Back*, though the boy with the grade school education relied on David 'Spec' McClure to write his manuscript (much thought to be fictionalized by McClure). The achievement, nevertheless, failed to exorcise his demons. Shell-shock, battle fatigue, military flashbacks, continued to haunt him, even damned him. He dreamt sometimes he was surrounded by the enemy and his gun fell to pieces in his hands.

He admitted, when he woke from nightmares, he often fired his weapon at items in the room: a mirror or a clock. Though hallucinations occurred less frequently as years passed, he never fully recovered from them. Yet, to his fellow soldiers, he had been an insurance policy on life: as one of them said later, "When Murph had his men in the front lines, we in the rear felt it was safe to go to sleep!"

Upon arriving in Hollywood, under a personal contract to James Cagney, Audie experienced a paternal care-giver. Audie lived on the Cagney estate in a remodeled farmhouse and received a salary which he largely sent to his orphaned younger siblings. Though Cagney discovered that Audie had a photographic memory and "tremendous powers of observation," he was baffled by his attempts to turn Audie into an actor. First, he decided not to "formally" teach Audie. Nor did he loan him out or "cash in on publicity."

Cagney hired a dance instructor to show Audie how to walk with proper movement and rhythm. He would have Murphy read aloud to a large empty room, telling the young soldier-turned-actor: "Let the voice come out from the top of your head." Overly self-critical, Audie's esteem plummeted when he couldn't learn Cagney's techniques. Audie wrote to one old friend: "James Cagney is trying to teach me show business, but I'm afraid he doesn't have much to work with."

Paid a stipend by the "Yankee Doodle Dandy," given attention and education a true father might have provided, their relationship faltered after two years. Cagney diplomatically refused to comment on his consternation with Murphy. Their metaphoric father-son relationship fizzled as Murphy's real one had. Neither ever gave an explanation for their falling-out. Spec McClure claimed they merely "drifted apart," though he hinted at some darker incident between them. Terminating his contract with Cagney, Audie moved into a gymnasium on La Cienega Boulevard. As a result of their breach of trust, James Cagney shelved a production especially designed for Murphy called *The Stray Lamb.*

Once during his movie career, on a publicity tour, a friend reported to Audie that his father who deserted their family years earlier, wanted to speak to him. Audie nonchalantly commented he had no father. With the same attitude he used to attack the enemy (whomever he perceived it to be) and which never abated until he secured a victory, he cut his personal commitments to a level he could control. He achieved what he sought: in love and in war, in family and in business. He tried to learn his new craft at classes given by a Hollywood drama coach.

Audie quit the training for acting over the left-wing political attitudes he encountered. "A complete realist," came the description from McClure who said Audie found it impossible to do acting exercises, such as pretending to sew up "an imaginary pair of gloves." Audie told his friend, "I went there to try to learn to act–" but he was constantly badgered to join political causes with which he did not agree. As Spec concluded, "Audie tended toward the conservative." On the other hand, in his later unpublished memoirs, McClure made a serious effort to explain Audie "was not frightened by Stanislavski or his self-doubt about learning to act. His sole objection was against being used for a cause in which he did not believe . . ."

Later he went to a psychiatrist to deal with his war-time traumas. When asked what the psychiatrist deduced about his patient, Audie answered: "He went to see his psychiatrist," after hearing Murphy's tale. McClure underscored this was "no idle statement."

Spec McClure used his influence with Hedda Hopper to win some respect and needed acting roles from the studios. Audie did a few bit roles, but suffered "his eternal restlessness . . . driving aimlessly about when the black moods were upon him." Cagney firmly believed Audie was not ready for the big time: "He never learned to handle his meat," by which Cagney meant theatrical concept about the unobtrusive handling of arms and legs while performing.

Audie admired the beautiful movie star, Wanda Hendrix, and after he charmed her, she married him. It was a mistake. McClure thought they typified the Hollywood story of *A Star Is Born.* One's career rose; the other's tumbled. She immediately recognized the threat "his war-jangled nerves" presented to their happiness. She lamented: "Audie's worst fault is his pessimism. He has been through an awful lot . . ." Years later Wanda told of how he claimed to have envisioned his father's face on every German soldier he killed. She realized he believed in nothing and had deep uncertainties about life. The marriage soured shortly thereafter.

One factor out of their union was that Wanda understood, upon seeing *Bad Boy,* how much Audie had a knack for whatever he undertook. She commented, "He had proven himself to be a good actor and proven he had everything it takes to make a great actor." She was being kind; she knew better. She admitted he "had to learn to adjust to civilian life" and the task was overwhelming in many ways, "a challenge . . . to learn to live life over again." Unfortunately, their marriage couldn't stand the strain. It ended with Audie saying he should never have burdened her with his problems.

From Wanda came revelations about Audie's darker personal behavior. She told McClure that "he slept with a pistol beneath his pillow, often awakening from nightmares to seize the gun before he was fully conscious of his surroundings. He played with death as if it were a toy, once shooting out a light switch." At one time Audie pulled the gun on his new wife "his face seemingly dead and white with some nameless rage." She witnessed him with the barrel of the cocked and loaded pistol aimed at himself, "thrust into his own mouth."

In 1949, when *Bad Boy* went into distribution, James Dean–the icon that eclipsed Audie, making the western hero an anachronism–finished his high school education and gave his first thoughts to an acting career. If he saw this movie while growing up in Indiana (entirely possible as it was a midwestern hit), he would have presumed the role exactly right for him. Audie assayed all the right hostilities expected of a delinquent, though Dean may have played him completely deranged.

Audie and Jimmy, in real life, could have matched each other, hour for hour, on the therapist's couch. Ben Cooper said, "There was a tenseness about him. He was always in total control–too much so. I often tried to get him to relax. He was always on guard. Sometimes I wished I could just get him to smile." Jan Merlin took the assessment a bit more to the edge. He believed, "Audie was a tight-wire. His gentleness could vanish in an instant if something irritated him. One had to walk carefully around him."

Filming in May and June of 1949, Audie starred as Billy the Kid in *The Kid from Texas*, and it convinced Audie Murphy that his metier was the Western. He subsequently made forty more just like this. In color, action-packed, and short on psychology and motivation, it was a genre staple. Playing it with some originality, the role proved Audie was not likely to accept stereotyped roles. Serious about performing, and so secure in his real life reputation, he easily played less than heroic film characters to bring an ironic realism to the screen.

On the set of *The Kid from Texas*, Audie first encountered Willard Willingham, one of the steady bunch of cowhand types Universal International kept on tap. Sue Gossett, in her book notes on this film, wrote: "On the first day of shooting, Audie's double broke is collarbone and Audie had to do most of his own riding throughout the picture. Subsequently, Audie did most of his own stunt work. During his career, he used only two stand-ins." Because of Willard's vague resemblance to Audie, he evidently inherited the job on that day, although his present recollections don't refer to it. With Audie's reputation as a powderkeg, Willard stayed clear of him all during that picture.

Audie's stunt-double and personal assistant, Willard Willingham, is seen here around the time he first worked with Audie Murphy. Later he helped the war hero and star prepare for his most daunting role in Graham Greene's pot-boiler. Photo courtesy of Willard Willingham.

"He was pretty strange in those days," said his future friend. "He was difficult for everyone." Despite the fact he was a native Texan, Audie hadn't owned a horse, nor had he ridden one. For one who developed into a superb horseman, he began the initial work "with great difficulty," according to Willard. "I saw that he watched me in my approach to the horse. He was observant and copied me." Willingham had grown up on one of the early "movie" ranches during the silent days, learned to break horses when he was twelve and had early on became a stuntman, or as they called the job: "Selling hide."

Audie's Billy the Kid was nearly a catatonic killing machine, but as one co-star discovered when he worked with the man as Billy: "He just couldn't reveal himself even playing a character." When he was with his gang members, he appeared alone and solitary—truly alienated. Yet, what proved acceptable and taken for granted as a standard western performance belied the fact that Audie was from East Texas. Thus, the quintessential movie cowboy stereotype developed from Audie's sheer willpower. Whether his one-note performance was a sign of bad acting, or deliberate, it made him more frightening in character.

As an interesting contrast, had he lived, James Dean planned to be the next Billy the Kid. The role went, finally, to Paul Newman, but James Dean's quirkiness and Audie's menace were palpable. Though they might seem at the opposite ends of the scale, their kinship presented a perfect example of the road not taken. Both were shorter than average, and both matured in the heartland of America. Of course, too, the differences were glaring: Audie, the totally masculine war hero; Dean, the allegedly bisexual draft dodger. Yet, each could have tapped into the other's film roles. One symbolized a teenage icon of rebellion; the other the staple of American conservatism.

As for the character they had in common, it was the concept of Billy the Kid, not the historical personage. The scarier question was why America, after World War II, cast and acknowledged its greatest war hero as a psychopathic killer. Audie accepted the role, according to McClure, because he had been offered nothing else, and he desperately needed the money.

By the end of April, 1950, his first marriage collapsed in divorce.

Little more than a year had elapsed, and Audie had lunch with Spec McClure on the day the divorce was decreed. "Amazingly unconcerned, even relieved that something had happened to relieve him of the responsibility of marriage," wrote McClure of that day. Audie then proceeded to give away all their furniture, a piece at a time, until their honeymoon abode was empty. Wanda had taken only her personal effects, wanting nothing else. As his career began its rise, Audie tended to "spend his evenings shut up alone in his apartment."

Audie's third unusual casting was in John Huston's adaptation of the Stephen Crane classic, *The Red Badge of Courage*. "Audie read the book, grasping the overall story as well as the most minute details to an amazing degree." One of the few films of which he was finally and still proud at the end of his career, Audie shared the critical judgment that the picture had been slashed and ruined by Metro. The director's intended version remains edited beyond recognition. In an odd turn, Dore Schary was opposed to casting Audie in the lead. "He was in favor of using a Metro contract player or going all out for somebody with the star status of Montgomery Clift." To this suggestion, Huston took his "turn to blow a gasket."

Audie appeared as a cowardly hero in *Red Badge of Courage*, but for a man of action of Audie's status to accept such a role and do it convincingly, must require that he receive some credit for his work. Surely, Huston cajoled an amazing performance out of his "killer." After all, Audie was still a novice to the acting business. In the hands of a great story-teller and film-maker, he gave the audience something they hadn't seen before. Yet, McClure remained stunned by the "dearth of publicity that was coming out on the film." Instead of being a press agent's dream, "nobody wanted to touch the picture with a ten-foot pole."

Hated by Louis B. Mayer, poorly defended by Huston and its producer Dore Schary, the picture was immediately re-cut: shortened from seventy-eight minutes to a skeletal sixty-three. It chopped out of its final release the most powerful scene from the novel–and, most important, for Audie as a fledgling actor. In this extraordinary scene, his Youth discovers a dead body that sits, regal and horrifying, in the beauty of a natural setting, like a king in his court in the clearing in the woods, as the Youth runs from battle in cowardice and from the image of the dead soldier. If one studies at the surviving version, one can briefly see the dead figure far in the distance as Audie races by it. Audie learned how cruel the cutting rooms of Hollywood could be. He blamed the film editing room repeatedly for other devastations to his film work.

One day, a crew member used harsh language at the genteel Murphy. He confronted the intensity of Audie's fury, that deeply hidden monster he had unleashed in his German battles. Ben Cooper who witnessed the episode remarked that: "I saw his eyes blaze. It was the first time I ever saw someone's eyes shoot sparks." After seeing this, Ben vowed never "to ever make him mad at me." A similar response came from another co-star, Jack Elam, who said: "He had a shorter fuse than anybody I've ever known. And he didn't like bullies."

Critic Lillian Ross dubbed Audie something less than heroic in her classic depiction of Hollywood's ruthless and smug producers in her book, *Picture.* She described him as having a "wan smile," inclined to say nothing much. "A slight young man with a freckled face, long, wavy reddish brown hair, and large cool eyes . . ." She reported without comment that he wore high-heeled boots. Her Audie complained of a sunburnt lip and forlornly spent time, "looking sadly out the window."

Ben Cooper noted Audie had "the most narrow and small hands." Adding to this assessment, Audie's occasional co-star Jan Merlin recalled, "Audie's hands had a characteristic I found curious. He displayed an odd curled palm. It was always noticeable to me when we worked, an unconscious habit of his hands which made me wonder at its image of vulnerability, as if he couldn't quite grasp what he was after."

Merlin recommended, "Look at some of his films and you'll see what I mean: an almost soft use of his hands, so strange for a man with his reputation." By this account, Audie presented the image of an ineffectual, near man-child, incapable of any actions, let alone heroism. For all Miss Ross's scathing interpretation, Audie's screen presence struck a chord with movie audiences, even if he (as Ben Cooper felt) "seemed so embarrassed to be doing acting."

By 1951 the solitary star of *The Red Badge of Courage* developed rapidly into a full-fledged movie star, and still a would-be serious actor. As one who observed Audie up close, Cooper decided, "I think he knew he was supposed to play the hero, but he was too uncomfortable to act like a hero. He was certainly aware of what people expected from him." As Ben concluded about his amicable co-worker, "There was nothing matter of fact about Audie Murphy."

Spec McClure also disdained the public image of Audie being "shy." Said McClure: "In reality he was about as shy as a keg of gunpowder with a fuse lit. Most people, particularly talkative ones, bored him. But when he relaxed, his facial muscles and brooding eyes gave a portrait of eternal sadness." All in all, Spec thought Audie "essentially remained a loner." For the most part, though, Audie came across as affable and pleasant, enjoying the camaraderie of acting and always willing to make a small wager with friends on the set. In this he did not often win. As John Huston said later, "He was always unlucky, always. Not unskilled, mind you, just unlucky."

Over the next few years he continued to make westerns of a low caliber for the most part. He didn't like doing love scenes. His films seldom, therefore, called for them. Throughout the Korean War era, he also felt unhappy about the "strange jerking back and forth between make-believe and reality." Audie complained about his discovery that "it's all a game." He hated the Hollywood hype and publicity.

After his divorce from Wanda Hendrix, he told Spec: "From here on out, I'll be the poor man's Howard Hughes." McClure believed the young veteran's life "looked as bleak as ever. Audie didn't care much for reading or socializing. He disliked the company of most people. But he fought loneliness rather than accepting it as part of life."

This dichotomy with acting could not be bridged: "Of course, acting is a game," countered Jan Merlin. "That was his problem. To him, life couldn't be make-believe. He was too reserved to be a true actor; he kept all inside. He wouldn't dare let anyone know what was inside." Veteran character actor Marc Lawrence concurred with this assessment: "The camera chooses what it likes or dislikes. In Murphy there were too many hidden qualities that rarely surfaced." Lawrence believed the refusal to be free with his feelings gave a falseness to some of Audie's performances. To him, there was nothing worse for an actor than to be "caught in a lie" by the camera.

Haunted by all those who did not come back from war, he wondered constantly why he received such adulation. He expressed irritation that he played with "swishy 4Fs" while real soldiers died in real battles. "I don't even like actors," he told Spec. "I don't want to spend time with them." Audie added, "I have seen too many good men die to humble myself before people whom I do not respect." His hatred of Hollywood grew dramatically; many in the film world saw him as a sad person, drifting aimlessly. Not everyone liked Audie.

Some Hollywood stalwarts, like Kirk Douglas, saw him as a "vicious little guy." Tony Curtis also held him in low esteem, citing his dangerous and puerile pranks. After one such incident, during *Kansas Raiders* Curtis never spoke to Audie again. In actuality, the term "actors" to Audie meant those people whose lives centered only on movies, to the exclusion of all else. He tended to accept the company of actors who had service records with the military in the World War.

As for Willingham, he and Audie worked together on four movies in less than two years. "I'd leave him alone and never spoke to him." Finally, one day Audie strolled to where Willard sat between takes. Since there was an empty chair next to his stand-in, Audie sat down and said, "Hello." He did not say another word. They sat next to each other in abject silence for a long time. According to Willingham, "it was the beginning of our friendship." Ten years older than Audie, Willard's cultured manner and eclectic interests soon won Murphy's respect. As they grew accustomed to each other, Audie asked his stunt-double "to evaluate his scripts. He wanted me to read them and tell him what I thought about them."

Audie found evidence that his career, sabotaged by the politics and intrigues of Hollywood, cast itself in unchallenging and stock characterizations in his movies. Ben Cooper who made both *Gunfight at Comanche Creek* and *Arizona Raiders* with Audie believed, "He always looked as if he'd rather be somewhere else." He didn't play their games, and he suffered for it. Audie himself assessed the problem, "No

65

one at Universal International cared if I got any good or not, as long as my films made money. I didn't hide that I had no acting talent and told directors that. They knew it. But they didn't help me. They used me until I was used up. I only got to make three films with quality people, and these were the only ones that got quality acting out of me. They are the only things I've done in Hollywood that I am proud of."

As another associate put it, "His acting didn't change over the years. What changed was his level of confidence. He was more aware of having star billing." As a result of this, he might dig in his heels when he wanted to play a scene a certain way. "He became more and more stubborn about doing it his way. He knew when something wasn't right for him and refused to do anything he thought would make him look like a fool."

As far as Jack Elam was concerned, "There was no change in him. Not even the slightest, from before he'd ever done pictures, before he became a star. Not even the tiniest change in his personality. Because he was what he was. He was Audie Murphy."

Audie Murphy and Associate Producer Vinh Noan during a break in filming The Quiet American. Photo courtesy of Vinh Noan.

Throughout the early 1950s many producers feared taking a chance on Audie. "A vicious rumor had got around town that Audie was a killer," revealed McClure–and the meaning of that phrase was not metaphoric. "And that number of men he had slain in the war reached a ridiculous figure in the report." Looked upon as the reincarnation of the character he had played with chilling accuracy, Billy the Kid, directors balked at working with him.

"What director would want to tell Billy the Kid what do to?" asked McClure. One of the great directors of Hollywood was not afraid of Audie, and Ernest Lubitsch wanted to use him. The Lubitsch Touch was a well-known phrase, a kind of movie Midas. If only that luck had rubbed off onto Audie. Unfortunately, again, the spectre of death took a hand in Audie's life. Lubitsch's sudden death closed that avenue. Producers simply repeated the refrain: "The Kid's too nervous." And, he made other film people nervous.

Despite his solitary nature and disdain for the concept of marriage, Audie married a second time, four days after his divorce decree, to Pamela Archer, a girl from Texas. However, their honeymoon didn't last long, despite the many tabloid essays to the contrary. Marriage burdened him. With his second wife, Pam and, in a few years, two adorable little boys, as well as a modest house, it was a time for him to be a "colossal success." In a haywire state, he spread himself in many directions: to make money, to create an artistic identity, to be an American patriot, and to be finally a complete and whole man to his family and friends. His family deserved it, but he believed his road to success ran though Vietnam by way of Graham Greene's map to trouble. Before long, he took up living separately from his wife and children. Audie partitioned himself in his home, moving into an in-law apartment within his own residence. One of the problems Elam succinctly and diplomatically emphasized: "Audie liked girls. I mean he really liked girls."

McClure believed Audie actually liked his westerns, but finally wished for more. If Audie Murphy found a consistency in his movies, it eventually bored him. By the mid-1950s he hoped to escape the usual oater hero parts, by playing variations on those stock roles. He sought comedy, villains, or contemporary stories, to prove his versatility.

Professor John Lenihan, in his assessment of the movie heroism of Audie, labeled the new approach an attraction to the Caspar Milquetoast character. Certainly Universal-International Studios was responsible, but to some extent during these years Audie too had a choice in his film roles. The reference was to a comic strip character who epitomized the timid, recessive, reluctant, small, ineffectual man. Audie played the Milquetoast as a variation on "Clark Kent": a mild-mannered, low-key individual for whom no one has initial respect, but who can burst into Superman at any moment.

This cycle of odd characters arose with *Destry,* a remake of the successful James Stewart/Marlene Dietrich film of fifteen years earlier. Carrying a parasol for a lady and wearing no gun, he was ripe for the snide verbal attacks of the movie's villains until he displayed his mettle and embodied all the Cardinal Virtues. Yet, the movie's worst quality was its lack of originality.

Producers showed some hubris by re-making a Western classic with another actor's definitive portrait (James Stewart in 1940). Murphy followed this movie with additional copycat films like *Walk the Proud Land,* a variation on James Stewart's *Broken Arrow.* Again, Audie played a mild and non-violent man, but suffered the comparisons to the laconic and likable Stewart. No matter what role he played, Audie revealed an edginess under the ease. His work in "comedies" like *Joe Butterfly* failed again for the pale photocopy style it took from *Teahouse of the August Moon.* Someone at Universal-International decided Audie was the key player in low-budget versions of other studios' opus productions.

If Audie had a way of revealing his attitude toward these poor pictures, it was that "he never kept a clipping about himself," observed McClure. Audie's attempts at depicting the unsympathetic characters proved far more successful in capturing his duality of good and bad. As James Stewart's bad, younger brother, resplendent in a black leather vest, in *Night Passage,* Audie held his own with a cast of wily scene-stealers. His variation on Ingmar Bergman's *Seventh Seal* took place in *No Name on the Bullet,* in which "the kid" is Death come to take one of the town's hypocrites. Of course, Huston cast him as the racist brother in *The Unforgiven*, showing off Audie's passion and zest about life in less than desirable fashion. Audie's bigot also happened to be a man destroyed psychically by witnessing horrible violence in his life.

This period convinced him that, to avoid typecasting and to win respectability, he must associate himself with classic literary properties. Audie announced he wanted to perform in adaptations of Dostoyevsky or Ibsen, which only served to make him an industry joke. Of the producer who sued him for selecting inappropriate character roles for the putative purpose of breaking his contract, Murphy complained: "I resent Mr. (Harry Joe) Brown's attempt to dictate my future in the industry." Yet, he showed bad judgment in the selection of the literary works he did finally film: *The Gun Runners*, like so many of his films, was a remake—and one that did not bring anything new or respectable to the story. Ernest Hemingway, never overly fond of movie versions of his novels, found this one among the most insipid of his stories done on screen.

If scholar John Lenihan asked the question: "why did Hollywood not exploit Murphy's war heroism with stories and characterizations ... ," the answer clearly lay in Audie's attitude. Yes, he was a standard contract player for a lesser studio and others decided for him what was appropriate, but Audie by the mid-1950s was tiring of the film roles the studio handed to him. With the advice of "literary" friends like McClure and Willingham, he felt confident to express his opinion on scripts. When he played himself in *To Hell and Back*, he exploded into a box-office sensation.

But *To Hell and Back* disappointed Audie for its falseness about death, lacking blood and horror, treating the killing of Audie's friends with a happy-go-lucky music score. He deplored the changes in death scenes from the corny truth to something inanely machismo. The life blood of the movie was anemic as well. Audie fought over the salty language being omitted. To the real soldier, celluloid heroes in pressed clean uniforms and smudges of "Fuller's Earth" on their faces, that dark powdery make-up used by actors to simulate dirty faces, showed phony bravado and false hearts, maligning the heroism of his fallen comrades.

69

Over the next few years he made a series of westerns and war movies. What Nazi soldiers encountered on the battlefield was still present in Hollywood in the person of Audie Murphy. Ben Cooper related that the movie version of his life couldn't portray the true bravery of his actions–because it appeared like mere motion picture hyperbole. "He ran directly into a machine gun nest, which would look phony on screen."

As for Audie's motion picture career, in the movies that followed he worked successfully as himself. Yet, the opinion lingered: "He was far better than most and should have received more credit," remarked one co-star. Personal foibles created a strain which dulled his sharpness in some respects, but not when doing a movie. Willard Willingham believed Audie was "brilliant, but eccentric." In his friend's eyes, Audie "had charm. He really had it." It was one of the keys to his personality. "He was always in total control. He was always aware of his surroundings, what was on his left, his right, or behind him." He had survival skills galore and needed them more and more in Hollywood. Ben Cooper said, "The trouble in Hollywood for Audie or any actor is you never know who your enemies are."

Yet, Audie had no basic theatrical foundation. "He didn't know the mechanics of acting. For instance," said veteran actor Merlin, "He couldn't discuss technique at all. He didn't consult with his director about his character's motivation. All he knew was how he felt. If a scene or line didn't ring true for him, he'd argue. His best performances came only when he trusted the director to stop him when he was wrong."

Another professional movie actor claimed that: "Audie could learn the lines and hit his marks. Anything else about acting was a mystery to him. But, untrained people like Audie can become quite expert as film actors, but they just die once you put them into a live show or stage play. In movies you only have to learn the lines for the next day's shoot on the night before, usually a scene or two. It's nothing like learning an entire role at once and having to perform it without stop at one session."

Despite personal worries, Audie always knew his long term Universal-International contract for two movies per year through 1964 remained in effect. Though he wanted out of the deal by the end of 1957, within a few years he'd feel grateful to have the coverage. His two major movies of 1955 did more than anything else to secure him, but his box-office reign would be short.

Audie used to say he knew his popularity just from his fan letters. He believed in his heart that he was a special symbol to the youth of America. It may have been true in 1956, but certainly it was not a mere decade later. He couldn't know how dark the future would become. The reputation he never capitalized upon finally deserted him. Murdered in Saigon was his screen character's fate in the Mankiewicz movie; Audie never fully realized how his fortunes started to mirror Art.

Then, of course, there was the enticement of being *The Quiet American*. In fact, despite the strong urgings of Willingham, at first he shied away from the chance. Of all he did in his fertile days of the 1950s, this showed the most originality, the most daring, and proved most different from whatever he had done previously. In no way did the proposed Mankiewicz film mirror the tired retreads of his Universal-International years. Audie was comfortable in his effortless westerns, and though he yearned for better, the idea of going to Vietnam did not grab him as irresistible.

Though Audie never wanted to be the poster boy for jingoism, *The Quiet American* addressed that issue head-on. Irony underscored every detail of the character in Greene's novel. In the film, the hapless American character was patriotic, but a dupe; he was heroic, saving the life of a man who would kill him; he was doomed, unable to escape communist assassins. He was an all-American "movie marine" type, who contrasted badly with a worldly British elitist.

As for Audie, he had always been revered by more people in Germany or Japan than in the United States, said Ben Cooper. "People from those places always tell me how lucky I was to work with him." Now, he acted out a character not so heroic. "And his biggest fans were in Japan and Germany."

Audie's biggest mistakes were always in being too candid, too upfront, with those who ran the town of Hollywood. To listen to him you'd never believe this glamour Mecca was merely a game of bluff, Gomorrah-style. In retrospect of forty years–his sobering anxieties, for the 1950s were the years when his talent was freshest and when, as an actor, he tried his best before the audiences in blackened movie halls.

Years after the experience, Ben Cooper still waxes eloquent: "He was so easy to work with. He listened. That's the secret of his acting. If you listen well, you must be able to deliver the next line convincingly." Learning from the best character actors, he starred in a series of roles in which he matched wits with a friendly villain. These characters could be played by Walter Matthau or Darren McGavin, Vic Morrow or Barry Sullivan.

Many fans admired his simple, good old-fashioned westerns; nothing less was contestable. Some objected to Audie going "arty." He had pushed the limits of his audience. The Boy Scout hero of World War II had usually been cast as "the Kid," a reprobate anti-hero in half his movies, the bad brother, the wayward boy, the psycho Western villain of mythology (Billy and Jesse among others). No ingenious theories account for Audie's success in these different westerns that Randolph Scott, on no account, would play.

Industry insiders acknowledged an old Hollywood law that, if a particular goal was desired, one had to adopt a logical and diabolical ruthlessness. His own limited success served Audie well so far as he took it. For a man lacking training, with a voice that fell short of the heavy macho basso of a John Wayne, for a man with the size and frame of an adolescent, with the looks of a choirboy, he had parlayed these deficits into assets. Audie needn't brag about success. He learned in battle that it was just dumb luck. He had no fear the string of luck could end with *The Quiet American*. It couldn't occur to him that those "inadequacies" of being an amateur actor–cited by Graham Greene for years thereafter–might have held him hostage.

Audie's hatred of Hollywood grew by leaps at Universal International, each film done there convincing him that he made an easy living effortlessly, while he yearned to work hard and create something genuine. By the time he played himself in the film version of *To Hell and*

Back, his life was in upheaval. His gambling habit reached the point that he could drop $5000 at the racetrack in one day. He indulged this habit from the days he first arrived in Hollywood. Actor Jack Elam first made his acquaintance, not at a studio or doing a film, but met Audie because "we had the same bookie."

Reports circulated that he'd drive around Texas, finding himself in roadside fistfights. Spending time at gyms working out, he had a penchant for the friendship of boxers. He compartmentalized his life and friends: wranglers, starlets, boxers, soldiers, congressmen, and executives. All befriended him. Yet, he remained aloof. "He was somebody I wanted to know better," said Ben Cooper, "but, back then, I wasn't mature enough to know how to do it."

Few of Audie's acquaintances knew his other friends in other professions. All knew that under stress he suffered from dyspepsia and nose bleeds. His stomach was always sensitive; he called it a "trick stomach." McClure explained Audie first would exhibit a grimace, "followed by a clutching of his abdomen with his hands, and bending double. This would often happen in the middle of a meal."

More often than not, those who met him were singularly unimpressed. He sometimes detonated like a hand grenade. At other times he found himself accused of being callous with his practical jokes. As the epitome of the returning veteran of World War II, he suffered by comparison and fell short of expectation. "He's not macho at all," or "He's a pip-squeak" were standard comments.

Well past forty years of age, Audie still portrayed the "kid" in many movies. Later in his career, he complained he "kidded his way through the West." He was either the Cimarron Kid, the Silver Kid, the Utica Kid, or Billy the Kid. If he wasn't the Kid, someone called him kid. If they didn't call him kid, he answers to names such as the "Youth" as in *Red Badge of Courage*. On his television show, *Whispering Smith*, produced and written for the most part by Willard Willingham, the villains scoffed and asked him if he shaved yet. He was 35. In the Graham Greene novel, he played an adult whom others dubbed, repeatedly, "a young American," and even re-emphasized by the police inspector, "a highly young American." If Audie were to play these stereotypes, he played them against the grain of the stock character.

Jan Merlin, also a veteran of the World War and an astute observer of the Hollywood scene, recalled: "I did an episode of *Whispering Smith* television series called 'The Blind Gun' with Audie, the premiere episode, I believe. We also acted together in two movies (*Hellbent for Leather* and *Gunfight at Comanche Creek*). My first meeting with Audie Murphy went so well that he asked me to do other films with him. Jan continued, "He wasn't an actor and tried his best to do an honest job of it. but an audience would have been very disappointed to discover he couldn't be Errol Flynn on screen. He was a helluva nice guy. Neither of us ever talked about the War, his with the Germans, nor mine with the Japanese. I think Audie actually hated the concentration on his war history . . . one of the reasons we got along so well was that we never mentioned those things at all in any of our conversations."

Most of the women co-stars were actresses one never saw again in a movie. As far as his leading ladies in his western movies, there was Sandra Dee, Gia Scala, Barbara Rush, Susan Cabot, Joanne Dru, and his agent's daughter, Susan Kohner. Cast in so many movies of the era, they were in Audie's movies too. In this way, *The Quiet American* stereotyped him like all the others; they paired him with a novice actress, one whose timidity and gentleness suited him and whose screen presence might not be too threatening. Her name was Giorgia Moll. Thrown together, they exemplified a perfect match, likely to fall in love and find safety with the other. Their pairing made them seem like forsaken and lost children in a sinister world.

One of the other key elements of Audie's life would be dogs. He loved hunting dogs, in particular. Only in one movie–*No Name on the Bullet*–does a dog bark menacingly at Audie (well, he is a dubious hero in this picture). Usually, the mutt rides, tossed over the saddle, together with the actor. In real life, Audie had a Weimaraner, a gift from John Huston. At least, that was the official story.

According to McClure, Audie stole the dog from the Huston ranch during filming of *Red Badge of Courage*. Audie had a history of bad dog affairs, losing animals to disease, neighbor complaints, and his failure to discipline the animals. Most amusing dog in any Audie movie was the Boxer named Duke in *The Quiet American*. This one's script name had to bring a smile to Murphy: after all, his arch-rival in westerns and war movies was the man whose nickname was Duke, none other than John Wayne himself.

No record exists of these two legendary figures meeting each other–the real hero and the reel hero. Actor Marc Lawrence noted how strange he found in that the "real hero doesn't come up to the off-screen accomplishments, while Duke Wayne, who never participated in military service, has the distinction of owning the designated signature of the American heroic figure."

The distance they maintained from each other spoke volumes. As if to illustrate their careful disdain for one another, many believed John Wayne resisted much pressure to cast Audie Murphy in his epic western tribute, *The Alamo*. Many Texans, in particular, were miffed at Duke Wayne for by-passing Murphy and putting the British fop, Laurence Harvey, into the seminal third lead at Lieutenant Travis, a native Texan hero. If Audie had feelings about this injustice, he never spoke publicly about them.

Marc Lawrence worked with both men. As the seminal villain in both gangster films and westerns (*Key Largo*, 1948, and *Ox-Bow Incident*, 1943), Lawrence shared the screen with John Wayne just as he made the bid for superstardom, expanding his acting repertoire from the field of Westerns. Their picture together was *Shepherd of the Hills*, a tale set in the back hills of the Ozarks with feuds and other hostilities within families.

Lawrence recalled, "Duke was coached by great character actor Paul Fix for ten or twenty years–pointing out the secret of acting." What Lawrence detected as the key difference between Audie and the Duke was "knowing what you're doing. You can't act if you don't know what you're doing. As we all know, Duke caught on and became the giant star he remained for many years."

Audie didn't make quite the same impression on Lawrence, though he freely admitted that the reason had more to do with the long, drawn out production of a movie (with Wayne) versus the short, chaotic few days on a television show in the 1950s (with Murphy) provided. A guest villain on Audie's television show, *Whispering Smith,* Lawrence did have strong opinions: "Murphy was a sky high schoolish personality that never graduated. The camera failed to give him the dignity he commanded in real life."

The irony of Duke Wayne's success on screen and his transition to non-western roles, contrasting with Audie's inability to do so, struck a chord with Marc Lawrence. "I don't know if Audie ever took acting lessons—and if he did—his screen appearances never grew as it did with Wayne." As Ronald Davis stated in his biography of John Wayne, Duke, the box office king of the westerns and war movies, saw himself as the "symbolic equivalent" of Audie Murphy.

Audie regularly played a sheriff, marshal, or ranger. He always represented the government, whether overtly or in secret. If he was in the army, he limned the role a captain or lieutenant. As a result, he brought with him to each role the connotation that he worked for the government, officially as a rule, sometimes on his own. In *The Quiet American,* he left the feeling that he did represent the United States foreign policy of the age, no matter what the Mankiewicz script said.

The unsuccessful pictures of Audie featured him in completely uncharacteristic roles. Twice he played privates. He performed in *Red Badge of Courage* as a cowardly soldier. In *Joe Butterfly* he played a shirker. Those roles were too ridiculous for his fans to believe; so, those films were box-office disasters, to no one's surprise. If he were to be a salesman for plastic toys in *The Quiet American,* not the renegade freedom fighter selling plastique as a tool against the Communists, he bordered on violating the audience's belief in his symbolic value as a government representative or as the rugged individualist citizen-soldier of American lore.

By consistently playing a man of law and order, his roles showed little variety. No wonder too he always claimed his films were so similar; he joked they only changed the horses. Often, he told variations on his self-deprecating image. One of his favorite devices to disarm directors and critics was the chestnut that he was operating under a handicap–

"no talent." This, amusing as it may be, was simply untrue. His talent, unexplored and misused, had few worthy outlets during his career.

In *The Quiet American,* his character allegedly is a covert agent of the U.S. government—as much a symbol as a sheriff or marshal in any western movie. As a poster model for the United States military, Audie made no secret of his patriotism in real life. It made all the more real the possibility, denied throughout the script, that Audie was the agent of his government. It was his symbolic value, not his acting, that probably won him the best role of his career in his most intellectual movie.

The controversy over Greene's story centered upon the de-fanging of this quiet American agent. The character nearly admitted his involvement in covert activities when he told Fowler that his government had called him home. This, of course, would not have been the likelihood had the young American merely visited Vietnam privately as a humanitarian citizen.

If a web had been spun to ensnare Audie in a quality picture, the offer of *The Quiet American* exemplified the spider's trap. He was hooked by unequivocal urgings of his two associates, McClure and Willingham. Once signed and committed, he learned his co-star would not be Laurence Olivier, but rather the equally elite stage actor, Michael Redgrave.

No matter to Audie: available, eager, hopeful, he'd go to Vietnam without hesitation if he might win that long-sought industry respect. Additionally, location work would take him from California and his squabbles at home. He was in need of an extensive respite. For all the pretense of artistic motives by the Figaro people, the choice of Audie boiled down to his box-office appeal and marquee name. With the ballyhoo around his potential film with Mankiewicz, Audie seemed hopeful his saddle-hopping days were now behind him.

4

MANKIEWICZ PURCHASED THE rights to Graham Greene's literary masterpiece, *The Quiet American*, for his production troupe in the late summer of 1956; Figaro vice president Mike Mindlin labeled this decision the beginning of two years of "self-destruction" in the life of the great film-maker. More than a few industry insiders thought the idea of making a movie out of Greene's controversial and anti-American novella was ill-advised.

Board members of Figaro, Incorporated, however ambivalent about the story, all firmly believed in the brilliance of Joe Mankiewicz. If anyone could produce artistic success, it was Joe. His producers did not mind artistic success as long as it didn't impede box-office receipts.

Robby Lantz remembered that Mankiewicz, "at one point may have even consulted with Greene about a script on the novel. Joe had great respect for writers." The man in charge of publicity, Mike Mindlin, also recalled during an interview that he had "a dim memory of such a meeting, but I could not tell you where or when it occurred." In all likelihood, it happened during the negotiation process for purchase of the film rights.

Joe's closest aide, Elaine Schreyeck concurs, stating that "it is more than likely" that both men met during negotiations over the film rights. After that, the rancor between the two made a consultation, or a civil word, unlikely. Mankiewicz and Greene's differences over the tale of *The Quiet American* resulted in stormy and hostile relations between them for the next thirty years, the remainder of their lives. Rumor also stated that Greene put a provision into his Last Will and Testament to purchase all copies of the film in order to destroy them.

Graham Greene was, arguably, the foremost living British novelist of his day–who occasionally wrote film treatments, notably Carol Reed's *The Third Man* (which starred Orson Welles). Having a keen interest in movies, he often "slummed" as a film critic. Greene's participation in the movie version of his novel would be negligible since Mankiewicz wrote his own scripts. Greene was simply unnecessary to the film Mankiewicz envisioned. Nowhere in the pressbook of *The Quiet American* was Greene noted–except for an obligatory "based on a novel by . . ."

That omission symbolized how unquiet the movie set would be– and how disquieting would be the results of filming. Had Mankiewicz told Audie Murphy, as he told others, "I can't produce blockbusters. I don't want to make safe, ordinary little pictures . . ." then Audie would have been advised he had met his Mephistopheles.

The British novelist owning the property known as Greene-Land was both condescending and ethnocentric. The biting irony of titling his collective literature "Greene-Land", paralleled the sly joke perpetrated by Leif Erickson a thousand years ago when, having discovered an ice-encrusted land, he named it Greenland to entice settlement. Like the geographical place, the British writer's *milieu* of the imagination was also a barren, de-valued place in philosophical terms. Cruel, terrible actions combined with the incongruous motivations of desperate characters. Their intelligence or sensitivity never helped overcome their fate.

The world of Graham Greene often epitomized black comedy–but laughs were hard to find. The most humorless inhabitant of this *milieu* was Greene himself. Yet, Greene's writing often seduced Hollywood with the Anglophile notion that somehow it was truer art than home-grown American novels.

Though Greene claimed to write with the eye of a movie director, following his characters like a cameraman, he could also say: "My books don't make good films. Film companies think they will, but they don't." His primary example of this for the twenty years after *The Quiet American*'s production was the Mankiewicz version. Invariably, supporters of Greene called the movie "deliberately adulterated."

Always willing to encourage the savaging of the film, the author wrote: "The most extreme changes I have seen in any book of mine were in *The Quiet American* . . . but the book was based on a closer knowledge of the Indo-China war than the American director possessed . . . Again, why should one complain? He (Mankiewicz) has enabled me to go on writing." It was a begrudging admittance of gratitude to the cinema. As late as 1980, Greene referred to the "treachery" of Joseph L. Mankiewicz.

He explained, in some interviews, that he felt totally surprised by the changes made when his novel became a screenplay." . . . the story was completely reversed. Instead of being a story with Communist sympathies, the story of an Englishman followed a dupe of the Communists, and the girl at the end of the story goes off nobly in a kind of Girl Guide fashion to fight for President Diem.

America at that time not having decided to have President Diem assassinated." Such distortions of the scenario by the author raised the possibility that Greene had not seen the movie. He candidly admitted how much he disliked America and Americans; it had nothing to do with the version of *The Quiet American*. "I think my anti-Americanism can be traced right back into the thirties, you know. A long, long time."

One of Joe Mankiewicz's sons later offered a new theory that some changes in the script were payable to the cooperation of the United States State Department. Secretary of State under President Dwight Eisenhower was John Foster Dulles–who was a Princeton graduate, and reputedly had discovered a student at Princeton who later became President of Vietnam: Ngo Dinh Diem. As a consequence, suggestions changing Harvard to Princeton developed when the fact emerged that Diem was a graduate of the New Jersey Ivy League school. This is yet another variation on the script alterations, yet on a minor point.

When Eric Pleskow who produced *Mississippi Burning* and *Silence of the Lambs* answered questions about authors disliking the film versions of their works, he dismissed the breed. "A writer is never happy unless he writes the screenplay himself. They seldom realize there is a big difference between written words and film, from the train of thoughts in the story and on and on." This experience, he said, frequently happened and often angered producers and directors, himself included, but it was part of the territory of film-making.

Pleskow recalled one of his films having suffered a condemnation before it finished production. (*Mississippi Burning* suffered a serious critique from Mrs. Martin Luther King.) As far as Mankiewicz having written the script of the film, he admitted in an interview that "Joe was no slouch," showing decades later another strong support for and total faith in the Mankiewicz mystique that was typical of the Board of Figaro, Incorporated.

Giorgia Moll offered a kind and sympathetic consideration for Graham Greene's mean-spirited attitude: "A writer is jealous of his creation," she attempted to explain the hostility of the British author. "Normally a writer imagines something different than what finally goes up on the screen. So, of course, he is disappointed." Greene certainly did not reciprocate her compassion.

Indeed, the only film versions of his novels that Greene truly detested came from American studios, directed by Americans (often the "great" American directors). He cited how much he disliked John Ford's version of *The Power and the Glory*, which he called "intolerable." The second director he attacked was George Cukor who did *Travels with My Aunt.* He admitted seeing five minutes of the picture on television, and "I turned it off." Saving his most savage assessment for Mankiewicz, he blamed the auteur for debasing his novel and making "it into a propaganda film for America in Vietnam, when it had been an attack on the American influences in Vietnam."

Seeing a large pot of money in American movies, Greene sold the rights of the novel outright to Figaro, Inc., the Mankiewicz production company. Julian Smith, in his highly political book, its tone closely tied to the anti-war movement of the age, indicted Mankiewicz in *Looking Back: Hollywood and Vietnam.* The author accused Mankiewicz of having "a cold war rule-book" and buying the novel's rights to undo Greene's damaging views on America.

The director "plunked down sixty-five thousand dollars for the privilege of correcting Greene's calumnies on the screen." He charged Mankiewicz with writing a script that was "full of people who take their identity from the West . . . and did not create a single important Viet-namese who is not defined through his or her relationship to Ameri-cans or (in the case of heavies) by a scriptwriter's notion of how a confirmed Marxist sounds."

Before the film director had embarked on a script of the book, Greene insisted Mankiewicz intended to misrepresent the author's mes-sage: "I don't suppose they can film it in the way it is written. They'll probably make it so that it looks as if the American was being bam-boozled all the time by the Communists or somebody."

The troubles started when Mankiewicz and his crew arrived in Saigon on the first week of January, 1957. One London correspondent for *The Times* claimed: "Some commentators are mildly shocked that Mr. Greene should permit this travesty of his work, others are saying it serves him right for writing such an anti-American book."

Greene was in New York City at the end of January and responded to the early reports from Saigon by showing his resignation to being trashed by Mankiewicz: "When you sell a book to Hollywood, you sell it outright. The long Hollywood contracts—sheet after closely printed sheet as long as the first treatment of the novel which is for sale—ensure that you have no 'author's rights'. The film producer can alter anything . . . if he wishes. He need not even retain your title, though that is usually almost the only thing he wishes to retain."

Still in a furious state of mind, Greene then penned a scathing letter to the London *Times,* reinforcing his righteous anger." . . . perhaps a Machiavellian policy is justified—one can trust Hollywood to overbid its hand . . . ". Of the purported alterations to his book, Greene concluded, "they will make only the more obvious the discrepancy between what the State Department would like the world to believe and what in fact happened in Vietnam. In that case, I can imagine some happy evenings of laughter not only in Paris, but in the cinemas of Saigon."

By the Ides of March, 1957, Greene resorted to using derisive ridicule in his attacks on the film. He wrote to *Time* magazine: "Why do American moviemen require pith helmets, salt tablets, quinine pills to visit the Cao Dai capital, Tayninh. The climate is somewhat similar to a Washington summer. Perhaps the inhabitants were mystified by their strange attire and eccentric diet." To some extent Greene was correct. American tourists of the day from Nairobi to Cairo often turned into objects of ridicule for their "safari" attire. Mike Mindlin, in fact, brought such a jacket to Vietnam, a gift from friends.

According to Graham Greene expert A.A.DeVitas, the novella fictionalized a true incident of terrorism in Saigon in 1952 at Place Grenier by the Viet Minh, and created a story about existential values and ethical dilemmas. No character was completely without guilt; the story hardly met the definition of a political treatise. Greene's irony and satiric delineations blurred the meaning of good and evil. With an American do-gooder named Pyle, considered a fool by some (apparently the author too), the British protagonist (Fowler) hardly compared favorably to the term "hero". Fowler was foul, a ruthless, atheistic, and morally bankrupt man who betrayed the American because he wooed and won the love of the British reporter's Vietnamese girlfriend.

How was the story anti-American in the days of the 1950s? In essence, the American was a dupe or forerunner of his government, involving himself in arms and political machinations. This bad behavior contrasted with the good "objective" nature of a British man with no values, and the French who have colonized and exploited the people, and the Communists who terrorized innocents.

None of these characters or larger forces allowed the Vietnamese to have individual choice and freedom. Why then was the American worse than the others? The novel hardly gave a firm answer. Its most un-American quality apparently rose out of the suggestion that the American character stuck his nose where it did not belong. He paid a price with his life.

Alden Pyle was the American: a Harvard educated fool who was silly, young, exceedingly eager to become involved in political intrigue, idealistic, and full of life at age thirty-two. In a Graham Greene world, this indicated stupidity. "He had no more notion than any of you what the whole affair's about. . . . He never saw anything he hadn't heard in a lecture hall, and his writers and his lecturers made a fool of him. When he saw a dead body he couldn't even see the wounds." Greene went on to say this character was "a dumb leper who has lost his bell, wandering the world, meaning no harm."

The Asian woman, Phuong, saw these qualities as charming, especially compared to her staid and effete British boyfriend Fowler. Older and dissipated, he was without allegiance, values, or expression. Yet, he was the ostensible hero of the tale. He avoided all entanglements and commitments, but expressed rage when his girlfriend ended their half-hearted commitment.

Consequently, he blamed Pyle for selling munitions that led to the death of innocent children during a terrorist attack, though Fowler's motives were muddy. Perhaps he simply resented the man who stole his girlfriend. He had some complicity in the assassination of Pyle who dies, not of his knife wounds, but from falling into a riverbank puddle and drowning. With no one to whom to ask forgiveness, he returned to the Vietnamese girl who had no other option but to take him back. We presumed she played at subservience, as colonized victims often do.

Phuong made no separation between Westerners–French or English, they were the colonial bosses. Since she spoke French as her first language, with Fowler, Greene may have concluded this was the native language of Vietnam. If anything betrayed the Greene colonial attitude, it was a detail like this. Yet, the most obvious examples of Greene's problematic attitude were thrust upon and blamed on Joseph Mankiewicz by many critics of the movie, including Julian Smith's book. The American director borrowed this detail directly from Greene and his novel.

When Mankiewicz authorized his pressbook plot summary, he boiled the story down to fewer details: The story began in 1952 where the murdered young American floated, face down, in the river. Seemingly a police investigation story, the Inspector suspected British journalist Fowler of some complicity in the crime. In flashback, the audience learned the American had political involvement with a mysterious "third force" to win freedom for the Vietnamese. He had fallen in love with Phuong, Fowler's girlfriend. Fowler fingered the American for communist attack. In the denouement, the Inspector indicated that Fowler was the real dupe, having been used by the Communists. Alone, friendless, his lack of values gnawing at him, Fowler epitomized alienation; his girlfriend dismissed him.

The few liberties Mankiewicz took with the story enraged Graham Greene. A quondam film critic, he unleashed a series of scathing comments about Mankiewicz having ruined the novel. The chant, unchallenged by those who probably never read the book, repeated the ridiculous claims. Among the notable was critic Pauline Kael, not one easily fooled. She called the changes at the end "offending compromises of the final reel."

Apparently, her view–shared by the Greene–was that the Vietnamese woman, a victim on all sides, should resume a subservient role and continue a relationship with a man she despises. In no serious fashion could that improve the film other than to underscore the victimized role of being a colonial of the French and British. It appeared to be the call of an elitist who believed in caste systems. No lesser or inferior being could express independence. If this was Greene's message, then Mankiewicz's democratic perceptions required he modify the ending. But, this change only altered human motivation, not the political meaning of the story, unless one was saddened to see the "happy days" of colonialism end for England and France.

Greene had served as a reporter in Vietnam. Like Fowler, Greene ought not to be called a journalist. Pretending objectivity, Greene expressed strong feelings on the political situation there, taking umbrage at United States economic aid. He wrote for the *New Republic* that "when a gift is permanently stamped with the name of the donor," it undercut the gratitude of the Vietnamese "peasants." Such conclusions hardly typified objectivity: The Vietnamese peasant hardly read English, or his own language. By calling these people "peasants" he displayed his elitist and condescending sense of value; Greene expressed the essence of *noblesse oblige*.

Whatever name appeared on a gift cannot possibly diminish its use or value, unless the recipient was vain and proud, a deadly sin in any moralist's worldview. In another scene, *The Quiet American* offered a pack of cigarettes to Fowler, who scoffed: "I asked for one cigarette, not economic aid." Not in the book, this example disturbed Greene devotee, and defender, Rev. Gene Phillips greatly, in his supportive book on the British author, entitled *Graham Greene: His Fiction into Film*, because th dialogue was symptomatic of how Mankiewicz slanted the audience's sympathies to the American.

Rev. Phillips apparently decided Fowler's habit of adultery (he has taken a marriage vow with a Roman Catholic woman) and begging his spouse to violate her religion by divorcing him (and lying to his Vietnamese girlfriend about his marriage and his job) did NOT slant the audience's feelings. Since Fowler also had complicity in murder (for whatever reason), one may wonder why a Jesuit priest overlooked these monumental violations of the Ten Commandments. The audience reacted to Fowler's objective and outright dishonesty, and their dislike of Fowler had nothing to do with slanting the goodness of the American.

Other changes were equally trivial in terms of the larger meaning of the story, yet raised the hackles of some temperamental types ancillary to the film. Mankiewicz felt Greene didn't comprehend the American earnestness and desire to help oppressed people. So, he softened the political views of Pyle. He removed the offending name. The publicity machine ran with the idea that the American "hero" was a nameless figure, just another typical everyman. Americans, in this picture and in Mankiewicz's view, were objects of violence and assassination on one side, and deportation on the other. The American cannot win, he seemed to say. When Greene protested, it became clear that no one took the American's side—except other Americans.

In Greene's world, the British journalist and the French police inspector, both symbols of their nations' exploiting colonialism, were somehow superior to the well-meaning American whose only motive was to help people achieve freedom. Vinh Noan argued to his countrymen frequently that Americans wanted only democracy for their land, unlike the French or British colonials. "Once democracy is established in a country, America withdraws and the nation thrives. Look at Japan and the Philippines." Not seeing this, nor accepting it, Mr. Greene maintained a resentful and defensive perspective in his story—and for the remainder of his life.

Julian Smith, in less than scholarly fashion, used his book to become another in a long line of Greene apologists and Mankiewicz bashers. Smith believed the Greene novel rightfully depicted Americans as "pompous or foolish." He chastised Mankiewicz for allowing Bruce Cabot to depict Granger as a sober observer, apparently missing the fact that Cabot's scenes occurred mostly in bars. Smith may be correct that the Americans appeared sanctimonious in the screenplay, but Smith also ignored the fact that the French and British represented rampant colonialism. Then, again, Greene also avoided this point.

Another oddity differing from Greene in the picture was the change of Pyle's educational background from Harvard to Princeton. In some instances, stinging blame stuck to Murphy for this alteration of the text–owing to claims that Audie could not pass as an Ivy League Harvard man. In fact, Murphy was completely innocent of the changed name of the alma mater. After all, Princeton is just as Ivy League as Harvard, though not as pompous (Greene's reason for the choice).

The President of Vietnam was a Harvard graduate. He was the one who protested the naming of the college in the film. Of course, Mankiewicz gave as good as he got. When protesters in his film carried a few placards that demanded the downfall of the Vietnamese government, Mankiewicz refused to cut the scene–much to the chagrin of the Vietnamese President.

In another instance guaranteed to upset Graham Greene, Mankiewicz had Fowler, in character, dismiss using the poetry used in the novel as "cheap melodrama" in the climax. One can imagine that Mr. Greene took umbrage at the rejection of his selection of poetry–which epitomized pedantic rationalization at best. The substitution picked by the director better suited the situation: Mankiewicz chose lines from Shakespeare's *Othello*–a man duped, tricked, and coerced into the murder of his innocent wife. Perhaps Greene's fury increased because Audie Murphy's nameless character, a boob of an American, immediately recognized the passage–though he was not smart enough to understand the aptness of its selection! It was a speech given by Iago, known for his treachery.

> *"Though I perchance am vicious in my guess,*
> *I confess, it is my nature's plague*
> *To spy into abuses, and oft my jealousy*
> *Shapes faults that are not . . ."*

The original passage in Greene's book proved appropriate for a betrayer's elevated sense of self. Greene flirted with the existentialist's meaninglessness by using such a light and trite verse. The poem's author was Arthur Hugh Clough. The line Fowler read he attributed to a minor nineteenth century poet of whom *The Quiet American* expressed disapproval. Interestingly enough, Clough spent his childhood in America, but chose to live his adult life in England where he became friends with men like Matthew Arnold. One of Clough's poems would have intrigued Audie Murphy. It features a discussion between a man on the road to hell and his encounter with Mephistopheles.

The poem dismissed by Mankiewicz included these lines, cited in the novel by Graham Greene:

> *"I drive through the streets, and care not a damn,*
> *The people they stare, and ask who I am;*
> *And if I should chance to run over a cad,*
> *I can pay for the damage if ever so bad."*

Mankiewicz also found some misdirected dialogue in the novel, which he refused to use in his script. Pyle, at one point, used a peculiar British phraseology that Fowler spoke earlier in the text. Acting as script writer, the director ruthlessly had the American point out to Fowler how often he used the expression. Again, that somewhat snide critique hardly would sit well with Greene.

Mankiewicz also filled the movie with ridicule of the novel and its film equivalent. Throughout the picture, the character of Fowler spoke caustically of Audie as a "movie Marine" or someone with "widescreen appeal." As a consequence, the director saved his most savage barbs for a discussion at the climax of the film between the police inspector and the British journalist over the difference between political reality and the kind of "entertainments" one finds in movies, using the exact word the British novelist condescendingly applied to his allegedly less serious novels.

Mankiewicz clearly expressed his contempt for the pretense Greene had put on this story; the man from Hollywood saw through the novel as "cheap melodrama," and had the Fowler character tell Audie's quiet American bluntly and with some satisfaction that he will "not get the girl at the end" as in American romantic movies.

Greene's vehement anti-Americanism may have many roots. Two reasons explain why he so frequently bashed Americans in his books. He had first interjected himself in American politics in the early 1950s with his public defense of Charlie Chaplin, a man banned from the country unless he willingly testified before the House on Un-American Activities as to his putative communist allegiances. Greene wrote an open letter that berated "witch-hunters," especially hypocritical Americans who "wound freedom throughout the world."

Greene's second experience with the American government also left him with a sour taste for the country. Though awarded the Catholic Literary Award in 1952, Greene learned the United States government would not grant him an eight-week visa (Congress citing the McCarran Act that banned foreign visitors with communist affiliations). This incident took three days to unravel before Greene gained the right to an entry visa. Nonetheless, he was unforgiving about the embarrassment—and refused the invitation. He held the resentment toward America for the rest of his life.

Rev. Gene Phillips called Greene's anger with Mankiewicz "quite understandable." He saw no connection between Greene's dislike of American government, his hostility to American film directors like Mankiewicz, and his antagonism to Americans in general. Phillips begrudgingly allowed Mankiewicz to defend his changes in the script of his version of *The Quiet American* by citing the director's one-time argument with F. Scott Fitzgerald over dialogue adapted from one of the American novelist's works. Mankiewicz gave an interview many years after the incident and said: "Writing dialogue for a novel and writing dialogue for the stage or screen are two different crafts."

According to Rev. Phillips, this statement proved the ultimate hubris of the film director.

Because Mankiewicz left much of Greene's dialogue in the film of *The Quiet American,* Phillips considered Mankiewicz's statement about his altering of F. Scott Fitzgerald's verbiage proved his hypocritical and untrustworthy nature. Yet, what Mankiewicz went on to say is that exchanges between characters often must suit and match the abilities of the actors who are playing the roles, especially in star driven movie vehicles. Actors have limits or ranges that a script may need to consider.

The consensus of all Greene defenders centered on the final interplay of dialogue in the movie of *The Quiet American.* The closing point that most damns Fowler, far beyond the fate that Greene stamped upon him, was his unrepentant attitude. Here, in the film, the Redgrave character spoke: "I wished there existed someone to whom I could say that I was sorry." Greene purists decried that Mankiewicz left out the prelude to the line: "Everything had gone right with me since he died . . ."

To incense Greene, Mankiewicz gave the last line in the movie to Inspector Vigot, who offered to take Fowler to the local cathedral. An atheist to the end, Fowler declined with a shake of the head. For those who believe devoutly in God and eternal judgment, Fowler has damned himself for all time. Greene, of course, was a devout Roman Catholic, and this ending of the movie vanquished Fowler in a definitive and complete way, capturing the flavor of the novel, yet presenting another dimension to the ramifications of condoning a murder. This too seemed to bother Graham Greene.

The writer said: "This is Indo-China . . . carefully and accurately described. I have been a newspaper correspondent as well as a novelist." Of course, the two connected in Greene's mind—though one deals with fictionalizing and embellishing reality, while the other "reports" on it. Yet, Greene has also stated: "That film was a real piece of political dishonesty. The film makes the American very wise and the Englishman completely the fool of the Communists." One may well question the wisdom of a man who saved the life of a man who is plotting to kill him. *The Quiet American* hardly showed insight into human nature when he accepted a dinner date with Fowler who was, at the same time, signaling the communists to assassinate the man.

Rev. Phillips cited one particularly galling moment in the film when Mankiewicz allowed the American to have the last word in a debate, which differed from the novel. He repeated the comment of Fowler, "I wish you had a few bad motives–" from the book, and the missing line, "and that applies to your country too, Pyle." Excising this line, he theorized, may have de-fanged the anti-Americanism that permeated the book.

Rev. Phillips did not see the shooting script, which featured many of these lines, but had undergone radical excisions to keep the film to the traditional two-hour length of motion pictures. Had Mankiewicz kept every line of dialogue from the novel in his script (most were there originally; most were actually filmed), the picture would have run for close to four hours in length!

On one rare occasion, when a critic found something laudable in Mankiewicz's script, Julian Smith rose to the attack. The *Saturday Review* explained that the depiction of Vietnamese were "more credible and true to the earnest, hard-working, apolitical types that (Mankiewicz) found in Indo-China . . ." Smith hastily pointed out that this proved "a remarkable compliment in that Mankiewicz had not been to Vietnam before he wrote the script." Of course, Smith ignored the fact that Mankiewicz had to revise the script after events unfolded in Saigon and had tinkered with this script up to the time of filming. He often changed the storyline during the editing process.

Nearly every critique of the picture qualified it as "flawed" or a "failure," often for unfathomable reasons. Some cited the picture is "loosely based" on the Greene novel, which is blatantly untrue. The film followed the novel more closely than most Hollywood treatments of well-known novels. The biggest complaint was the deviation from Greene's alleged opposition to America's involvement in Vietnam. Unfortunately, the text of the novel didn't bear out this "opposition" because Greene was a tightrope walker who hedged every opinion and obfuscated his characters' views. Was Fowler really an atheist? Was

Pyle really an American agent? Was Phuong really a victim? The book abounded in contradiction, reflected cleverly in the screenplay.

The most serious charge against the film and its performers, apart from suffering from miscasting and upending the story, was that Mankiewicz turned Fowler from a weak protagonist, tormented by his ill-deeds, into the fool of the story. The British journalist had no convictions and suffered from a moral lapse of fatal proportions. It was the more sympathetic role in both the film and novel. Since Greene wanted Pyle to be the fool, and Mankiewicz turned the character into a nameless American, the film lacked any hero. The audience must tolerate then unsavory and unpleasant characters, however tragic and pathetic they may appear to be. Apparently, in the dominant critical view, an American movie cannot be devoid of heroes. In the end, the lack of box-office receipts proved the critics right.

Years later, disapproving advisor and loyal friend of Mankiewicz, Robert Lantz gave an interview in which he called the decision to tamper with the Greene novel's ending: "unpardonable arrogance." Lantz felt himself in a quandary: caught between his abiding affection for Joe Mankiewicz and his fear that his friend tossed aside all good judgment. That was typical of the opinion of Joe Mankiewicz's friends. The movie's doomed fate seemed apparent before it shot one of its location scenes.

As a *coup d'grace* in his dismissive way, Graham Greene pronounced, "The cast is appalling." Whatever other problems the production might encounter, the author, in his public condemnations, doomed the movie before cameras rolled. Unable to desist, Graham Greene issued a series of unpleasant pronouncements about "Mankiewicz's impertinent picture." He claimed the director had set out to "deliberately attack the book and its author." Calling the film dishonest, Greene aimed his cruelest barbs at Audie, labeling him "incapable", and "without talent", or "looking even worse than usual next to Redgrave." All this derision came from a man who never met an American he liked. Greene further complained, "The most extreme changes I have seen in a book of mine were in *The Quiet American*; one could almost believe the film was made deliberately to attack the book and the author . . .

and I am vain enough to believe that the book will survive a few years longer than Mr. Mankiewicz's incoherent picture."

No way about it, Greene despised the entire cast, including Michael Redgrave who had once before done a Greene story on film (*e.g., The Man Within,* a version which Greene accused of exhibiting "real treachery. ") He wrote scathingly of *The Quiet American,* again picking on a young and vulnerable member of the cast, "and the Vietnamese girl was played by an Italian." Rev. Phillips seconded this opinion and accused Mankiewicz of trying "to reshape material to his own specifications, and all of the considerable technical and artistic skill was spent in turning out a rather ordinary film" instead of the great art that a dutiful copy of the Greene novel would have produced. A study of the making of the motion picture helps to answer the question of how accurate the thesis of Rev. Phillips and Graham Greene might be.

If the movie of *The Quiet American* was an important one for Audie, it was more so for this young Natalie Wood lookalike actress making her American film debut. The actress she resembled was far too busy and unobtainable, if considered. One of a spate of Italian actresses to reach the screen and try the cross-over the American mainstream, only a few, such as Sophia Loren and Gina Lollobrigida, succeeded. Not as voluptuous as the standard might expect, her willowy frame and darkly exotic looks could help her pass as Phuong, a Vietnamese woman. At twenty years old, Giorgia "bowled over" the director with her "linguistic ability"! She flew in from Rome to Saigon and learned some Vietnamese immediately, undergoing some arduous training.

Miss Giorgia Moll had appeared in *Nero's Mistress* in 1955, an Italian film, with a fascinating cast including Brigitte Bardot, Gloria Swanson, and Vittorio de Sica. Her career in European films included such movies as *The Thief of Baghdad* with Steve "Hercules" Reeves in 1960. She called it "a picture that would appeal to little boys." She acted in the remarkable and brilliant film, *Contempt,* by Jean-Luc Godard in 1963, second lead to Brigitte Bardot. She felt justifiably proud that it had been re-released thirty-five years later to greater acclaim.

In costume, but out of makeup, Giorgia Moll in Rome during the filming of The Quiet American. Photo courtesy of Vinh Noan.

Since actress France Nuyen, an Asian, was eagerly hoping to do the picture, it seemed a great expense to try an unknown in the part who did not have the prerequisite racial heritage. It appeared Miss Nuyen had, in fact, conducted a campaign to win the coveted role of Phuong. Mike Mindlin informed the author during an interview for this study that he had discovered Miss Nuyen, based on a tip from actress Suzy Parker and her sister model Daria Leigh. "I had some photos of France taken up in Marseilles that showed how gorgeous she was, and I showed these to Joe." According to Mike, Nuyen "was breathtakingly beautiful." He also felt she was the answer to the film production company "desperate search for someone to play" the Asian girl in the picture.

Believing that avenue may not be enough to garner the lead role, Miss Nuyen sprang into action, looking for other entrees into the picture. She sent a photo of herself to Vinh Noan in Saigon when she learned he was influential in the casting of the film. "It was a nude picture in which she held a small handkerchief in a strategic way." Noan, not knowing she had also used contacts to reach Mindlin, sent the picture on to Mankiewicz. By now, she had covered every angle to win recognition. It may well be that Mankiewicz felt besieged by the actress. He certainly didn't give her a screen audition in a happy state of mind. Mindlin added, "I know Joe was not a visual director, but he made her look like Minnie Mouse in the test."

One common belief over the years was that Mankiewicz tested Miss Nuyen for the lead role in *The Quiet American*, before her discovery and success in the stage version of *The World of Suzy Wong*. This led to most of the criticism of Mankiewicz for by-passing an Asian actress to cast the role with an Italian. When contacted in 1998 for her opinion, Miss Nuyen couldn't recall testing for the specific role in the Graham Greene story. Up for a role in Mike Todd's *Around the World in 80 Days,* France Nuyen believed this was the picture she tested with Mankiewicz.

Unfortunately, Mankiewicz did not have anything to do with the Mike Todd picture. "The only test I remember doing for Mr. Mankiewicz was in Rome when I was fifteen years old," commented the Asian actress. It was doubtful Joe Mankiewicz tested actresses for the picture in 1954 or 1955 before he decided to do the movie version of a book that didn't appear until 1955, and he did not purchase the film rights until mid-1956. Mike Mindlin countered Miss Nuyen was about eighteen at the time of her test.

All this was complicated by another fact, "Alas," said Miss Nuyen to the author, "I did not speak English at the time and did not do the film." Since the director did test France and the test certainly occurred in Rome, it seemed likely that she had a test for *The Quiet American*, but may not have understood the film's title or plot. A nervous adolescent, doing a test for a major director, might have confused her about which film she might be doing. Since Joe wanted a multi-lingual actress, France may have been disqualified because of language alone.

In character as a Vietnamese, France would require several different language coaches and extensive training. Joe Mankiewicz recognized it as another major problem in France Nuyen's ability to perform, regardless of any test. Denied her chance with this director, she went on that year to succeed in films like *In Love and War*. Mindlin later worked with her on the play version of *The World of Suzy Wong*, and her greatest achievement remained, *South Pacific* under the aegis of Joshua Logan.

Figaro's publicity vice president Mike Mindlin also disputed the possibility that Mankiewicz may have deliberately done an unflattering test of the Asian actress. However, he theorized the entire production of *The Quiet American* was a controlled exercise in colossal failure. The director apparently made failure his goal and blithely went ahead to create a self-fulfilling prophecy. The reasons remained inexplicable to Mindlin.

If Nuyen looked mousy according to some amazed observers, Mindlin believed Mankiewicz must have had his mind already made up about the casting of Miss Moll. What some presumed was an unflattering screen test could have been the result of Miss Nuyen's bad make-up and poor lighting. However, as Mindlin aptly assessed the situation, "You have to be a great film director to make a test that bad." France believed she was not the mature and exotic creature of later years. Of course, whatever the results, Joe expressed no interest in any other actress.

Interestingly enough, Miss Nuyen still spoke only rudimentary English during the filming of *South Pacific* in 1957. She communicated in French on-screen with her co-star John Kerr as Joe Cable. When Mindlin worked as a producer with her as Suzy Wong, a year later, her English was greatly improved. Her character's English, or lack thereof, in *South Pacific* paralleled the scenes in *The Quiet American* when Phuong spoke only French to her American boyfriend. During a pivotal scene she needed a translator to understand his proposal of marriage. How then did the language barrier prevent Miss Nuyen from playing the role? It didn't. As Mindlin said, "It simply wasn't an acceptable excuse. We had dubbing, you know. It was done all the time."

So, of all Mankiewicz's decisions, the one casting Giorgia Moll raised a question far beyond any other casting controversies that spun around the selections of either leading male roles. An unknown actress, her birthright was an ethnic mixture, not any part of which was Vietnamese or Asian, and her performance required coaching, though not nearly as much as Nuyen would have requested. "I always had my language coach near," said Giorgia. The young girl arrived with one point in her favor: she would work as hard as necessary to do the job correctly.

With a few Italian pictures to her credit, and experience as a model, she felt delighted when Mankiewicz signed her to a personal film contract: a move that raised a few eyebrows for its daring. It was a huge commitment. It may be that his deep involvement in the career of Miss Moll precluded France Nuyen from serious consideration in *The Quiet American* role of Phuong. In all likelihood Mankiewicz wanted an elder unknown to play opposite Murphy, in order to prevent his performance from being overshadowed by a veteran actress, since having Murphy and Redgrave play against an adolescent would have risked complications involving pedophilia, which the film did not need.

The selection of an Italian to play an Eurasian girl disturbed some critics, especially Graham Greene. Miss Moll concluded about her playing the role, "This would never happen today. Back then, it was expected." At that time, the mid-1950s, producers didn't often allow casting of pictures with Asian women in the leading roles (Jennifer Jones played an Eurasian doctor two years earlier in *Love Is a Many Splendored Thing*; one year earlier Rita Moreno played a Siamese girl in *The King and I*). Many producers believed casting had a correlation likely to risk box-office appeal. As a consequence, the role of Phuong went to a European in order to pander to racist feelings in the audience of the age.

The criticisms disturbed Giorgia Moll after she reached Saigon. So, she buried herself in her work. Of course, the attacks were hurtful. She felt, with make-up enhancing her genetic Oriental qualities, that she could be convincing. Letters posted from many quarters called the casting "ridiculous," said Giorgia. Though she had come half-way across the world for a chance to prove herself, controversy swirled around her

97

and her inclusion in the picture. As a consequence of the choice of Giorgia, the connection between Moll and her director sparked rumors during the shoot in Vietnam when the director spent inordinate amounts of time rehearsing her. Nothing, as the pressbook informed, could "interfere with his daily study sessions with Giorgia." The actress insisted she had a dialog coach, and Mankiewicz didn't do such work.

Giorgia Moll entered upon her odyssey with the picture in October of 1956 when Mankiewicz visited Rome at Cinecitta to conduct screen tests and to audition actresses, looking for the right quality in a woman to play Redgrave's mistress. Having a British theatrical agent who believed she had Eurasian features, an audition was arranged when the role in *The Quiet American* became available. She recalled, "We made a test and shot a few pieces of dialogue." It was a long shot.

Mankiewicz told her he planned other tests in New York, especially with a young actress who was Marlon Brando's then girlfriend and soon-to-be-wife, Anna Kashfi. Because of the connection between Brando and Mankiewicz after the movie *Guys and Dolls*, Giorgia Moll presumed she wouldn't be hired by the great director. "I didn't hear a word until December." She had been on a ski trip in the Italian Alps when a cable arrived from her mother. "He has chosen you!" That left her with a perilous short period for all her inoculations and preparations; yet, to her, it was the prospect of a lifetime.

Clearly prepared to do her homework, the first thing Giorgia did upon hearing the news was to find a copy of *The Quiet American* novel. Reading it avidly, she looked for clues to explain the character and develop the screen persona that she hoped to express. She found she enjoyed reading the entertainments of Greene. She said: "Then I read some of his other spy stories–all so very amusing."

At first Miss Moll thought to invite her mother along on the long shoot, but chose to go it alone because she was partial to "adventure" in those days. The trek to Vietnam by itself qualified as one: the journey, before jet travel, took her two and a half days. It was a schedule that would have exhausted and irritated anyone else. Filled with joy and excitement, riding a high over her selection for a big break in a major

American movie, Giorgia saw every element of her experience, every day of the production, as a fairy tale come true.

She had seven stop-overs in Turkey, Iran, and Pakistan, before reaching Saigon. Delighted with her new opportunity, she enjoyed the hardship of the long trip by treating it as a wonderful all-expense paid holiday. Veteran actors usually grow disenchanted with conditions, even if all was entirely paid for by the production company, and travel is first-class. For Giorgia, everything was amazing and thrilling.

When she deplaned in Saigon, her official greeter was the "jack of all trades" in the production of the movie: Associate Producer Vinh Noan. He did everything asked, and was happy to do it. The duty he especially enjoyed was the job of meeting Giorgia Moll upon her arrival. Immediately, as she stepped from the airplane, she won a big fan. He found her beautiful, exquisite. "I was so impressed by this lovely young lady," he admitted decades later. Having such an admirer from the moment she landed in Saigon did much to bolster Giorgia's confidence too. When the production ended, she autographed a photo for Vinh Noan—much to his delight.

Because she was "so fearless," upon reaching Saigon, she immediately roamed about the city, eating anything and everything she could find from street vendors. "I was young. I was never afraid of getting sick!" Besides, she would bear anything, do anything for her big break. She took great satisfaction that she was working with an elite organization like Figaro, Incorporated. For quite some time she lived in the clouds, feeling like an enchanted figure in a storybook romance.

5

WILLIAM HORNBECK
STARTED work in Saigon immediately upon de-planing. During his
first full day in the city, he visited the locale Production Manager Johnny
Johnston selected as the production company's temporary headquarters while on location in the downtown area, not far from the docks.
Hornbeck's major concern focused on, of course, a good site for his
cutting room, the place to install his splicing machine and projector and
store other sundry equipment in the perpetually humid atmosphere.

For Hornbeck, and later proven to the director, Johnny Johnston's
organizational skills were amiss during this production. Hornbeck, usually circumspect, found himself dissatisfied with some of Johnny
Johnston's decisions, but believed that the arrival of the company's leader
would put things right quickly. Because they had such a long-standing
professional relationship, Mankiewicz opened up on Johnny whenever
the urge came upon him. For the unfortunate Johnston this time around,
he tended to find himself at the wrong end of Mankiewicz's attention.

"Directors like Huston, Kramer, and Mankiewicz," said one person
who frequently witnessed such behavior on productions, "often pick
out one susceptible person on the set during a film's shooting, and that
unlucky individual becomes the object of torment. It seems they serve
the role of scapegoat for the director." It was Johnny's fate to suffer
chronic blame for all ills on this picture.

On Hornbeck's mind was the imminent arrival of the director,
traveling on Air France, the slower of the two carriers of personnel to
Vietnam. Joe Mankiewicz was due to land at Tan Son Nhat airport, its
low structures painted with bright yellow and white colors, reflecting

the Saigon sun, early the next morning, January 6th. Air France used at least seven stops–in Turkey, Iran, and India.

The Pan American Clipper's long trip to reach the exotic Oriental setting had three lay-overs, one overnight, tracking along the Pacific Rim from Seattle to Alaska, then flying down the coast of Asia to Vietnam. Using Air France to his advantage, Joe worked on the storyboard for *The Quiet American* script. Whatever its pro-American stance, Mankiewicz believed in letting the on-location ambiance tailor the scene's style. According to Elaine Schreyeck, "he may have had a number of drafts before he settled on a final script . . ." though she believed he would have settled this before his arrival in Vietnam.

After watering down all the anti-American cracks, the script still hinted that the Communists caused intermittent bombings, including the ruthless killing of children, and slimy double-crosses. The frustration of the director over how he could deal with the novel's snide anti-Americanism certainly contributed to his growing irritability during the long flight from the United States to Vietnam. Greene's public criticisms constantly spurred Mankiewicz's decision to excoriate Greene through his own novel.

Joe Mankiewicz's flight arrived at eight a.m.. Deplaning into steamy and unpleasant heat, the director looked worn, rumpled, and visibly irritated. Giorgia Moll reminded that this long excursion preceded jet travel, and the arduous journey required hours of numbing and sometimes nerve-wracking flight. "Was he dead!" exclaimed Hornbeck. Mankiewicz told his old friend, "This was the roughest trip I ever had coming East."

Vinh Noan had also been at the airport to greet the director. He conveyed to Mankiewicz how much the Vietnamese people felt flattered that the American movies had come to them. According to Noan, they felt only goodwill toward the idea of filming the Greene story. Vinh offered a perspective of a staunch anti-Communist. Early on he informed Joe that the people knew Greene "had used us like in a game of chess. So had the Communists. The citizens of Vietnam knew that, if we go along, we could gain independence. That was all we wanted."

The next day, to Hornbeck's delight, the Vietnamese newspapers published pictures of Joe Mankiewicz landing at the airport, and the city expressed delighted to cooperate with the Americans who had come to their land to make a movie. Mindlin had done his job with the excitable press attention to the project. It cheered the film company.

Mankiewicz now claimed to have hired for this film the perfect symbol of *The Quiet American* in Audie Murphy. Obviously, he knew enough to adjust his public observations after the drastic substitution of star, but he still harbored a delusion that he could use his original script. As Joe's friends and allies attested, once set in his decision, nothing could dissuade him. Of course, deprived of his dream cast, he should have made suitable revisions.

Mankiewicz didn't intend to change any of his dialog to suit the actor, though he had so promised Audie. What he wrote was what the actor must speak on film. Mankiewicz presumed, once in Vietnam, once committed to the picture, Audie would simply knuckle under to the situation. The director had made a fairly brazen assumption about his star. Audie often joked he could barely wend his mouth around the few easy lines in his westerns. So, he faced a double whammy in a Mankiewicz script of a Graham Greene novel.

Ignorant of his own temerity, the director stepped into a minefield, not understanding Audie Murphy's explosive temper. He was ready to call Audie's bluff, a big mistake, though Mankiewicz did add a minor script exchange between Redgrave and Moll that made *The Quiet American* a native Texan who happened to attend Princeton for some courses. Overall, however, according to Giorgia Moll, Joe never felt reason enough to change his script for anyone on the picture. Yet, by these small assists in the scenario, Audie Murphy's credibility in the story increased, and he could easily meet the director's standard. Joe took for granted this would satisfy Murphy.

Mankiewicz chose several other well-known faces for the supporting roles of the cast. First and foremost, he selected Bruce Cabot to play a crude American, in contrast to Murphy's quiet one. Unable to live down his starring role in *King Kong* over twenty years earlier, Bruce Cabot had settled into small, supporting character roles. For many years a close pal of Errol Flynn, he had engaged in numerous hijinks, including filming a movie with Flynn for three weeks he summarily abandoned when indigent Italian producers could not meet payroll.

In *The Quiet American* he played Bill Granger, an American journalist. Having moved to Rome in the 1950s, he was dubbed the "unofficial mayor" of the American expatriate community. Though he tried to engage Audie, he found him to be distant and distracted during the movie's filming in Vietnam. It was otherwise with the friendly Italian starlet. Like a fan, Giorgia Moll gushed about Bruce Cabot, finding him enchanting and helpful, "and always quite nice to me."

Third billing in the movie went to Claude Dauphin who signed to play Inspector Vigot. Originally a behind-the-scenes man on the French stage, Dauphin started as a set designer, but in the cliche tradition of show business, stepped onto the stage to act when the lead became ill. After that, he enjoyed a meteoric film career in France, filling in the void of Charles Boyer after he departed for America. Dauphin also had his admirer on the set. "I loved him very much," co-star Giorgia Moll admitted. "He was just a fantastic actor, who always was willing to give me advice. He was so protective because he knew this was my first big picture." When Hollywood movies used more international locations in the 1950s, Claude Dauphin was generally cast as the classic French police inspector.

Enjoying themselves between scenes, left to right, Claude Dauphin, Mrs. William Hornbeck (Babe), and Bruce Cabot. Photo courtesy of Willard Willingham.

For *The Quiet American*, Dauphin played a French detective in Saigon, and was the catalyst for the narrative flow. He spent a good deal of time with Noan, mainly because they could converse in French and reminisce about Paris. In the Greene book, the police inspector behaved as a father confessor, but Mankiewicz made him a symbolic image in the movie. It was a role he continued to play in movies, typecast for the most part thereafter.

Kerima played Phuong's sister. Another actress well known for her exotic roles, especially as the quintessential Oriental temptress, Kerima had won her biggest accolades in *Outcast of the Islands* nearly seven years earlier. An Algerian, the actress was reportedly a medical student when she discovered the joys of acting. Another of the budding generation of "international" film personalities, her multi-lingual abilities helped her win the role of the young Phuong's spiritual advisor and older sister in *The Quiet American*. Giorgia Moll considered Kerima to be most famous of the cast in her homeland of Italy and felt thrilled to work with her.

One of the most intriguing bits of casting, raising nary an eyebrow among the all-knowing Figaro troupe, was that of Fred Sadoff as Dominguez. Though a workmanlike actor, his signing for the picture was attributed to reasons other than his acting abilities. It was standard practice for an established star to receive personal service, as did Audie, by having a preferred standard double or assistant placed on the payroll.

Redgrave's perk ranked higher than usual on the list of star favors. As personal traveling companion to Michael Redgrave, Freddie was granted the role of Dominguez, a treacherous spy of the Communists to gain some advantage of the additional expense of having him with the company. Having become close to Redgrave within less than a year, they remained involved for the next twenty years. There often was a part in a stage play for Sadoff, if Redgrave had a say, but his career in movies never took off. Freddie played guest roles in a variety of detective television series, ranging from *Toma, Rockford, Baretta, Harry O, Mannix,* and had a continuing role on *Streets of San Francisco* throughout the 1970s.

On and off the set in Vietnam Freddie maintained his affable personality for those around him: Miss Moll recounted how "he taught me English and was very kind and patient." As she had her own problem with the role of Phuong, Freddie recalled his own experience years earlier to help her deal with the criticism and controversy around her casting as the Asian girl. Those who knew Freddie from the New York days said he was a "charmer." It was a role he played to perfection. And, indeed, Vinh Noan also called him "a nice guy," and enjoyed his gregarious nature.

Another early arrival, William Hornbeck, met Freddie on January 17th when the actor showed up at the hotel, and they found good company in each other. "He is a nice fellow," Bill Hornbeck informed his wife. During one of the lulls on a hot afternoon, the two met and took the ferry across the river. "It cost less than one cent to go over and very few tourists are ever seen there." Both enjoyed this leisure time to sunbathe and relax, rare on any location.

Richard Loo played the urbane but deadly Mr. Heng. Born in 1903 in Hawaii, this actor was a familiar face to film and television audiences. Starting in the years of World War II, he made a virtual career out of playing despicable Japanese soldiers. "Die, you Yankee Dog!" was one of his famous lines, as he appeared in *Purple Hearts, God is My Co-Pilot,* and other memorable films.

Later, he did respectable roles in films like *Love is a Many Splendored Thing*. However, in his elder years, he found himself cast in television shows like Kung Fu. In *The Quiet American*, the connotation of his appearance carried much weight to convey easily the villainous nature of the Communist who arranges Murphy's murder. He was the last of the featured players to arrive in Saigon.

Accommodations for the film group were in the heart of Saigon at the Hotel Majestic, a grand lodging done in exquisite French manner, slowly going to seed. Its palatial door was only one step up, and the decor was a natural colored marble. Each room was done in a "French essential" style. Vinh Noan called the rooms "small but well furnished." The colonial French, now gone for about two and a half years after their defeat at Dien Bien Phu, left a typical paint-peeling, non-luxurious hotel. Tropic hotels, worldwide, didn't have air conditioning in those days—and still don't for the most part. It was the norm to have ceiling fans or none at all, just open the shutters. A ceiling fan cooled rooms at the Majestic—if one imagines stirring hot air around refreshing. The air seldom moves under conditions like those in Saigon: "It is more like swimming in sweat," complained one of the visitors.

Temperatures in Vietnam during this season seldom drop below 100 degrees. Most of the troupe generally ignored the heat, though the elder actors like Bruce Cabot, suffered badly from the experience. Nearly everyone from Figaro created a card-playing clique. Because many did not comprehend the volatile politics of the area, their isolation owed nothing to fears about wandering the city without body guards. Many members of the crew and cast took to heavy bouts of drinking alcohol to numb themselves to the discomfort of the tropic location during the erratic hours when they were not filming. Mike Mindlin and Bill Hornbeck were non-drinkers and stayed away from the overindulgent members of the crew.

One of the director's first duties was to hold a series of production meetings in Saigon with his staff. He insured that all was in order and told what was expected of them. After this, Hornbeck and Mankiewicz went off to scout locations for filming. They had a particular interest in the facades of local churches, visiting Cholon, which is part of Saigon on the right bank of the city's central waterway and river. In the mid-1950s, Cholon was far more segregated from the larger Saigon. One major avenue about four miles long connected the two boroughs. A largely immigrant Chinese population lived there. At the end of hot days, Mankiewicz and Hornbeck had dinner at the Hotel Majestic, whose culinary delights were cheap and varied.

On Thursday and Friday during the first week the director was in Saigon, Hornbeck spent much time visiting docks, junkyards, and temples in and around Cholon. It was only when Mankiewicz scheduled a day full of meetings with everyone except his Film Editor that Hornbeck found free time. However, during these moments, Hornbeck had an eye for detail. He took a boat up the river on Sunday and took pictures for his amusement and to send home, but kept notations of any possible locations for the picture.

Sunday was also a work time for the director. When alone, he pretended to tinker with the script. Mankiewicz, at heart, believed himself to be a talented writer, beyond any associate's critique. Days on which he did not shoot scenes, he celebrated for the opportunity it gave him to re-read his script: From constant readings, he further reinforced his self-appreciation, or it allowed him a chance to cogitate about how the words were to be acted out. If he made revisions, they were in longhand, and his habit was best indulged on weekends. Elaine Schreyeck who followed him from movie to movie personified the dedicated assistant during all script sessions. Producer Walter Wanger had observed their rapport: "She transcribes her shorthand notes in rough form. He corrects and edits them in long hand. Then the material is mimeographed," and it was a system that served them well. On *The Quiet American*, Miss Schreyeck doubled as Mankiewicz's continuity editor.

Mankiewicz preferred complex flashbacks in his movies—as in *All About Eve* or *The Barefoot Contessa*. He made subtle but noticeable changes from the novel to create his shooting script. This time, after the rewritings, the narrative tale was simplified: Audie was dead when the film opened, and Fowler (Redgrave) remembered *The Quiet American* who befriended him in Saigon when no one else would. Then, his Asian girl fell for Audie, creating a triangle in which the deceptive Briton presented himself as a witty, cavalier gentleman, but out of his sour bitterness, he blamed Audie's American for supporting terrorism and held him responsible for the Place Grenier bombing of 1952.

When the opportunity arose, the British reporter turned Audie over to the Commies who ambushed and killed him. Fowler complained to the Inspector when questioned about withholding information about the American's murder: "I am not an informer." Instead, he proved far worse. Fowler had a revelation that Audie was innocent and Fowler's Asian girl finally left him, wishing to be a prostitute than to stay with a Judas.

Whether he was a persuasive patriot or not, Mankiewicz disliked the anti-American biases of the novel and wanted his script to reflect anti-Communist sentiments. He judged the cold-blooded killing of the American appalling. The self-righteousness of the novel wallowed in the murder. If the British journalist of the story started out hating American heroism, by film's end he must come to a begrudging admiration of it. That was the essence of his American interpretation of the novel. Mankiewicz knew that no film could be truly successful in America if it thumbed its nose at the audience. Immediately upon the film crew's arrival in Saigon, Graham Greene angrily expressed disappointment that his theme had been gutted.

Misinformation had filtered back to Greene about the script–and incorrectly disclosed the American lived at the end of the movie and married Phuong! At the least, Greene spoke out too soon–condemning the movie before the film was in the can. From then on, the movie could never recover from his scathing and widely reported opinion of the movie.

Related to another pre-production issue, rumor incorrectly indicated Audie refused to accept the name of the character in the book. Actually, this was a director's decision. Joseph Mankiewicz had no problems leaving the character nameless. He pointed out this broadened the metaphoric impact. Later publicity for the movie highlighted Audie as "the man without a name." The rest of the story was fleshed out with the phrase, "a girl without a future, and an adventure without equal." On top of that, the first name of the character presented a problem. In the book, he was "Alden." It sounded too much like Audie could be the sobriquet of the character. The *London Times* demanded to know if Mankiewicz had realized that Audie was NOT Graham Greene's concept of the title character.

On January 14th, Mankiewicz led an early morning entourage that drove up the highway toward North Vietnam. The group included Film Editor Hornbeck, Publicity Veep Mike Mindlin, Project Manager Johnny Johnston, Art Director Rino Mondellini, and Technical Advisor Vinh Noan. Mindlin thought they went as far as ninety miles from the capital. "On the road all you could see were rice fields–as far as you could see, in every direction." They scouted locations for one of the big scenes, later recreated in Rome. "The British crews refer to this kind of tip as a reccy–short for reconnaissance trip."

Standing outside the Continental Palace Hotel, Production Manager Johnny Johnston consults with Vinh Noan and came to rely on him for many tasks. Photo courtesy of Willard Willingham.

On this lonely stretch of highway built for two lanes of non-existent traffic, Mindlin noticed, "I saw two men squatting near where we stopped the car. They were probably Vietcong at night, no doubt. They were naked, except for loincloths, and those conical straw hats. They watched us with amazement. We all stepped from the car, and Joe was looking in every direction with his viewfinder. You could tell from their expressions that these guys probably had never seen a movie, and they had no idea what we were doing."

Mindlin often had a running bit of business with Mankiewicz, playing gags to make him laugh; every tyrant being entitled to his tolerated jester. "So, I had an idea while Joe was looking here and there at the rice fields. I asked Vinh who acted as our interpreter to go over to one of the squatting men and have him come up to Joe and make a bit of a speech." Then, Mindlin explained what else he wanted. Noan followed the instructions, and Mankiewicz suddenly found, under the conical hat, the short man in the loin cloth standing directly in his line of view, speaking vociferously. The director turned to the young and trustworthy face of Noan who explained: "He wants to know if you are the great American director, producer, and writer, Joseph L. Mankiewicz, who has made so many literate and award-winning pictures for the American cinema."

Flabbergasted, Joe turned to his straight-faced staff, and he exclaimed, "What the hell! Did you hear that? He knows who I am–" immediately he knew from the expressions of his traveling companions what a put-on he had fallen for. Many years later, Mankiewicz pointed at Mindlin when they met in a restaurant and told his daughter: "He's the one! He's the one who pulled that joke on me!" Mike fondly reminisced that, "I had a lot of laughs with Joe. I could always get a laugh out of him. We had a good relationship."

A second key location was scouted on January 14th when the entire Figaro crew went up the road for another hour or so to Tayninh where the Cao Dai procession and temple scenes later were staged. A religious and political sect, the Cao Dai numbered about two million adherents, anti-Communist in outlook and Buddhist, in many ways it became a state within a state. Residing mainly northwest of Saigon, the group maintained its own army, seen proudly marching in the parade sequence of the movie. In years ahead that army would be slowly destroyed.

The cathedral Mankiewicz and Hornbeck selected for the film is notorious as one of the most bizarre places of religious worship in the world. Failing to do the picture in color defeated the best reason for location shooting: the church is decorated "in brilliant birthday cake colors" and has molding displaying fanciful, if not gaudy, plaster dragons and cobras. Mankiewicz was fascinated with the symbolic giant "One Eye" staring out from the various rococo designs of the temple and featured prominently in the film. Noan explained a Cao Dai tenet was predicated upon the idea that no one culture or religion having all the answers. "They took the best from all cultures and religions as the basis of their philosophy. That was what the Eye symbolized. They were always looking out for the best." Its Big Brother symbolism, used by anti-Communists, best typified the irony of everything in the Graham Greene story.

Hornbeck took the following days to inspect rustic sentry towers and sought the best locations for one of the most arresting and dangerous scenes in the movie: an attack by Viet Minh, the Communists, upon a lonely outpost along the road where the characters found refuge after their car ran out of gas and the Communists attempted to assassinate them. The weekend kept the film editor busy for he had to work the following Friday night at the Dakow Bridge, and on Sunday, he hosted a party for a group of executives and visitors at the Hotel Majestic.

Most of the technical people came in from Rome on the days right before Tet. This included such people as the grip and painter, and several electricians: Edemondo Saglio, Giorgio Pasqualini, Nunzio Coluzzi, Vincenzo Balducci, Romolo Romangnolo and Giovanni Mayer. Also arriving on the same flight, but leaving from London were George Frost, a last minute signer to the contract with Figaro as the make-up man—and his primary hairstylist, Ida Mills.

Though the picture was about to start, and cast arrived daily for the shooting, certain members of the Figaro crew in Vietnam continued to be indignant over the hiring of Giorgia Moll. Some had more clout than others; few had the inclination to breach the subject with the director. Yet, if one could find the onset of the film troupe's slow poisoning, those muted mutterings behind the scenes about the lead actress in late January might be the moment.

This bit of controversial casting had remained a thorn to Hornbeck, and he expressed dismay that the issue still hadn't been resolved before principal photography began. The central role of the Eurasian beauty named Phuong (meaning Phoenix) was the flashpoint for the rivalry between the cynical British journalist and *The Quiet American*. The role also triggered a schism of sorts within the Figaro troupe in Vietnam, according to Hornbeck. It was evident that Mankiewicz knew whom he wanted and that decision was unshakable, though he may have given lip-service to the comments of his closest aides. The actress was to represent the motivation for a man to order the death of the lead character, a result of the romance when politics took advantage of personal jealousies.

When Hornbeck arrived in Saigon, he learned the female lead still remained to be cast. Mankiewicz hadn't told his film editor the role was filled. "The leading lady has not been picked as yet," he complained peevishly in a letter to his wife. "A girl from Italy will arrive on Tuesday for some more tests." The director, rather than face questions about his judgment, had misled Hornbeck. Giorgia Moll's hiring was a done deal. Another person to offer his strong opinion to Mankiewicz about choosing this actress was his *aide-de-camp* Robert Lantz, advising she was "not very good." However, these complaints fell on deaf ears. As Lantz pronounced decades later, "Joe was stubborn."

"We are not very happy about her," commented another staff member of Figaro about the casting of Miss Moll in the key role. But, they were in no position to do anything about it. Mankiewicz too full responsibility for any Figaro, Incorporated, decision, much less his own. Perhaps he knew something about her which they didn't, and they had to trust him.

The only outside factor that might damage the starlet's chance at the role was if she happened to be taller than Audie Murphy. Miss Moll admitted she unable to wear heels because of Murphy's height; she stands five feet seven inches. A diplomatic woman, she wouldn't say whether Audie wore lifts in his shoes for their scenes together without having to point out the common solution to height problems in movies. She'd wear flats, and he'd stand on what is called an "apple box."

Later, Audie Murphy did indeed complain to a friend–in jest–that during his dance scenes with Miss Moll, he found himself constantly looking into her bosom, not her face. Mike Mindlin recollected she was taller than Audie and had to wear slippers without heels to match his height. "This is the picture business," commented Hornbeck about the Moll situation, which plainly told of the resignation many had to the "magic" of film production.

During the making of *The Quiet American*, Bill Hornbeck confirmed some of the height issue: the Vietnamese actresses were ideal for Audie because they were formed so petitely. Some problems arose from the use of Giorgia Moll in the part of Phuong, the love interest. Hornbeck graciously acknowledged Audie stood "only five feet ten inches"–generally thought too short for a leading man. However, in their scenes together Audie and Giorgia are about the same height, owing to judicious camera angles used by the director.

Nevertheless, Hornbeck—one of the few with the courage to do so—stood up to Mankiewicz to tell him of his fears about the Italian actress: "I do not think she is right for the part." It may be testimony to how much respect Mankiewicz had for Hornbeck that he made a show of postponing the film start and going to Hong Kong to do a star search at this late date in the pre-production phase. However, owing to the pressures of finances and convenience, he would make further film tests with Giorgia Moll to learn if she had the ability and screen presence to carry the movie.

Hornbeck bought the lie. Mankiewicz was the boss. Though her casting won no approval a generation later, Miss Moll had Mankiewicz's total support. He explained they simply couldn't fight the viewpoint that American audiences would refuse outright to accept an Asian lead in the picture, and this especially was true with the Figaro backers.

Though Giorgia sensed the disapproval of her casting, she set aside her feelings of rejection and hurt. The lack of support from Figaro staff and crew gave her stronger reason to immerse herself in the role. She learned the actors and other people on the picture fully supported and wanted her to do well. Among those were Vinh Noan. He defended the director's choice. "There were no actresses in Vietnam who had enough English proficiency to master the role."

For this reason he gave Giorgia his total commitment, knowing also how much the opportunity meant to her. What really mattered and remained paramount to her years later, was that she had the full confidence of Mankiewicz. As long as he expressed his belief in her, she charged ahead. Like Audie in more than a few ways, she used the disdain she saw as a fuel to spark her performance.

Crew sets up for the big explosion scene in the center of Saigon which depicts a 1952 terrorist attack that is central to the plot of The Quiet American. Photo courtesy of Willard Willingham.

Film tests were made of Moll, occurring on January 23rd on a day when the heat "was something fierce," according to production crew members, but those tests were for make-up and costumes, which had arrived two days before. At the worst time of day, in the notorious Saigon sunlight, the staff of Mankiewicz "worked like fools," said Hornbeck. The actress went through the motions of a screen test; a sham for the benefit of the disgruntled.

At this juncture of the film production, Mankiewicz had no inclination, nor time, to import an actress from Europe or the United States. To some extent, local actresses may have been interviewed and found wanting. Since dailies for the test would not be available until mid-February, the preliminary work on Miss Moll occurring in Saigon in late January was obviously a waste of time. It was too late to replace her. Anyway, Joe expected to see the rushes the day before shooting Giorgia's first scenes, as she would not appear in the opening Tet sequence.

As for her preparation and rightness for the role, Giorgia's posture and deportment were decidedly European, not the recessive personality usually encouraged in women by Asian societies. Willowy as Miss Moll might appear, she was an ample girl with attractive figure. "I looked like an elephant next to Asian women," she said years later in self-deprecating fashion, though no one ever accused her of being elephantine. Her concern centered on trying to emulate the "graceful and gentle" demeanors of the Vietnamese girls she met once in Saigon. Miss Moll herself felt self-conscious about her height, noting how "tall" she was in comparison to Vietnamese women.

Willard Willingham expressed the strongest views against Miss Moll. He called her "too tall, too powerful, too athletic. They needed a fragile girl. She was totally wrong." As always, Willard's opinion delineated his protective streak when it came to Audie. If an actress did not enhance the deification of Audie, she received the first stone cast. Of course, Hornbeck's comments on the hiring of Moll were the kind of shameless overstatement that he knew conveyed its ironic meaning. "We could not find a Vietnamese girl who could act," he explained to those who questioned the director's judgment. Hornbeck told his wife, "People are very upset with us over this" casting of a European girl instead of an Asian. "Can you imagine that?" dead-panned Mike Mindlin. "We could not find an Asian actress in Vietnam."

If any character from the novel had undergone transformation from novel to the script version, it was Inspector Vigot (played by Claude Dauphin). In the novel the cat and mouse game between the police and their culprit is a narrative cement of story-telling. In the film version, the Inspector served more in the role of a Greek chorus–though to no one's knowledge has anyone protested about how Dauphin's role had been subverted. Of all the participants, the French actor did his job with no fanfare and no complaints; he arrived on January 20th, as scheduled, knew his lines, and gave the director all he asked. Dauphin required the least amount of attention from the Figaro production team; he gave them pure professionalism.

The main wave of British contributors to the picture also arrived on the same day as Dauphin. Among this group were the camera operator, John Harris and his two assistants Ronald Maasz and Godfrey Randall. Among this entourage were two key women of the project:

Elaine Schreyeck, listed on the manifest as Script Clerk, but also the most significant and close aide of Mankiewicz, and also Doris Spriggs who worked as the publicity secretary with Mike Mindlin.

At 6:00 o'clock the next morning after the arrival of the first major star, Mankiewicz and Hornbeck took a small boat up and down the river, looking for locations that appealed to the director. They felt satisfied by January 21st that they had found all the major sites for filming. It was again "terribly hot," much like every other day. Yet, at disembarking their boat trip, their lungs swam in the moist torpor of an air that they gulped, not breathed. Damp and steamy with a peculiar odor of urine and something antiseptic. "Such a different life!" Hornbeck spoke to his director. To his close friends, Hornbeck expressed abject horror. "I will never forget the sights . . . the most terrible conditions . . . the way those people live. It is unbelievable. The water smells bad and is so dirty. One can hardly stand it–and a few feet away from children playing you will find sewage pouring in."

With just a few days to go before the Tet celebration, Mankiewicz had many other problems to occupy him. Planning to use the local celebration for colorful backdrops to the killing of *The Quiet American* and the boiling political situation behind it, Mankiewicz needed the cooperation of the authorities to carry out his movie script on the Chinese New Year. Most of the early shots, used under the opening credits, were of the Tet parades in Saigon squares, featuring magnificent dragon costumes and the faces of awestruck children watching the festivities. Hornbeck expressed delight and amazement with one parade prop: an eighty foot paper dragon.

Noan regretted that the audience couldn't see the colorful detail of the accouterments which the citizens brought to their celebration. As for the long dragon, its head fell into the river and floated downstream, which quickly culminated in the discovery of *The Quiet American* star (a mannequin standing in for Audie and his absent double), face down on a muddy riverbank under the Dakow Bridge. "A most unnatural death," reported the police inspector. It was a prophetic start for these pioneer Americans, the first of a great wave in the forthcoming decades who were to arrive in Vietnam on far more serious business.

6

SLICED IN half not quite at the mid-point, Vietnam's partition created two countries—North and South—thereby making an artificial peace that pleased no one. Ready for violent demonstrations and possible terrorism in the hotbed of southeast Asia, the crew composed of about sixty: actors, production people, technicians, other assorted talents and friends of talent, braced themselves for an adventure of a lifetime.

Word had come before the Figaro film company landed on the tarmac in Saigon that Viet Minh were unhappy with Graham Greene's book, and their outrage that the novel's alterations branded them the unmitigated villains made them all the more hostile. The press office of the studio let all know of this prospect ahead of time. In fact, Mankiewicz received death threats and, naturally, these threats extended to the quietest American: Audie Murphy.

Back home, before departing on the longest journey of his life, the star, reluctantly packed to go with and his traveling companion. Audie and Willard encountered enough signals to alert them that the sojourn would dump upon them a tale of woe. If Audie believed in premonitions, there developed an ample array of reasons to cancel out of the picture. The fact remained, when Willard picked up their tickets, they read: "LAX to LAX" which simply meant, like Phileas Fogg and his companion Passepartout, Audie and Willard were about to embark on a voyage around the world, in somewhat more than eighty days. They would cross the Pacific to reach Saigon, and the return would cross Asia and Africa to reach Rome, thence across the Atlantic and back to Los Angeles. Upon realizing that the film would require about 28,000 miles in the air, Audie considered deserting the film on the spot: Willard again applied his persuasive techniques. "Audie agreed to go, solely based on pressure from me," Willingham related, "or he would never have gotten onto the plane."

Figaro had provided two round-trip tickets for a rickety-looking Pan-Am Clipper departing Los Angeles Airport. The plane itself didn't encourage them about the comfort of the trip. "We had bunks on the plane. They folded down from above the seats, like an upper berth on a train." Though the flight seemed endless, the two men enjoyed kibitzing with the friendly stewardesses who made one leg of the journey pleasant. Part of the way, they were delighted to discover yet another celebrity on their flight. Brenda Marshall, who had played Jane to Johnny Weismuller's Tarzan, happened to be travelling to the Orient as well. In real life, Brenda Marshall was married to William Holden; she was flying east to join him in Burma where he filmed *The Bridge on the River Kwai*.

The captain of the clipper appeared as grizzled and experienced as any B-movie character. To Audie and Willard who fancied themselves sophisticated professional gamblers, the flight tested their sense of probability. On the way to Midway, the plane developed engine trouble, and they had to make an unexpected stopover. What worried the two men was not the sight of the captain with wrenches, conducting his own repairs, but the addition of the Filipino cook who worked as his assistant mechanic. After some labor, they announced the plane was fit again for the trek.

Gulping hard, Audie and Willard boarded again. Onward they flew, hearing next the announcement that a typhoon was dead ahead. The captain went on the intercom to state flatly that the storm was too big to fly around and the plane was unable to fly over it. So, the Clipper went into the teeth of the wind. A fugitive from the law of averages, Audie came through yet another ordeal unscathed. Here again Willard proved his long-standing adage, "Luck is for losers."

Not long after his arrival, Mike Mindlin noticed some odd details about various tourists who had come to Vietnam. "I remember meeting guys from the United States Air Force in Saigon. They told me who they were since they were all in civilian clothes. Since I was once in the Air Force myself, I struck up a conversation with them." Not considering himself political or attuned to the nuances of government, he did sense something wrong in the country.

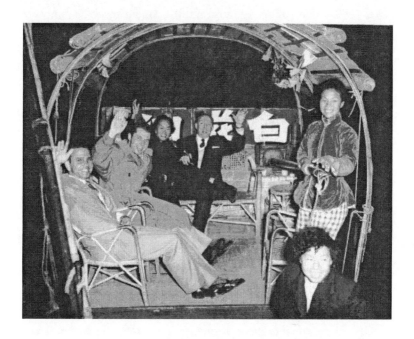

Before reaching Saigon, Audie Murphy landed in Hong Kong, where he was met by Dick Guardian and his wife from the Asian bureau of United Artists. Willard Willingham (far left) and Audie Murphy were entertained lavishly and reluctantly left after a four day layover. Photo courtesy of Willard Willingham.

"I realized that Americans had been sold a bill of goods about Vietnam. The government in Vietnam was reprehensible," stated Mindlin. When he seriously questioned the various young American airmen who were in Vietnam in January of 1957, they told him "we are doing aerial mapping of the country." His conversation left him "feeling uneasy." In years to come, he knew why.

To some, like Vinh Noan, the presence of American soldiers in civilian clothes was not unusual. He bluntly commented, "They were advisors, even as early as that. They did no fighting. There were many American military advisors in Vietnam at that time," although official American policy indicated these "advisors" did not arrive in Vietnam until 1959. Noan confirmed most of these Americans in Saigon were, in all likelihood, members of the Central Intelligence Agency.

One of the small trucks that often clogged the streets of Saigon greeted the film company as it scouted locations for the movie. Photo courtesy of Willard Willingham.

Before the excitement of Tet and the start of filming, all the supplies shipped from the United States cleared customs; and, even better, nothing appeared damaged during transit from Los Angeles. More traveling around the countryside firmed up various sites for the camera. In fact, Hornbeck's worry about the language problems improved slightly when Mankiewicz hired an interpreter, based on Vinh Noan's recommendation, to partner the Vietnamese cameraman. Hornbeck expressed delight to his wife in their correspondence when the director told him that he'd be used in many of the crowd scenes as an extra.

"Only long shots," he wrote to his wife. As part of the deal for placating the South Vietnamese government, Mankiewicz had also hired some "interns" who may or may not have had film experience, and who may or may not have been government observers.

Another major frustration, thought minor at first, was language. Mike Mindlin reported to the American press proudly that eight nationalities worked on the film: English, French, Italian, German, Australian, Polish, Vietnamese, and American. What he failed to note: none of the principals of the staff spoke French, one of two common languages in Saigon. No one from Figaro spoke Vietnamese—which precipitated the hiring of Vinh Noan as an Associate Producer. Worse yet, few local technicians and advisors in the fledgling film industry in Vietnam spoke English. A completely unexpected need of the Figaro company was someone who could speak Chinese.

No one thought Saigon had hundreds of thousands of Chinese living there. It was difficult enough to find bilingual people. The movie company was in dire need of quadra-lingual employees. Translators and interpreters had to be available for every phase of production. It played like farce; a Chinese translator spoke to a Vietnamese translator, who explained in French to someone who could talk English to the Figaro production staff. Many of the actors were bilingual, but hardly felt prepared to serve as consulting linguists for the production team. Vinh Noan couldn't be everywhere at once and do all his duties as well, though the Figaro troupe fairly ran him ragged because he was the bridge to all components of the culture, the language, the production.

After problems emerged with communications on the set, Vinh Noan hired translators to expedite the production with its multinational cast and crew. This translator spoke three languages fluently and worked closely with Audie Murphy. Photo courtesy of Willard Willingham.

Producer Walter Wanger reported a traditional pep talk that Mankiewicz delivered to his location crew members about the language and culture wherever they filmed. "Please bear in mind," the pipe-smoking director intoned, "that if it is difficult to communicate, the reason is that YOU do not speak their language . . . NOT that they do not speak yours!" Wanger's view conceded Joe's insights were appropriate to any time and any place film crews gathered at home or abroad.

Moments of early tension were dissipated by Joe, with his usual dry wit. One of the Vietnamese translators presented an Oriental beauty contest-type to Joe for possible use in the film. Because of the heavy accent of the girl, she introduced herself "Miss Phuog" in a way that sounded like, "Miss Fuck." Mankiewicz pulled the pipe from his mouth, tapped it on his wrist, and looked up: "What year?" Mike Mindlin was there to savor the humor.

The four days and nights of filming the Tet celebration required marathon strength. In terms of noise, crowds, and firecrackers, the Chinese New Year in Saigon is equivalent to a combination of American Independence Day, Rio's Carnaval, the New Orleans Mardi Gras, and an Easter Parade, going on and on for nearly a week. Sleeping during the day proved impossible, owing to the distant din of rockets and firecrackers of varying sizes. Many citizens, with long experience of the holiday, could sit at the curbside during the festivities and play Mah Jongg with full concentration. To prepare for the shoot, the crew went to the city's central Market Place to select angles for shots. With large crowds expected, Mankiewicz had to arrange well beforehand the placement of his cameras, their height above the streets, and decide where he'd perch on ladders to gain an overview of the square.

Noan busied himself with the logistics of set-ups. As he knew, the people in Vietnam were thrilled to have an American movie company doing its business in their community. "Everyone cooperated fully. I think many of the Hollywood people were surprised at how nice and accommodating these huge crowds of people could be." Vinh laughed to recall how the Figaro crew behaved in typical movie production fashion. "Oh, we acted like we owned the city. We'd close off streets and stop traffic. We'd tell the police what to do." Like movie fans everywhere in the world, gawkers and fans didn't mind a bit. After all, they never before had an opportunity to appear in a moving picture.

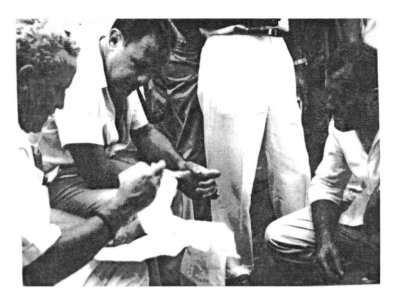

Joseph L. Mankiewicz prepares to film on a street in Saigon with Johnny Johnston (left) and Assistant Director Piero Mussetta. Photo courtesy of Vinh Noan.

Hornbeck took charge of the sound engineering. With Basil Fenton-Smith handling sound equipment, they went out with a 16mm tape recorder to make tests of cathedral bells at night. These tests went back to Rome for processing, and they had to wait to learn whether the effect was as Mankiewicz wanted it, or whether the equipment was not up to par. One of the problems immediately apparent was the poor sound quality when they used interiors in Saigon. This made them assign to Cinecitta nearly all the interior scenes (*e.g.,* Fowler's apartment, the Rendezvous Club, the Continental Hotel bar, and some of the military posts).

Sound recordings made in Vietnam utilized the services of Radio France at their Saigon studios; one indoor scene filmed in Vietnam has extremely poor sound quality, but was left in the final print, inexplicably, without being re-dubbed.

A few days before Tet, one unnecessary glitch particularly infuriated Mankiewicz. During night shoot, special effects wizard Rocky

Cline and his assistant George Schlicker tested his equipment; his most arduous task was to recreate a deadly terrorist bombing in downtown Saigon which had killed many innocent bystanders and children just a few years earlier. *The New York Times* reported the resulting practice detonations made the residents of the area "jumpy." Once again, the press spin on the facts tended to downplay the angst among the native Vietnamese as well as cast and crew.

One of the unreported incidents involving special effects supplied by the pugnacious Cline involved a near-fatal casualty. During set-ups of the explosions, one charge inadvertently went off in the hands of a Filipino technician. He was literally blown open by the charge and flown, by emergency crew, to Hong Kong for medical treatment. "He was quite badly hurt," commented Noan. The young man did recover from his injuries, but couldn't work again on the picture.

President Ngo Dinh Diem's government expressed concern for the noise and verisimilitude to past terrorist explosions. "Saigon's mayor was even summoned . . . to explain what the shooting was about. The country, after all, has been at complete peace for only a little more than a year, and nerves are still a trifle frayed," stated the report. Recreating this traumatic historical event on the exact location where it happened caused such consternation for locals that the authorities arrived. Just as Cline and Schlicker set off his rockets, "The police came and arrested Mr. Mankiewicz." The incident went unreported by American media.

In downtown Saigon, the famous Cathedral of Our Lady was not in the finished picture, but its bells were used for sound testing–and many cast members visited it as tourists, including Audie Murphy and Giorgia Moll. Photo courtesy of Willard Willingham..

This particular screw-up fell on the shoulders of Johnny Johnston, which was no surprise to Hornbeck. When the authorities wanted to haul Mankiewicz to jail, he was unable to produce the proper permits sanctioning his rehearsal. Johnny Johnston kept them locked in the hotel safe, and they were not readily accessed. Hornbeck sneered, "That's a fine place for the permits." As a consequence, according to Hornbeck, "Mankiewicz was fit to be tied." What made the entire episode more odious to the director was that Johnston didn't arrange to have an interpreter on the set. With the police speaking Vietnamese, and Mankiewicz speaking English, the resulting fracas bordered on either low-comedy or an international incident. The result was that the director relied heavily on Vinh Noan.

To no one's surprise, Mankiewicz became ill-tempered over every detail of the preliminaries. Later in the week when the police informed him that, when he climbed the director's ladder to survey the area he made himself a target of snipers, he cavalierly dismissed the dangers. "I can't see a frigging thing if I don't go up the ladder," he said. "I don't think they're going to shoot me. It would be stupid. Besides, there should be some way of protecting the ladder." He initiated a habit of retreating into his location trailer after each scene was shot; some speculated he worked on the script, ever evolving. The less kind hinted he hid from assassins.

If he were sequestered from the rest of the troupe, Mankiewicz maintained his contact to the social life of Vietnam through his Associate Producer. The director called on Vinh Noan to perform some duties of a personal nature. He requested Noan find him a young Chinese girl who was adept at performing oral sex. "Find some girl who gives a good blow job," he ordered Noan. Ever concerned that the head of Figaro received only the best of what Saigon offered, Vinh manfully interviewed each of the perspective girls with the same zeal he gave to his other hiring practices. Of course, to be certain of product quality control, Noan personally tested each girl to find just the right one to give Joe Mankiewicz his requested service before sending her over to the hotel room.

Because communist agents threatened Mankiewicz, Saigon authorities spread plants among the crowds to observe for dangers. Police briefed the director by playing tape recordings indicating a plot against the American who refused to be intimidated. He vociferously announced his plans to continue the movie. If he believed the rumors, he was courageous to pursue his film. If he didn't believe them, he took a reckless chance.

The night of Mankiewicz's arrest was also the date Audie Murphy's contract specified his arrival in Saigon. Though his appearance during the Tet festival would be similar to that of an extra, seen milling about and interacting with the locals, Audie didn't show up on the appointed day. With teeth already grinding over small and inconsequential problems, nothing surpassed the absence of the star of the picture. Redgrave had received permission to show up in Saigon at the end of the first week of February, which left the movie without either principal on the set for the Tet opening sequence. Mankiewicz was forced to alter the scene, by foregoing appearances of the major stars, except Claude Dauphin who showed up with sundry guards to discover the body of *The Quiet American.* Noan revealed the jeeps snaking their way through the thick crowds of celebrants in one of the early scenes of the picture were actual security forces doing their job, a newsreel view of the Tet.

As far as daytime filming, expert Robert Krasker recommended scenes commence at sunrise and stop filming by noon-time. As cinematographer, Krasker had jurisdiction over this issue. He feared the fierce sun and Saigon latitude made for too much heat–and light. According to Mike Mindlin, "The midday light was too flat for photographic purposes. It is impossible to describe the expressions of complete consternation on the faces of Vietnamese spectators when they saw Krasker using enormous arc lights in the brightest sunshine imaginable."

Krasker had worked on *The Third Man,* the most successful of any versions of a Graham Greene story made into movie; Krasker had won an Oscar for his brooding and Byzantine photography in Am Hof under Carol Reed's direction–but no such recognition came from his depiction of Saigon, though several sequences used in the film provide a sense of a lost culture, exotic and idiosyncratic. His Cao Dai temple pictures and images of the desolate Vietnam highway, as well as the shots of downtown Saigon, have his visionary stamp upon them.

Academy Award winner, Robert Krasker, selected by Joe Mankiewicz as his cinematopgrapher, had also worked on The Third Man, the most successful of all the Graham Greene stories made into movies. Photo courtesy of Vinh Noan.

American movies and their stars were wildly popular in what Hollywood might consider a backwater. Though Tet attracted many people under normal conditions, the word that a movie with American stars would be in town certainly contributed to the throngs. At 5:00 a.m. Hornbeck reported over 100,000 people were in the square in the center of Saigon. The numbers impressed Noan who had seen several

Tets. Hornbeck wrote in his diary: "We had lots of police and soldiers and at times they had to get rough." Because of the Chinese New Year holiday period, shooting occurred without delay.

Vinh Noan arranged much of the Tet shooting schedule. He had recommended the crew film in Cholon where the Chinese had a more public and social display. "The Vietnamese in Saigon tended to have small, private celebrations with their families, but the Cholon event was spectacular. The colors of the dragon's design cannot be counted. The fighters wore red and yellow satin clothes, all making for a bright display." At this point in the production, Vinh Noan approached Mankiewicz about the use of black and white photography when the city, its dynamic and exotic culture, cried out for color. As a director himself, Noan certainly would have opted for Technicolor and more action-oriented scenes. Mankiewicz had the money to do a color picture, but made the artistic decision to go with the shades of gray. "Black and white makes for a more dramatic story and image," he told his Associate Producer. And, that settled that.

The first night's shooting occurred at the Market Place and continued until 3:00 a.m. The biggest crowds witnessed the dragon dance, a colorful paper creation that stretched for eighty feet. Filming in black and white lost the brilliant aspects of the costumes, decorations, and fireworks. As unnerving as gunfire, the report of firecrackers startled members of the Figaro crew each time they exploded, no matter if in daylight or at night. The fear of Communist terrorism had the Chief of Army's security force on tenterhooks.

A few examples of police control seemed harsh to Americans, not exposed to depictions of African-Americans being hosed down by police on television news from the American South because they had demonstrated for Civil Rights. If nothing else, the intermittent racket of firecrackers proved to be maddening and obstructive, a redundancy, if that was possible in a city where life was measured by disruptions. No one on the Figaro crew wanted or expected the fireworks and local color to cease. After all, the noise and hoopla was the reason for being in Saigon.

The second night's shooting lasted till the crack of dawn. What pleased Hornbeck most was a privilege awarded him by the director: "Mank is letting me shoot the camera by myself. . ." This was perhaps the most spectacular of all the celebration. "They really put on a good show," an elated Hornbeck reported. Years later Giorgia Moll could only marvel at the dragons and press of crowds. Caught up in their excitement, she never considered security an issue, now attributing it to her inexperience.

The largest and most congested crowds turned up in the Chinese section of Saigon, Cholon. Here, however, could be heard some occasional anti-United States outbursts accusing Americans of attempting to take over the country by the bribery of their aid. Vinh Noan provided the perspective that the security force he hired to protect the cast and crew was the best in the business. One of his friends, having supplied the "private" force several years earlier for Noan's picture, was the Chief of the Army, a general under Diem. He willingly took charge of the safety issues. Their cordon around stars was so tight and so unobtrusive that many, like Giorgia, never knew the reason they felt so safe and secure was owed to the plainclothes guards that enveloped the Figaro people.

The third night's shooting continued in Cholon. With the press of crowds and heat, the experience heightened the growing fatigue. The toll touched nearly everyone in the film company, and Mankiewicz called it a wrap around 11:30 p.m. "When I finish work," Bill Hornbeck wrote his wife, "I am dead." The Film Editor was bothered by a growing sense of jealousy and pettiness of feeling that washed over the Figaro group. The testiness was not helped by the alcohol consumption of the film company. Hornbeck lamented this as he felt "on an individual basis" each person was "quite nice"–but the tension and stress distilled a bad mix of people; the shoot had become abrasive. Vinh Noan himself said, "I never liked the humidity of Saigon, and it was hard to work in those conditions."

Mindlin observed that people, after constrained proximity, tended to play on one another's nerves. "Bad habits become magnified. After a while, irritation sets in. I used to have lunch with one British member of the crew who drove me crazy. He'd push back his plate every day when he finished eating, then taking a toothpick would pick his teeth, while covering it with his other hand. A kind of European thing."

The English auditor of the film troupe, K.J. Richards, was the culprit. Mindlin had the idea that he would react in the only pleasant way an American could; he searched through the junk shops of Saigon for an old-fashioned harmonica. "Not an easy thing to do in Vietnam back then," he proudly boasted, "but I found one. Next time at lunch, when he started his usual post-meal activity, I cupped the harmonica in my mouth and began playing." Everyone at the table laughed appreciably, but Richards never understood the point–and continued with his fastidious habit.

The fourth night of Tet was a Wednesday and the scenes scheduled was to be directly in front of the crew's hotel: the Majestic. More dragon dancers showed up and employed in the film to great effect, but the only saving grace at the end of Tet was the notion that the crew and cast could quickly step into the hotel for a good dinner. As for the constant heat, people lost weight, having made booze the main course of their diet. Not being used to the cuisine also affected the American company. Everyone looked desperately for a means to cope with the unceasing humidity and discomfort. Personal hygiene became a lost cause to many of the crew. Hornbeck laughed it off by noting, "I just run with the perspiration."

One of the points of great pride for Vinh Noan when it came to his countrymen was their professionalism when it came to making the movie. Mankiewicz pulled him aside at one point to admit he was truly amazed by the fact that he had only to give instructions to the milling crowds once–and they did the actions perfectly. "They never look at the camera!" he told Noan with great relief. Having expected to need dozens of takes because of mugging extras, the director managed to complete work in efficient time. Such small successes helped a crew that found its energy drained by the heat, the frenzy, and the culture shock.

With phone service and other communications out of Vietnam highly unreliable, Audie's absence had created a visible sense of "tension" with the director. Mankiewicz may have wondered where his star was, but, as it happened, Audie simply chose to remain in Hong Kong for four days, not arriving in Saigon until the Tet festival was well underway. As he told his fellow traveler, Willard Willingham, "We'll wait in Hong Kong till they call for us," because he so loved the city.

Audie was in no hurry to reach to Saigon. All happy pictures of Audie in Hong Kong were taken by Willard. Though he continued to be apprehensive about the work in Vietnam, snapshots showed Audie good-naturedly walking the streets of Hong Kong while in transit and accepting the greetings of Asian diplomats, fans, and movie people. Audie knew he had no major scenes during Tet and hardly felt like hanging around the set doing nothing for a week. Besides that, as Willingham indicated, the star continued to express mixed feelings about the picture and the long stay in Saigon.

During the stopover in Hong Kong, Audie Murphy changed his mind about doing the film and had to be persuaded to continue to Saigon. Photo taken by Willard Willingham and courtesy of Audie Murphy Research Foundation.

The layover in Hong Kong seemed a well-deserved reward for the arduous trip. For that reason primarily Audie chose to skip his arrival date in Saigon. Besides, they had fabulous accommodations at the Peninsula Hotel on the tab of United Artists. Greeted at the airport by a contingent of executives, they were wined and dined in style. "Oh, we had a great time," recalled Willard. They were given a two bedroom suite with a view of the harbor and neighboring Kowloon. Under the circumstances, they remained in Hong Kong for four days until someone from Figaro put in an inquiry to the United Artists office, asking if the star of the picture had arrived. Once again, Audie was tempted to dump the picture and return to Los Angeles.

At last, to the delight of all the Figaro crew in Saigon, Audie Murphy landed in time for part of the festival. He flew in during the day when, in all likelihood, Mankiewicz and most of the crew were sleeping, as they had been up till early morning filming the festivities. At the tarmac, when he disembarked, the greeting contingent included a representative from the United States Embassy to Vietnam and Johnny Johnston who was ordered to be on hand when Audie landed, as well as a large contingent of the press. The star's doubts changed to expectations and hopes as he reached Saigon. Usually taciturn and glum, for a man who had traveled half way across the world, he positively glowed, brighter than the Vietnamese sunshine at midday.

Unfortunately, the press corps clouded the tarmac. When Willard looked out the window of the plane as it taxied to the terminal, he saw the "vast array of reporters."

This was not one of his favorite duties when it came to helping Audie, but this time he fulfilled it unknowingly. When the plane came to a halt, Audie moved along quickly, but Willard remained in the rear of the plane, seated, gathering his and Audie's belongings, when a "bumptious" reporter somehow forced his way onto the plane. He ran down the aisle and hemmed in Willard, peppering him with a dozen questions. "He was interviewing me, thinking I was Audie!" Willingham glanced out the window and pointed to the crowd chasing Audie on the tarmac. "There's your quarry," Willard indicated.

For Audie the future looked brighter upon his arrival in Saigon: his first prestigious role with one of the all-time great directors. Willard was there, a Passepartout if ever the role called for one, a man who could allay Audie's apprehensions and serve him with a steady stream of inventive solutions and grounded advice. Though he was not billed as Audie's double or stand-in for the Figaro manifest, his usefulness centered on such duty. He provided Audie with the Man Friday a star needed while coping with tiresome location work.

Audie was well aware of the early news dispatches about possible assassination attempts upon the principals involved in the movie. Fearing kidnap or worse, Audie purchased pistols and ammunition for his protection while in Hong Kong during his prolonged layover. Nothing dampened his optimism, certainly not Viet Cong terrorists who slunk around the countryside in black pajamas. He told a reporter several years later that he kept 500 rounds in his hotel room at the Majestic, just in case the communist terrorists tried to take him out. "The Commies were only sixteen miles from Saigon at that time, and you never knew what was going to happen." Willard confirmed, "It was a dangerous city to those who knew what was going on."

Mike Mindlin told about going into Audie's hotel room at the Majestic one time to visit. Upon entering, he found the star brandishing a weapon. "He always carried a .45." Since Mindlin had a peaceful nature, he chastised the actor: "Audie, would you put that thing away?" Probably amused at the nervous executive, Audie did so without objection. It was the kind of incident that left Mindlin with a "vague sense of danger and quite uneasy" about the world they had entered. Yet, like most confident Americans of the age, he remained largely impervious to the potential terror and violence which was the hallmark of Vietnam during the years between the French war and the hapless American intervention. In the movie the Viet Minh communists do "get" Audie, which makes him represent the first American casualty of the Vietnam War. Needless to say, in January of 1957, the nation had no idea of the protracted American combat to occur within a few years.

Life on the set grew complicated in Saigon by a reporter's false news stories that the production was to be a "travesty" of Greene's artful novel. This led Greene, in England, to savage a picture that had not done its principal photography, let alone be released as a finished product. Greene suggested the version underway would prove to be a laughable commodity. As expected, Mankiewicz took offense and expressed his umbrage to actor Claude Dauphin who played the Inspector. The director of the picture defended changing the novel because its content seemingly served as a diatribe against the United States. Among those agreeing with him was Noan who simply believed, "Joe bought the book, paid for it, and now he could do what he wanted with it."

Once settled in his hotel room, Audie looked for the new script with all its promised changes. When the Figaro people delivered his new copy, Audie's bad temper exploded. There were no changes he requested. Audie saw at the same script he had read in Los Angeles. Mankiewicz explained he hadn't gotten around to making the alterations Audie wanted. Within minutes, Audie had a telephone in hand and called Los Angeles. Before much time elapsed, he fired his agent, Paul Kohner, his lawyer, and anyone else he could think of blaming. Willingham knew enough to lie low during the turmoil, and Mankiewicz and the Figaro people had to rely on Willard's ability to soothe Audie into a calmer frame of mind.

The only solution to an explosive situation was for the director to capitulate. If Audie was a stick of dynamite with a lit fuse, then Figaro itself was the target. "Audie was malleable," concluded one co-star. "He was learning all the time. That was the best part of the fact that he was not a real actor." This characteristic motivated him to proceed with a picture out of his usual scope, but he still knew what he could and could not do on screen. "If you wanted Audie Murphy, that's who you got," insisted one associate, "You didn't expect Audie to turn into Brando or Clift."

Mankiewicz quickly made a few cosmetic edits in his script. What was important to Audie were two vindications. First, the character's name was now "anonymous" and, at the end, over his corpse in a mortuary, the police explained he was not an American spy or agitator. Redgrave's Fowler allowed himself to serve as an accessory to murder by the Viet Minh to cause the death of an innocent man. If Mankiewicz had a mission in this movie, he wanted to expose the falsity of Greene's politics. It was the American director's position that Greene was not such an intellectual, but had simply penned this "serious" novel out of bilious humor and pure pique. Nonetheless, Audie couldn't be called "mollified" in any sense. He had been lured half-way around the world betrayed, and now all bets were off.

At the Hotel Majestic, Audie's room overlooked the square, absorbing the noise of traffic on the streets below. To him, the constant turmoil interrupted sleep, but as he said: "I probably won't sleep much anyway." In those days Saigon was constantly chaotic; its cacophony of sounds allowed for no respite. Audie's suite also had a verandah upon which he stood, watching the crowded, mad confusion down below. "Someone could toss a hand grenade up here," he announced, explaining why several windows and French doors had mesh coverings on the outside, according to Jim Kirkwood who questioned Audie about it several years thereafter. A few window panes used tape to prevent shattering glass from flying in case of an explosion.

Also a traveller to the Third World, Jan Merlin confirmed, "I can understand Audie preferring to stay in his room or look at the city from his balcony. When I did a film in Manila, I spent lots of time at the window of my room. I didn't like going out, nor walking through the city particularly because of the constant approach of beggars . . . so hard to refuse, but if you stopped to give one anything, you were inundated by a horde of other outstretched, grasping hands and had to fight your way free. It would have been even worse for Audie because of their recognition of him."

Between takes at the Tu Do Street apartment, Audie Murphy regards Saigon with a forlorn attitude. He returned to filming in Saigon shortly after nearly dying from a ruptured appendix. Photo courtesy of Willard Willingham.

Audie himself was quite diplomatic in a piece written for him by Spec McClure upon his return to the States. He said he found the people "reserved, unobtrusive and understanding." Of the horde at the airport to greet him, he noted they did indeed follow him to the hotel and congregated in the lobby, "waiting to look, but they wouldn't bother us." He concluded they were "very polite."

Perhaps Murphy didn't feel the discomfort of the heat, though a medical crisis was brewing within his intestines. Perhaps his years of knotted stomach, vomiting spontaneously, and myriad ills, simply went ignored. The symptoms of his ailment had to be growling in his groin from the moment he landed in southeast Asia. Had he taken heed, he would not have been ambushed by an attack of appendicitis. Willingham hinted the disregard could have been tied to Audie's desire to quit the picture. He wanted to pull out of Vietnam as soon as he saw the script unedited, unchanged, and unacceptable. But, for distraction, he looked for the nearest card game, a standard past-time on movie sets.

The view from Audie's window at the Hotel Majestic, beyond the square was downtown Saigon, with its main boulevards and dozens of tiny off-shooting streets; long vertical signs in Chinese character were displayed in abundance, outnumbering signs in French. English bill-boards were rare in those days; the names of streets still bore the French words: "Rue de . . . ", four years after the French had abandoned their colony. The square was also a patchwork of shops, vegetable and fruit stands, milk bars, outdoor barber shops, and an enterprising array of fortune tellers.

During one of his rare forays outside socially, Audie was surprised to learn that many fans had "passport size photos" of him. He discovered, "that there was a vendor outside who'd set up shop. This means he'd gotten some photos when he'd learned we were to location there, spread a handkerchief on a curb, and was in business."

Of course, cathedrals and temples speckled streets throughout the city. With the mossy black rot of smoke and humidity, stones of the buildings bore a slimy covering and appeared decrepit, prematurely aged. Most of the Catholic churches were erected during the French colonial period of the previous hundred years. Yet, many cathedrals had been newly constructed.

Some cathedrals were no older than their congregations. Another overall impression of Vietnam in the decade before the American intervention and war was that of a country-wide junkyard. Out of fear of shortages, or warped values, or spiritual equality of every person and object, the Vietnamese never threw away anything: rotting tin pans, broken chairs, spare tires, moldy cushions, carburetors, just about anything might be lying aside the road, next to a shop, next to a food stand; whatever garbage remained smoldered in ubiquitous heaps like neighborhood cairns.

Finding Vietnam unlike their homeland, Westerners suffered shock in the world of the Orient. Because fertilizers employed for farming came directly from gathered human excrement, a disagreeable odor hovered over the land. Lack of sanitation often allowed human waste to puddle or flow along curbsides, raising a pervasive aroma offensive to the nostrils of Western visitors. The Americans in the Figaro troupe felt deep revulsion; the Europeans seemed more tolerant.

Of the locals, youngsters were strikingly beautiful youths and maidens who darted among the crowd of aged people horridly deteriorated in comparison: toothless, shriveled ancient men and women rested on haunches everywhere, as if the adults, the middle-aged, had been killed in conflicts between the French and the Communists. The boys resembled Audie: eternally young, until that day when abruptly they became old men. Nothing in between in this steamy nation. Most of the children were Audie Murphy fans. Each morning they crowded around the hotel entrance expectantly, hoping to see "AUDEE!"–a name they cried out like teenagers anywhere.

Security hired by Figaro, Incorporated, need not caution Audie and other stars. Their rule of professionalism hinged only on one precept: keep the fans away from the set and performers. The only man in the picture with a recognizable face was Murphy. Though he was known as a war hero among the Vietnamese, his western pictures did play in Saigon–and he had a following. With the security force arranged by Vinh Noan, the stars never needed to stop and sign autographs. The public found itself far from the actors, owing to the Chief of Army's experienced troops whose specialty was crowd control.

Among those who enjoyed going out and never noticed the security ring around her was Elaine Schreyeck. "We all enjoyed riding around in the Tri-shaws or Pousee-pousses as they were called. There was an air about the place that time just didn't matter . . ."

Cars of the performers had chauffeurs and could not be left unattended. Mankiewicz had always insisted on having a driver for his personal limousines; a combination body guard driver made sense to him.

Unfortunately, the crew discovered these "drivers" exhibited careless skills. Their reckless driving generally was more dangerous than threats from the communists. "We were in an accident one time," Mike Mindlin remembered. "Their driving was a problem because they were operating big American cars, and the drivers were so short, they could barely see over the steering wheel. In addition, to that, we were helpless to speak to them. They didn't speak English and we didn't speak Vietnamese. Not being able to talk to them, we couldn't say things like, 'Will you slow down!' It was frustrating and dangerous." The streets were filled with cyclos, bikes, scooters, animals, and people. Vinh Noan claimed, "There were no traffic regulations. You were on your own. It was entirely up to pedestrians to avoid the traffic."

Another requirement of the Vietnamese government had private guards deployed throughout the hotel, and floor restrictions prevented the general public from gaining access to the stars and crew. "I think the actors could wander out in the streets if they wanted," Vinh Noan reflected many years later. "I do not believe they were followed all the time." Armed agents remained at their stations near the elevators to keep out unwanted fans—or terrorists. One of the universal sights in Southeast Asia in those days was the uniformed guard with his automatic rifle or sidearm at the entrance of every hotel, bank, or big commercial business.

In early February, shortly after the Tet celebration ended, Mankiewicz, Johnston, Hornbeck, and key staff went up the seacoast where they filmed exteriors for the most dynamic and dramatic sequence in the picture—near one of the army watchtowers which dotted the main road from Saigon to Hanoi. The perilous roadway required a drive of nearly one and a half hour. For dramatic effect, the scene was done at dusk. "It should make a wonderful shot," Hornbeck told his wife. For further protection President Ngo Dinh Diem ordered his Army of Vietnam to cooperate with the film company, with rumors that among the American Friends, proto-type Peace Corps sorts, were Central Intelligence personnel on guard.

This scene proved to be the most suspenseful in the picture, meant to feature Fowler and the American driving alone a desolate road dotted with look-out towers erected to watch for terrorist rocket attacks. When their car breaks down, they take refuge in one of these towers—but are soon set upon by the Viet Minh.

Trying to escape, the reporter fractures an ankle and the American assists him to a suitable hideout as the tower explodes behind them. They run into the rice paddy to avoid the barrage of gunfire. The scene ends with the American doing the "fireman's lift" on the taller and heavier actor. Actually, during that Vietnam filming, doubles stood in for both principal actors throughout since the company dared not risk taking Audie into such dangerous areas. Close-ups and dialogue for this sequence were to be done in Rome weeks later.

The shoot was enhanced by filters to seem nightmarish. Everyone was jittery about this because Viet Minh had allegedly threatened to kidnap Mankiewicz during the scene and kill Audie. Noan dismissed this possibility as he believed that the Viet Minh Communists in 1957 simply had not the firepower or manpower to conduct serious terrorist operations. Nonetheless, since the special effects done in Vietnam were nerve-wracking because of local misunderstandings, Rocky Cline knew they required exact synchronization, extra precaution, and plotted to the second. Noan was awed by the realistic effect in which the watchtowers exploded under mortar attack from the Viet Minh.

Not needed until after the Tet celebration, the key supporting actors flew in from Rome via Air France, arriving on February 1st. The group included a trio of actors to portray the members of the Fourth Estate in the picture: Bruce Cabot played Granger, Peter Trent as Wilkins, and Fred Colson played Morton in Vietnam, but by the time they reached Rome, his role belonged to Clinton Andersen who received the cast billing in the film. They were the same person; Colson used his stage name.

Newcomers found their director armored behind a tough guy veneer. Whatever had no direct connection to Mankiewicz—or to his film—had no relevance in his life. The barbs by author Graham Greene and his minions of the press had burrowed like ticks into Mankiewicz's hide. For an actor as sensitive as Redgrave, the negative media coverage unnerved him, and the attitude of the man in charge of the film was devastating. Murphy had for nearly ten years played up to the movie rags, giving banal interviews and opening up his home and private life to photo spreads and the like. He consented to the exposure as simply as another unavoidable vexation, something to do amiably as possible. Bad or good, the press didn't bother him.

In a picture hinting at complex, hypocritical, untruthful, and manipulative relationships between its characters, there were two galvanizing, violent scenes: the lonely road where *The Quiet American* and British reporter were attacked and nearly killed by Viet Minh on patrol and the grande finale, when a Saigon square was bombed, killing many innocent civilians. The picture repeatedly built itself to a powerful moment of irrational forces, between stretches of mundane exposition. The style of sudden punctuation of violence within placid caesuras appealed to Audie, who later observed he found his life and career a series of efforts "to keep from being bored to death."

7

SCHEDULED TO BE in Vietnam for eight weeks, the Figaro troupe felt it lasted much, much longer. Giorgia Moll expressed surprise upon learning, years later, how much time she actually spent in Saigon. She felt she had lived there at least three months. "Everyone suffered from acute pangs of isolation," concluded Mike Mindlin. He reported back to the United States that Joseph Mankiewicz "termed the prevailing emotion the 'But Are You Absolutely Certain The Rest of the World is Still There' trauma." Mindlin admitted the shoot was hectic, intense, complicated, imponderable, and rife with unexpected problems.

Nasty items appeared in the *London Times* about the production. A correspondent filed reports that the cast and crew insulted the locals. Worst of all, suspicions arose that Joe Mankiewicz pandered to the political machinations of President Diem in order to gain governmental cooperation. As Robby Lantz said, the entire filming had been "arranged" through the good auspices of the Central Intelligence Agency. Overseeing all "overseas" productions, Eric Pleskow vehemently denied that the CIA had damaged the integrity of the film. Graham Greene's novel required a reverence usually assumed by scholars who read the Dead Sea Scrolls–and Joe heard ludicrous accusations from abroad of trashing a holy book. Forty years later a historian called Greene's literature "a caricature" of Vietnam.

Michael Redgrave deserved credit for writing a rebuttal to the *Times,* defending the film: Greene later cut him for this. Joe took to calling his source book by Greene "cheap melodrama" at every opportunity. He asserted all the false moments in the screenplay were literal crossovers from Greene's book, blaming the book for any failure the movie might have.

If President Diem did not already regret allowing this film to be done on location, more reasons emerged later. Vinh Noan, however, believed that Diem barely knew little about the production and cared less about the movie beyond its propaganda and public relations value. "He was not exactly a movie fan, though he may have had a projection room in the palace. He was usually occupied with matters other than movies."

Audie too had other matters on his mind. After compromising with the humidity, aromas, and other cultural differences of Saigon, he hadn't lessened his anger about the deception Mankiewicz had tendered on him. The script was not to his liking. The country was not what he expected, and now he felt unwell. Though he had suffered his trick stomach for many years, the worsening of pains and discomfort led him to consult a doctor. As the United States martial presence in Vietnam was growing, unbeknownst to the world, Audie had these contacts available to him. He used them to find an American military doctor in Saigon. When he consulted with the U.S.Army major, the diagnosis was not good. In the opinion of the physician, Audie suffered from appendicitis, and it could become worse.

One of Audie's strengths was also one of his foibles. He had an extraordinary tolerance of pain and exhibited stoicism as his personal badge. "He was held together with wires, you know," commented Ben Cooper. The pain of the war wounds were continuous, and he learned to bear the intolerable. "He would fall on his bad hip all the time, off horses and during fight scenes. Yet, he never complained. He literally kept getting back on the horse."

On Wednesday, February 6th, the nighttime shooting was completed in Cholon, and a change of plans abruptly derailed the company's schedule. Audie called a meeting with Mankiewicz. In attendance were Willard, Audie, Audie's medical doctor, Alfred Katz, and the director. Since Joe Mankiewicz knew Audie was unhappy with the script, he was given his first inkling that he might lose the star totally. Any doubts Joe had that the crisis was not real, was undercut by the doctor's dire prediction. He wanted to fly Audie to Hong Kong for likely surgery as soon as possible.

One member of Figaro, Mindlin's assistant Alfred Katz, would be allowed to accompany Audie and Willard on the military plane out of Saigon. At this meeting, a decision to put a lid on the medical problem with Audie seemingly occurred. The knowledge of Audie's appendectomy would be limited to the key people in the room, with only leaks of it to slip out in later months. The official story was that Audie would travel to Hong Kong on holiday and "catch the flu," keeping him there for a short time.

A majority of colleagues, including Redgrave, Noan, and Mindlin, didn't know about Audie's condition, since the matter was hushed up as part of a mutual agreement between Audie and Mankiewicz. The matter never received accurate press coverage, and Redgrave's belief Audie had "a bug of some sort" echoed the official disinformation. The necessity for a cover-up ranged from protecting Audie's indestructible image to not alarming Figaro producers and insurance companies. Forty years after the event, surviving cast and crew members expressed astonishment that this medical crisis of the star hadn't been revealed to them when it occurred.

Prior to his appendicitis attack, Audie had been dismissing the bouts of vomiting and nausea as part of his long-standing condition. Audie surely suffered frequently and at length before his inflamed appendix brought him down. He never once complained of pain or discomfort, either before or after his surgery, to Vinh Noan who spent much time with him.

For the rest of the crew, the truth of Audie's appendicitis would be withheld. So, the story release was that his trip to the Orient included sight-seeing and picking up souvenirs for friends and family; a lapse in the shooting schedule provided time to leave the area for a side trip to Hong Kong after just a week, and Audie fell ill in that British colony. His "tricky stomach" had been acting up again. He was always feeling the heat, yet seldom without a tie and jacket in his scenes. Nearly all his movie scenes called for him to dress well, wearing a tie usually. After all, the temperature was over one hundred degrees, humid too. The extent of his feverish feeling failed to alarm others in the troupe, never thinking it could be prelude to something worse. After all, nearly everyone felt disoriented and whoozy from the abrupt change of time and culture.

In the States Spec McClure, so concerned with Audie's illnesses over the years, had sought medical advice on what was occurring to Audie. He was told that the solar plexus was "one of the most sensitive and important of the body nerve centers . . . A wild impulse striking the center can cause the feeling of nausea. The impulse can be started by a flick of memory; a sight or sound which, though seemingly innocuous, can associate itself with some buried thing in the subconscious, starting the chain reaction." McClure learned how this may have caused Audie's occasional violent shakes. Audie was often edgy, "tensing up as if ready to spring and muttering imprecations under his breath. This would happen, for example, if a waitress would be overly careless in setting down a glass of water before him."

No sooner did Audie—and his escorts, Katz, Willingham, and the army doctor—land in Hong Kong, he had pains in his lower abdomen and couldn't straighten up when he stepped out of a car. Hospitalization ensued immediately. Emergency surgery seemed to be the recourse. The nagging stomach problem he attributed to the cuisine doubled him over in pain, and he was rushed to a hospital where he heard the diagnosis of acute appendicitis. He was under anesthesia and into surgery immediately. As he was in a strange place and felt alienated, the experience seemed unreal. Yet, just as his days at war, his survival became his sole issue. He had a cable sent to Joe Mankiewicz from the examining doctor who predicted a four to seven week convalescence. Willingham hinted this extended convalescence was a ruse by Audie to end the connection to the picture.

"Audie was stalling," concluded Willingham. The star knew full well that, if he had such a long recovery, Mankiewicz would be forced to replace him in the cast. "Audie simply did not want to go back to Saigon." In the British haven, the U.S. Army major put Audie one of the best hospitals in Hong Kong, tended by nuns. He had hoped to solve the problem of apprendicitis with "a pill or something," but he found himself "at the Matilda War and Memorial Hospital, having my appendix out. Although I had excellent care there, I did wish at the time I was home in th San Fernando Valley with Pam and the kids." The hospital staff, of course, treated him with much deference and kind pampering which Audie found delightful. He announced to Willard, "I have a good excuse not to go back to the movie." Audie told him he hated Vietnam and was totally unhappy with the script.

Since Audie was the main character in the exterior shooting schedule, Mankiewicz hoped for a short delay. A longer delay without Murphy rendered the entire trip to Vietnam an exercise in futility. If Murphy were out of action for the entire time the troupe stayed in Vietnam, Mankiewicz would have to consider a replacement. Back in Saigon, the director was beside himself with agitation. His principal actor and absolute centerpiece of his film schedule being unavailable, they were limited to doing long shots with doubles and stand-ins. Using his imaginative talents, he was able to concoct twists to the script, but on the whole production practically ceased. Noan expressed admiration and amazement, "He always liked to find an idea on the set about how to stage his script."

While Audie was in Hong Kong, and for a week thereafter, no filming ensued, other than background photography, and Mankiewicz revised the script to make Audie's Vietnam scenes rather bland and non-physical, having him riding in a car or being pulled in a trishaw. Murphy was the pivotal part of the story-line exteriors, and much of the movie suffered as a consequence of his illness. In his own way, Audie extracted script changes from Mankiewicz which no one else had been capable of doing.

Mankiewicz hadn't counted on Audie's allergic reaction to drugs, the reason sent to the director for Audie's long delay in returning to Vietnam. The isolation and poor communication, not knowing how his star was doing in Hong Kong, provided Mankiewicz with many introspective moments. Though the director might feel sympathy for Audie, their relationship was tenuous. They were travelers engaged in a length journey together, but would be strangers again once it ended.

Decency motivated Mankiewicz's concern to a lesser degree than business. He didn't want to shelve the picture. Telephone lines to Hong Kong fell short of American standards or expectations, and the Figaro troupe found themselves severely limited in their ability to make phone calls from Vietnam, due to technical snafus, party line conversations, and a window frame of only an hour per day to reach the hospital.

Mankiewicz wondered if Montgomery Clift might recover his health enough to show up in Vietnam to take over the role, but Audie would not be hospitalized the four to six weeks doctors had predicted. Mankiewicz realized the advantages to replace Murphy were too few. When he weighed the options, the director chose to play the hand he was dealt. He stuck with Audie.

There was still a trump card for Mankiewicz to play: Willard Willingham. Acting as Figaro's intermediary, Alfred Katz had to appeal to Willard. Only he had the influence and ear of Audie. If Willingham could not convince Audie to return to Vietnam, or at least to stay on the picture, the production fell into jeopardy. To the great relief of Katz, Willard agreed to raise the issue with Audie. "I wanted to go onto Rome," said the stunt double. So, using his own disappointment with aborting their journey, he begged Audie to reconsider his opinion. "The advantages were that, when we got to Italy, Audie would again be able to see Anzio–which held a big place in his heart. He fought his way from there to Rome." Willard insisted he shouldn't give up the chance to return to those important places. It worked, and Audie relented. Mankiewicz and Figaro could breathe more easily.

Since Audie was a national treasure, the best way to protect their star and investment in the film project was to call on the American military services. One of the Generals of SEATO alliance cut through red tape to have army doctors sent to Audie's bedside days after his operation. The military immediately put Audie under its protection, flying him from the Hong Kong hospital to be placed under Army supervision while in Saigon.

According to the Hornbeck diaries, Alfred Katz returned from his Hong Kong mission around noontime on Friday, February 15th, nine days after Audie's surgery. The actor's condition was supposedly quite bad, and further reports indicated that he proceeded to lose fifteen pounds–which made him seem emaciated with his small frame. On top of this, he expressed no inclination to work after returning. Instead, he preferred to remain in his hotel room, avoiding the troupe, the crowds, the entire situation which he disliked.

In the hot and unpleasant conditions of Vietnam, Audie never truly recovered his zest, his health, or his commitment to the picture. Kept away from the rest of the Figaro crew, Audie rested in his Majestic suite. Several weeks after the operation, Audie wrote to Spec McClure about his illness and the pace of recovery. "My operation is still draining. If this keeps up, it will have a longer run than most of my pictures." His absence continued to be explained with false reports about his health, or with the excuse that he was not needed on the set. Audie's inactivity would impel him to report for work at the end of the month.

Though Redgrave stated on February 7, 1957, "I was eager to meet (Audie)," he was less than disingenuous. Right from the start, he had expected more of Audie than he should have a right. He peevishly expressed his annoyance that, after cutting short a New York TV commitment, and having agonized about the decision, Audie didn't deign to greet him at the airport in Saigon.

Upon de-planing, four weeks later than many others in the troupe, he discovered rather casually that Audie had been temporarily hospitalized in Hong Kong. He told friends back home that Audie contracted "some germ or other," leaving them to their own conclusions. He also disdainfully complained Audie's recovery was slow, probably to his overuse of penicillin during his recovery from wounds in World War II. Redgrave's characterization was petty, misleading, and diminished the dreadful seriousness of Audie's acute appendicitis. In all likelihood, Redgrave was spared the truth of the matter in order not to alarm him about the progress of the production.

When Redgrave arrived, the Cao Dai festival had begun and, lacking Murphy for the scene, Mankiewicz insisted the British actor hurry up to Tayninh immediately. Though he had not slept for two nights, during the arduous flight, the star "was rushed through customs and put in front of the camera before he was altogether aware of what was happening."

Then, Redgrave discovered he had plenty of free time. Murphy's illness closed the production, essentially, for an unspecified amount of time. So, his haste to leave America and another commitment had been for naught; he was not so desperately needed on the set of *The Quiet American*. Redgrave's feelings were downplayed by Mindlin in his dispatches out of Cinecitta when they reached Rome. He sent back to the United States a report that "Redgrave has some rather vague memories of being in Vietnam." Considering the dark future which awaited Sir Michael Redgrave, beneath the humor could be discerned the predictive truth. During Audie's convalescence, Mankiewicz decided to film a special major event, the pilgrimage of the Cao Dai: a quasi-religious/political group in the Tayninh area. This too was a celebration of several days' duration including processions, colorful costumes, cardinals of both male and female sexes, soldiers, and the installation of the "pope" of this particular sect. Since politics and religion mixed well, Mankiewicz expected he could take advantage of the exotic pageant.

In messages back to the home front, Mike Mindlin maintained assurances regarding the company's "innocent involvement" regarding political turmoil in the southeast Asian country. It would hardly do to have accusations about this group of American movie-makers stirring the pot or causing an international crisis. Mindlin reported: "The unit was in Tayninh, seventy-five miles north west of Saigon, filming what was represented as a religious procession. The impressive spectacle, in which 40,000 disciples of the strange Cao Dai sect participated, turned into an illegal demonstration for the return of their pope who is living in exile in neighboring Cambodia." He avoided mentioning that Mankiewicz meant to capture this pivotal moment on film, no matter what. "No one had any reason to believe this was anything but a religious procession," he argued. "The proceedings seemed a trifle lacking in spiritual quality, but then again no one in the unit had ever seen an Oriental religious procession before this."

As if to underscore how the Vietnamese took advantage of the city-slicker Americans, he went on to defend the indefensible: "The police, in the meantime, did nothing to stop the demonstration because they had been led to believe that all was being staged at the request of *The Quiet American*, which had gotten complete cooperation from the Vietnamese government."

As the crew filmed the religious procession on a Tayninh street, apparently some citizens took offense at the sacrilege of imitation, while others found easy political reason to riot. The protests and perpetrators were like summer thunderstorms, squalls that rose up suddenly and disappeared in a march of angry feet, just as quickly. The daily crises took a toll on Joe Mankiewicz: in two weeks he lost many pounds, and local reactions to him gained a new title, which could be translated as "Frog Face with Pipe."

The site of this event, earlier chosen for an important parade scene, was near a cathedral where Mankiewicz collected atmosphere, scenes not necessarily seen in the finished picture. Much of what was filmed never made it into the released version of the movie. Unfortunately, this situation called for an actor in the garments and official robes of the titular head of the local Buddhist sect in solemn procession down the avenue before the adoring masses. No one told the religious disciples it was make-believe; they had come to the conclusion that a new "pope" enjoyed a sudden installation ceremony, indicating political machinations.

The traditional mode of transportation around the city was the cyclo or cyclo-pousse, a smaller version of the trishaw or tricycle driven carriage. Photo courtesy of Willard Willingham.

Elaine Schreyeck confirmed "there was some sort of demonstration, people with banners, etc., and we may have recorded this on film, as the authorities wanted us to hand over the film—but we didn't surrender it—and we had to leave the area." At first the shouts and carryings-on resembled typical religious protest, standard around the Far East where Buddhist priests would, in subsequent years, douse themselves in gasoline and set themselves ablaze in city streets as protest.

During filming, mundane protests always cropped up suddenly and sporadically. However, the American envoys of peace and humanitarianism around Vietnam, as some analysts have concluded, were CIA (Central Intelligence Agency) people. Air America was largely made up of Agency people, from top to bottom. Hornbeck and others joined several groups in Saigon, including the International Rescue Committee. Noan revealed his opinion that it was rife with players from the United States secret agency. All the Figaro people were acutely sensitive to "political" demonstration. Somehow the two mixed during this latest protest. The volatile situation threatened to explode into a riot, and filming ceased. The crew dismantled sets and retrieved props.

Most of the crew spent Wednesday through Friday, February 6th through the 9th, at Tayninh. Whatever Mankiewicz wanted to shoot inside the cathedral, according to Vinh Noan, could not be accomplished, owing to misunderstandings, political unrest, and religious rules. "All the interior temple scenes were done at Cinecitta." Mankiewicz subscribed to a philosophy that drove his producers to madness: his dictum was to shoot long, and cut later. This, as Walter Wanger remarked about Joe's method, "was an expensive way to work."

On the other hand, Eric Pleskow, one of the most honored of all producers in Hollywood with over thirteen Oscars, dismissed the practice of overshooting. "It happens all the time. More today than ever, especially if a director has clout." Miss Moll had been used to lira pinching companies in Italy and marveled at the endless takes Mankiewicz required: "He took so many shots for one scene . . . left side, right side, all different angles." Vinh Noan also confirmed the director did each scene five times, at least, in order to keep his editing options at a premium.

Filming in the streets of Saigon was essentially no different from a typical location shoot. Crowd control always dominated security; curious by-standers wanted a closer examination of the unfolding events, so unlike what finally appeared on screen. Mankiewicz and Johnston, together with assistant director Piero Mussetta and technical advisor Vinh Noan, held endless conferences before shooting each segment of film. All wore lightweight cotton shirts, short sleeved with open collars, two or three buttons undone, depending upon the degree of heat each man could tolerate.

Only Noan, a native, remained crisp in his freshly ironed white khakis, though he too thought the humidity enervating. The director with his pipe always clenched between his teeth, even if unlit, sat and looked over Johnston's shoulder at the script. Like generals before setting foot on a battlefield, each key member of the team took notes as to where the deployed actors and extras would stand, move, or enter and exit.

Johnny Johnston took much blame from the producers of the film for the botched timing in regard to the use of one of the Buddhist pagodas where Mankiewicz wanted to film. "Weeks before the scene was scheduled, Johnston and Buddhist authorities agreed on a specific date. However, when cast, crew, and equipment arrived on the designated day, they were told it wouldn't be possible for them to work inside the temple because the moon was in its third quarter. The costly day was saved by some extremely hasty rescheduling," wrote Mike Mindlin. Yet, Johnston was dedicated to Mankiewicz, reported Noan, and the feeling seemed to him to be mutual. Another scene was filmed instead, at a different location.

In essence, Mankiewicz ran into a brick wall no matter which way he turned. Erratic deliveries made it problematical to see the results of what he had shot to decide if he needed to do his work over. The production, according to Giorgia Moll, had reached an impasse and fairly much closed down for two weeks, at least. Murphy didn't work with her on the film for nearly three weeks. It gave her, however, time to enjoy the culture of Saigon, but increased her worry and anxiety about how well she worked in "my first important picture." She claims to have spent long hours, not with Joe Mankiewicz, but with her dialogue coach and language teacher. "I had to learn Vietnamese. I still can

154

remember a few sentences, in case I ever go back," she pertly added. On the other hand, Audie's illness and hospitalization had a disquieting effect on the entire production: "It killed everything," said Giorgia.

Redgrave, during this delay in his own filming schedule, went off to enjoy the sites. He admitted cavalierly: "I left Audie to fend for himself." The tall actor flew up to Angkor Wat to photograph the ancient ruins. He later showed his daughter, actress Vanessa, dozens and dozens of pictures of the country and instilled her rudimentary hostility to American involvement in southeast Asia. As his plane crossed the jungles of Cambodia, he thought how much this experience in Vietnam reminded him of an earlier movie in his career: *The Night My Number Came Up.* Its title, unsettling, gave him more than usual pause.

On February 25, 1957, many of the crew took a daytrip to Angkor Wat. Here Michael Redgrave climbs to the top of one ruin, despite the intense heat. Photo courtesy of Vinh Noan.

Though struggling to overcome the numerous delays in filming, the director decided to inform the edgy production team of sixty people that they could be the subject of a bomb threat–or of a sniper attack. Their resulting caution could slow down the work, but not as much as the frustrations of Audie's absence and the inevitable technical glitches, broken equipment, delayed arrival of rushes, and the like.

During this hiatus, Miss Moll had little opportunity to become closer to Redgrave. Thinking of him as a great actor, she was shy about approaching him. He never encouraged her friendship. The rest of the troupe, even Freddie Sadoff, showed her great friendliness. Giorgia was eager to like Redgrave and learn from him, but he remained aloof from her. Everyone else recognized her novice status, Giorgia demurely purred that all endeavored "to give me all the help I needed." She continued to study her precious copy of the novel of *The Quiet American*. Again, because of her deep emotional involvement in the project and desire to succeed, she remained oblivious to some of the political and artistic controversy. She didn't learn of Greene's hostility to the picture until much later.

Then, and for many years thereafter, Greene was vindictive, especially toward those associated with *The Quiet American*. The author turned his hostility on fellow countryman, Redgrave, accusing him of turning the character of Fowler into a "buffoon." Redgrave had no defense to offer; Mankiewicz wrote the character of Fowler into a satiric version of Graham Greene! The innocent actor had his hands full trying make a self-centered and pompous prig the hero of the movie.

Hornbeck had his own problems and sarcastically penned a notation in his diary on Sunday, that a meeting with Johnny Johnston and Mankiewicz concerned his complaint he "had too much help." They had not noticed Hornbeck was wearing down rapidly in the stifling heat. He was the true fireman of the production unit, grappling with problems, day in and day out.

One of his headaches was the failure of the projection machine to work properly after the Vietnamese customs damaged (or vandalized) it. He spent two days trying to fix the machine so they could view the rushes. With the help of Roscoe Cline, the projection machine was ready. On February 14th, the film shot in Vietnam, processed in Rome, and returned to Vietnam, was available for Mankiewicz to check. The first batch only dealt with his first few days of filming during Tet. Five days later a second batch of film arrived, which was the footage staged before February 4th.

Mankiewicz wanted to depict this land that slithered off the South China Sea as a movie about political intrigue. One of the weaknesses of Joe's plan involved doing just exteriors in Saigon. Though they were quite atmospheric, the interiors of clubs, offices, apartments, all were recreations, done later in Rome, to the detriment of the movie. The director did not ignore the ambiance that existed inside of buildings in an exotic foreign city; any interior may be duplicated to perfection in a studio. One of the best set decorators or set dressers in the business was Dario Simoni who lent his talents to the character of the interiors in *The Quiet American*; many of his later successes included epics on the order of *Solomon and Sheba*, *Lawrence of Arabia*, and *Dr. Zhivago*.

What affected filming interiors in this foreign or local place was the unwanted sound interference. Hollywood studio productions invariably dub scenes when sirens, airplanes, or other outside noises intrude. In a location like Saigon, Mankiewicz had little or no control over ambient sounds. His decision to shoot interiors in Rome rested firmly a flawless production; yet, one scene remained in the picture in which a portion of the tinny and static-laden original soundtrack was evident. Vinh Noan said the country was riddled with an endemic clatter and chatter which made sound control nearly impossible. When he directed his own picture in the countryside, though miles from city life, along the Ho Chi Minh Trail, he had similar problems.

Political and religious strife had prevented Joe Mankiewicz from filming in the Tayninh cathedral, so its atmospheric touches had to be rescheduled and duplicated at Cinecitta because of the ruckus Buddhists and Taoists created. As a result of the Cinecitta Studio work, much of the indoor action looked fabricated, and could as easily have been filmed in New York or Los Angeles. Costs, higher in the United States, remained the key factor in the decision to film in Rome.

Fortunately for Audie, and not for the production, the hotbed of protests and problems with the local demonstrators forced Mankiewicz to jettison scenes he wanted to do on location. In Rome within a few weeks, the crew recreated several outdoor set pieces. One such scene, for instance, took place in a bright courtyard outside the Cao Dai Temple, where Audie discovered his car sabotaged, through gasoline draining.

So disagreeable was the experience in Vietnam, and so unsatisfying the film version of *The Quiet American*, that Corin Redgrave simply left the entire mess out of his memoir of this father. There is a simple unexplained photo of Redgrave in Cambodia at Angkor Thom on shooting break in Corin's book, but the film itself was never mentioned, not even in the chronology appendix of Michael Redgrave's career. Corin chose to make certain the involvement with Mankiewicz and Audie was completely ignored. Corin misrecalled instead that during 1957 he spent nearly every day with his father and Freddie Sadoff, which was impossible since they were Vietnam from the start of February through the first week of March.

Redgrave and Sadoff both took an interest in handsome Vinh Noan. Unlike many in the troupe, Noan always had a friendly word with Redgrave, chatting amiably about many issues. Redgrave sent Vinh Noan an autographed picture after the production finished. Yet, for all his friendliness with Redgrave and Sadoff, Vinh was somehow completely unaware of their sexual liaison–and never felt any sexual tension directed at him by the pair. He noticed Bob Krasker was far more open about his gay relationship. The Oscar winner had brought a young assistant cameraman to Vietnam who attended to the imperious Krasker all the time on the set, bringing him coffee or eagerly running errands, day or night.

Back in Vietnam either through Willingham's insistence or his own sense of duty, Audie finally was on his feet, a reluctant performer. As he admitted, he preferred to stay in his hotel room. "One evening I was in my hotel room, lying in bed, just about to drop off to sleep. My attention was divided between the book in my hand and the ceiling where I was watching three lizards snapping up mosquitos." Even in his room, he found life in Vietnam uncomfortable: "Suddenly," he reported, "one of the lizards fell, bookmark fashion, onto the page of the book I held.

My first reaction was that I was glad I'm not one of those fellows who sleeps on his back with his mouth open." He continued to suffer from his usual problems–like insomnia, bad dreams, nausea, and nose bleeds.

During his two week convalescence, having had so much time to think, his extreme views on Graham Greene's novel had worsened. He later told James Kirkwood, a young actor then and later a writer, after the film's release and lackluster box-office returns: "Greene never met a real American, I think. He believes a guy who goes to Harvard and lives in Boston is a real American. Did you ever meet anyone from Boston who went to Harvard? They all come from anyplace but . . ."

A few years later Audie also commented to Kirkwood whom he met on the set of a television western, about the failure of *The Quiet American*. Despite its long exposition and tedious moments, the movie might be called an intelligent, mature film: or, in Audie's words, "the biggest artistic flop in my career."

Redgrave's anticipation over working with Audie had led the British star to read *Picture,* the Lillian Ross work about the production of John Huston's *Red Badge of Courage*. In one of the first conversations with Audie, Redgrave inquired about the legendary problems on that movie. Audie referred to the "boys in the front office" as the culprits who ruined one of his finest performances. In some amorphous way, Redgrave realized that the "massacre" of Audie's early work might be a foreshadowing of their involvement with Mankiewicz. Later, Redgrave wrote that Audie's experience on the Civil War picture "should be compulsory reading for armchair critics who do not realise that 'Art Cinema' is to some degree . . . and to a much greater degree in the English-speaking countries, ineluctably geared to the statistics of the box-office and the distributing circuits."

Michael Redgrave had another reason why he stayed long hours at his hotel suite when not needed on the set. Most in the company had no idea that he was writing a book. Considered articulate and intellectual, Redgrave enjoyed the solitary creativity that came from writing. Several years earlier he had written *The Actor's Ways and Means,* based on the lectures he delivered at Bristol University in 1952. Yet, one role that intrigued him more as he reached the age of fifty was to share his understanding of theater and acting with younger professionals. In his latest work, he envisioned a broad book that would tell interested readers about his approach to Shakespeare, how he connected with his audience, and his insights into Stanislavski and modern acting.

Willard Willingham joined Fred Sadoff (foreground) and Michael Redgrave at the private excursion to Angkor Thom. Photo courtesy of Willard Willingham.

As he sat before a typewriter in his Saigon hotel room, Redgrave wrote in his forthcoming book, *Mask or Face*: "I would like to correct an impression which I seem to have made previously and assert now that I do not believe and never have believed that the greatest performances are those in which the actor becomes totally unrecognizable." He often consulted his colleagues about their approach to the art of acting. Though Arthur Kennedy once told him that the hardest job is to be oneself on stage, Redgrave resisted the notion about such an acting style. Mankiewicz and Murphy would severely test the idealistic approach to art that he so cherished. What he could not know just yet was that his work on *The Quiet American* would prove a turning point in his own life and career.

During the times that the theatrical star of the film did emerge from the hotel as a tourist, Vietnam filled him with dread. Whatever Redgrave saw on his forays certainly increased his strong views, eventually transferred to his daughter Vanessa, about the inappropriateness of American involvement in Vietnam. On one trip to Cambodia in a Dakota aircraft, Redgrave took many photographs, which he shared with Vanessa in Rome six weeks afterwards.

The British actor also related to his family the callousness of Mankiewicz, citing the incident he and cameraman Robert Krasker thought typical of the director. Their translator had begged Mankiewicz to stop filming the "religious procession" scene because the moment on film caused confusion and led to great distress among the locals and spectators. Mankiewicz reportedly refused to stop filming. Neither Krasker, nor Redgrave, appreciated the director's dilemma; for he was reluctant to re-stage these scenes unrealistically in studio and thus surrender his integrity.

Ever the diplomat, Redgrave conceded in his book that Mankiewicz was "one of the most talented men I have ever worked with." Indeed, the director firmly believed that he could make a great movie out of the Greene material that had brought the British thespian to Saigon, but the hope gave way to caveats about the Mankiewicz talent, referring to the "enviable American quality of making life seem as if it were happening as he has ordered it to happen." Their disputes about the direction of the story and their scenes slowly gave way to Redgave's recognition that Joe's "patience has a hint of thunder in it." He concluded that, although Mankiewicz wore three hats (director, writer, and producer), he did not have the "suggestibility" to be an actor of any sort.

Indeed, Redgrave quickly determined that his new director had no understanding of actors or their art. One of the star's complaints was that "he never praises, except inadvertently or by implication. When an actor would occasionally ask, after a final take, if it was 'really all right' he would answer: 'I wouldn't print it if it wasn't.' This pat response irritated Redgrave more and more as the shoot proceeded. If the difference in their attitudes could be found anywhere, it was in their respective opinions of the professionalism of Audie Murphy.

In Saigon, upset by Murphy's self-reliance and decision to carry weapons, Redgrave also allowed this idiosyncrasy of the American to influence his performance, further developing his antipathy for Audie. Michael Redgrave was a British actor of the sort who lived the part. If he played someone who disliked you, he had to dislike you off screen too. If his character hated Audie's character, the line between takes would be as contradistinguished. As the shoot progressed, the performances in the movie mirrored the behavior off the set.

During their combative and jousting moments on screen, Murphy simply fixed Redgrave in their scenes with a deathly stare, which completely unnerved the flighty actor and exposed the pretense of his cool professionalism (exactly what happens to the characters in the script). Audie proudly and sarcastically told Redgrave: "I've made the same film twenty times." Audie's view on acting that "it beats picking cotton," rankled the imperious British thespian. It was a line he used regularly with new acquaintances, reported Jimmy Kirkwood. For Redgrave this remark, at first, entranced him: "To do the same thing over and over again would seem to be an easy task. To do it over years and years and keep a world public fascinated by the spectacle is not so easy. That requires, if not genius, something more than talent."

Yet, after working with Murphy for a month, the idea of repeating the same performance in each film rankled Redgrave. Back in his hotel room, he added segments to his manuscript: "This may sound not a little smug. But it is all the same true that there are some dizzy dozens of film names who discover, too late, that the technique of screen acting is largely a matter of selection and that having no range of acting resources they have little from which to select. They then repeat the same performance which, according to their health, looks, and vigour, satisfies the public until on a certain date, after a certain not so successful film or films, and by the sortilege of fashion, they have to find something else to do."

Tension between Mankiewicz and Redgrave also was unavoidable. Michael Redgrave was certain the American director favored *The Quiet American* over the dry British journalist. In his suite in Saigon, Redgrave noted on the manuscript of *Mask or Face* that Mankiewicz "seldom tried to get more out of some actors than could be seen to be there . . ." referring in all likelihood to Audie's performance. And in regard to his own work on the film, he seemed to admit, "knowing how insecure most actors can feel, whether an occasional pat on the back might not have produced something which would have surprised him. But there is no knowing whether he may not have done this by another method which is the most stimulating of all: to receive praise through a third person."

During their earliest story discussions, Redgrave declared the script had bloat, being both overlong and windy, to which Joe Mankiewicz encouraged constructive criticism, despite his reputation that he never allowed tinkering with his work. In all likelihood, Mankiewicz had said what was expedient, knowing such problems are inevitable on location. Redgrave began quickly to believe that Mank was less of a genius than he had suspected, owing to the fact that this director tended to "accept ideas which do not immediately hit the jackpot of his imagination." Most damning of all, Redgrave came to conclude in Saigon "no praise at all can be as harmful as extravagant or faint praise if the actor thinks the director doesn't really care."

Redgrave's opinion of the director plunged more each day, as he concluded Mankiewicz was callous, a man substantially convinced of his self-righteousness. The British star later told his daughter, actress Vanessa, that Mankiewicz inflamed the politically charged air. When extras carried placards bearing anti-American slogans, he filmed it and passed it off as part of the local color. "No one back home'll know what they mean." This raised some hackles too with the local protesters.

In addition to the on-camera problems, Redgrave found his nightly sex life becoming overly complicated. According to one source, the mosquito netting around the hotel's bed had proven to be an impediment to his love-making. The British star subsequently went to pudgy executive Alfred Katz for advice on how to enjoy active sex without bringing down the mosquito netting as part of a curtain call. Katz responded seriously to the star on balletic technique, and then mentioned indiscreetly to a few other bemused members of the Figaro troupe of Redgrave's peccadillo.

Though Mankiewicz had agreed during their courtship period that Redgrave could edit the verbose script to his liking, by the time they were in Saigon, the director had changed his mind. The one pattern made clear during the preliminaries of the picture was that Mankiewicz made grandiose promises to all members of the cast and production staff about altering the script. He gave the impression he spent hours in re-write. In fact, the director seemed to have simply stonewalled all the requests. Mankiewicz never intended to change a word of his script.

When Redgrave criticized one of the lengthy speeches spoken by Fowler, he met a cool reaction from the director. There were to be no further incisions in the script, and Redgrave was not to take liberties with the script. "This is not some ninety minute movie," the director chided frequently. Redgrave stewed silently each time. Convinced that director and star were in cahoots to undermine his performance in the movie, Redgrave became more and more alienated from the process. The director allowed the actors to assume their characters and to live their parts.

At least one bit of news arrived to cheer the company. Bill Hornbeck received a telegram from George Stevens informing him of an Oscar nomination for his work on *Giant*. At once, the Film Editor's hot, dusty, hard work in Marfa, Texas, during the previous year, marred by temperamental James Dean in perpetual conflict with Stevens and feuding with his co-star Rock Hudson, looked as though that bitter production had been a picnic outing for Hornbeck in comparison to his current assignment.

8

DESPITE THE WEEKS of deplorable heat, the degrading poverty of the Vietnam, the political instability, and the mounting frictions among the crew and cast of the picture, Saigon did supply its moments of happiness and charm. Mankiewicz tried to capture the breezy boulevards of downtown Saigon at dusk and how the wind tended to cool their hot pavement. The tree-lined avenues had been designed by the French to resemble Parisian boulevards in summer. However, it was at the Hotel Majestic the company found local color tantalizing. Whether due to choices of three hundred varieties of menu items, or the charm of urbane denizens, the difference always beguiled the crew when they attempted to relax.

Mike Mindlin recollected, "Saigon–now Ho Chi Minh City–was an interesting place. First, you know, I flew 14,000 miles to get there, to experience an exotic place. I traveled so far and landed, to my surprise, in a French city. Here I come half-way around the world, and I'm in France. And, second, I felt immediately–and it didn't take me long to realize–that this country was no bastion of democracy, as I had been led to believe. It was a fascist dictatorship. Jesus, it certainly wasn't a bastion of democracy."

Somewhat in agreement with Mindlin, Elaine Schreyeck also called Saigon "a most interesting place." However, she was quick to add a few caveats: "Yes, okay, maybe the hotel wasn't the greatest and one had to cope with the heat and atmosphere, but there was a lot of French influence there and I certainly enjoyed the food, especially at a great Chinese restaurant in the Cholon area, where we as a group used to go on many occasions called the Arc en Ciel."

Willingham took this photograph which he called "fast food, Vietnamese style," but gave a sense of the street vendors and locals that populated Saigon and Cholon. Photo courtesy of Willard Willingham.

Giorgia Moll has said Saigon did not look at all like a city which a few years earlier had suffered war. "It was calm and pleasant. No one seemed distressed." She admitted her own view of the Asian country may have been affected by her memory of the sorry conditions existing in post-World War Europe. "I was so young and just interested in another culture and its habits." Her fascination led to the Chinese section of town whenever possible. "Cholon's restaurants were lovely. I tried all the Chinese restaurants and went only to those." Enchanted by the old-fashioned mode of the Majestic Hotel: "clean, well-organized, a delightful place," she remembered, somewhat at odds with Hornbeck's feelings about the decaying conditions.

Hornbeck related how one could see the big boats coming up the river for miles. He expressed surprise at the urban features, like cinema and other accouterments of civilization, which contrasted so drastically with the tart odors and third world nature of the old section of town. "What awful smells. It nearly made me sick. Well, it smells a thousand times worse than kippers." And, it was clear the Vietnamese knew better than their foreign visitors about the worst time of the day. The streets emptied for the most part shortly before noon; the natives tended to nap until three o'clock, outdoing a Mexican siesta ritual by a good hour or more.

An inveterate traveler, Willard Willingham rejoiced in the cultural differences in Saigon. Though Audie remained a curmudgeon who preferred to keep to his room, Willard was not so constrained. "It was the best time to visit–between the wars. Vietnam provided a good lesson if one was prepared to learn it. First, the French had learned theirs. Then we learned ours." Having grown up in Mexico on his father's ranch, Willard found the attraction of foreign lands always enticed him. "What I liked best about making movies was going on location." Neither cuisine, sanitation, nor language, could raise a barrier to Willard's enjoyment of the charms of Cholon and Saigon.

Mindlin agreed with some reservations. "The Vietnamese food was terrible. For anyone with a sophisticated palate, you couldn't eat it. They put this sauce on everything. I think it was made of decomposed fish. It was totally inedible." So, like Giorgia, he found himself visiting Cholon frequently. "There, at least, we could find French restaurants and Chinese restaurants, where the food was superb." Yet, the food issue nearly caused a diplomatic *faux pas.* "We had a few state dinners with the government leaders of Vietnam," Mindlin explained. "We couldn't eat their food, so we ate before we went to many of these functions. Once we got there, we'd fake eating their dinners–but wouldn't touch the food."

Whatever reason the cast was given for filming in Vietnam, all were on the verge of deciding it an ill-conceived venture. Redgrave wrote in his journal that he found Americans in the diplomatic service in Vietnam were in need of "distraction from the boredom." He had little respect (like Fowler, his character) for their profession or attitudes. In fact, he simply did not like, nor understand, American macho stoicism.

Giorgia believed walking along Saigon boulevards and visiting bistros for coffee and tea put a deep imprint on her, as she was the youngest of the Figaro troupe. She plaintively remembered the "Cholon nights, so wonderful in their atmosphere. It was a special place. I thought the people were warm and friendly. When I met them, I feel I knew the heart of Saigon." Of course, the stress and tension on and off the set sent her to a Vietnamese masseuse who regularly kneaded the strain from her shoulders and neck as she lay on a wooden pallet in one of the parlors she frequented in Cholon.

For the most part, however, Giorgia basked happily in the lime-light of a major American motion picture. Whatever else happened, it could never lose its luster as an important film made by Mankiewicz. Never before had she been treated so royally; everything about the Figaro budget was first-class. From accommodations to the airfare to the chauffeurs, all fed every expectation that she would emerge from this propitious employment a "Meravigliosa Stella" in the caliber of other Italian actresses of renown. No other possibility entered her mind, and she willed herself to focus only upon doing her best.

During his limited stay, Hornbeck noticed in the four years since the French "abandonment" of the coastal country that traces of French colonialism were rapidly disappearing. The new South Vietnamese gov-ernment determined to eliminate vestiges of the Old World. A civic effort was clearly underway to change the names on streets from French to Vietnamese. Billboards and business signs in French transformed overnight into Vietnamese.

This development perturbed the Figaro company only to the ex-tent that they were trying to make a film about the conditions in 1952, a scant six years earlier, and the times had changed so fast that the commercial life–formerly under French rule–underwent the term later coined by Americans: "Vietnamization." The troupe had to supply sub-stitutions of their own over the new signs wherever visible. Hornbeck concluded within a few years "there would be very little French left" in the country they occupied for a hundred years.

In terms of the shooting schedule, Mankiewicz was expecting an-other key member of the cast, enabling him to continue with the paral-lel political plot of the motion picture. Coming from opposite direc-tions, feature photographer Robert Landry flew in from Paris on Air

France, and Richard Loo took the Pacific route with Pan American. They left the same day, but owing to time zones and travel problems, Landry arrived first. As recalled by Mike Mindlin, Landry "took a taxi to join the company on location in Tayninh and inadvertently crossed the border into Cambodia!"

Character actor Richard Loo arrived on February 13th for his scenes and went to work immediately. He barely had time to acclimate or find his place in the Figaro troupe. As a result, if anyone in the cast was a lost soul, the one most disremembered by the others, it was Richard Loo. If he had a particular friend on the crew of the picture, it was Vinh Noan whose social group he joined for touring the city of Saigon and exploring its charms.

Mankiewicz discovered the perfect junkyard for the pivotal moment when Fowler becomes corrupted by a communist assassin, naturally enough in Cholon, the ethnic enclave of Chinese immigrants. Giorgia Moll's favorite haunt, she hadn't the vaguest idea she was among the famous Catholic Sea Swallows, expatriates who settled there after fleeing Communist China in the 1950s. Vinh Noan explained the Catholic population numbered fewer than ten percent of the people in Vietnam, but the Diem regime had a strong Catholic flavor. Most of the key positions were filled by Catholics; Diem's brother, a priest, was, in fact, a man ambitious to become the Cardinal who represented all Southeast Asia to the Vatican.

The minority power of the Catholic Vietnamese later led to much of the hostility among the South Vietnamese and the instability that permeated the government. American soldiers a decade later would label this part of Catholic Cholon as a haven for guerrilla attacks and dangerous snipers. The waterfront housed a haphazard labyrinth of shanties for the poor. Apart from the pervasive heat, the location generated its own blast furnace of temperature. The overpopulated section of the city, near the docks, was unsavory and perfectly suited for the moment in which Redgrave as the British reporter gives his soul to Richard Loo as Mr. Heng, the head of the communist assassination bureau.

If Mankiewicz wanted to know how his rushes looked from anything filmed after February 4th, he was out of luck again. Air France had gone on strike. The director thus had another reason for anxiety and worry. Paranoia showed on Mankiewicz. After shooting scenes which could never be replicated in Rome if the film negatives were damaged in processing, he chose to make two sets of scenes, put them in separate canisters, and then for added insurance, sent them to Rome on separate flights. "Just in case one of the planes crashed," Vinh Noan laughed. However, in light of previous problems, it was not a frivolous decision.

The company was booked to leave Saigon early in March. The director drove everyone to work harder and faster. Whatever they failed to shoot on location required expensive recreation in Rome, undercutting the point of the entire trip abroad. Yet, those who working with Mankiewicz knew, he wasn't being tyrannical. He had earned his reputation behaving calmly and wisely in a crisis. His patience and wisdom surely were taxed to the limit on this location shoot.

One of the busiest people on the picture was Vinh. He seldom had an opportunity to view a day's shooting. The nature of his production work required he attend to the next day's events. So, while the cast and director were in one location, Noan might check to see if his preparations were sufficient, but usually he went on to a future worksite. He had to arrange everything from having lunches provided to the crew when it was out on the road, to completing arrangements for the arrival of Figaro equipment. "Actually, food was the biggest problem for me. The Americans, in particular, were quite fussy about what they would eat, so we had to be certain that the meals pleased them when they went out to Tayninh or on the highway sets."

Vinh Noan also arranged for major convoys to pack up equipment after each day's filming–and have it in place, at the right locale, for the next morning. "There were huge generators that had to be moved everywhere. We had four. Two were spares just in case something went wrong. So we frequently had many trucks loading and unloading all the machines one uses in making a motion picture." As a director himself, Noan proved to have the best overview of what Mankiewicz needed, when he needed it, and where taken for any occasion that arose. Vinh reported delays were for other reasons. "In addition to all that, Mankiewicz began to do five versions of each scene."

Because the crew were made to work on Saturday late into the day, the director gave them the entire day off on Sunday. Having worked four Sundays already, the group used this special treat to take a side-trip. A number in the crew and a few of the cast hired a plane to Cambodia to view the ancient ruins at Angkor Wat. Among the tourists were Bill Hornbeck, Willard Willingham, and Michael Redgrave accompanied by Sadoff. When asked if Audie joined the group, Willard just laughed, "No, he hated the entire experience."

Willingham also expressed surprise at how active and exuberant Redgrave was during the visit, clambering over ruins and showing a wholly different side of his personality. "It was a miserable day, so hot, but Redgrave was all over the place, just loving it." Vanessa Redgrave reports that her father took over sixty photographs during this occasion. Sadoff also took many pictures of his lover.

Two other people who didn't make this trip were Mike Mindlin and Giorgia Moll. "I kick myself now for not going," the former Figaro executive stated. "I thought Giorgia and I go could over there at another time with feature photographer Bob Landry and do a publicity shoot. But, we never did." Owing to other duties and functions, they never again had the chance. So, they passed up an afternoon flight to Cambodia, instead taking a boat ride for several hours down the Mekong Delta–a pleasant Sunday, but nothing to match the extraordinary ruins they missed. Having remained at the hotel, Audie took the occasion to rehearse scenes with Giorgia early in the day, which was one of his priorities and pleasures.

It was during this week the dangers of Vietnam became politically real to the Figaro troupe. On February 23rd an assassin tried to take the life of the President of South Vietnam. Ngo Dinh Diem escaped unharmed. The people in the southeast Asian country were not told about the event for at least one day by official government sources. Vietnamese authorities soon informed the Figaro officials their operatives said how the conspiracy could be labeled "well-organized." It was a solemn warning of terrorism which heightened everyone's anxiety.

Audie probably felt confirmation about keeping his guns and ammo on the ready.

Vinh Noan, however, remained completely skeptical about such an attack on Diem. A long-time observer of the political scene in Vietnam, he expressed his sense that "the story was probably one from some reporter who wanted to make a name for himself. He accepted without question the disinformation from the Communists." Interestingly enough, Noan's interpretation of the report on the Diem attack paralleled the plot of the movie and novel of *The Quiet American*.

On Tuesday, February 26, a third batch of dailies finally reached Mankiewicz. These included everything up to the sixteenth of the month and would give him the best sense of what he had on his reels. However, the worst news had yet to arrive. Several scenes the director filmed were not among the rushes returned from Rome. The segments had mysteriously disappeared. It meant additional footage must be shot in Cinecitta which could never truly replicate the ambiance of Vietnam.

Feeling better, Audie attempted to go out on a sight-seeing tour on his own. He related later that he went no further than "six feet" when he experienced an agoraphobic's anxiety, overwhelmed by "thin reaching hands, outstretched for money." He couldn't abide the gleaming wide eyes of children who surrounded him with hungry and desperate stares. Another account, incredible to some friends of Audie, stated "he saw hungry kids again, begging in the streets. That was the afternoon he broke down, crying in the street." Murphy gave an interview in one tabloid report wherein he told about his epiphany: "That was the afternoon when I first found out that maybe, in some small way, there was a reason–for even me. And I could feel, well, I could feel like the road was a little familiar and I knew where I was going on it . . ."

According to Spec McClure, disclosed in his unpublished manuscripts, "In his entire life he (Audie) never learned to take care of money. In a sense he loathed money because the world put such great value upon it at the expense of higher ideals." Nonetheless, Audie sought money and needed it desperately to spend "recklessly and foolishly on things that gave him no pleasure." It may be that the urchins of Vietnam took advantage of a man who, at last, found a use for his money.

Audie surely was reminded of his own deprived childhood upon encountering the impoverished youngsters. In all likelihood, he had been thrust back to the days when he supplied his younger brothers and sisters with food. Ben Cooper knew about this: "He was a good shot because he had to hunt for dinner for his family. If he failed, they would be hungry."

In Saigon, Audie probably felt something had to be done for those hopeless children, of course, the myriad numbers thunderstruck him. He couldn't provide for all. If the reports of his depression are accurate, this could explain that highly uncharacteristic epiphany in Audie Murphy's life: when he lost all control of his emotions and unnerved himself with his own public display of weeping. Willingham, the nearest witness to Audie's behavior, confirmed only that the stay in Vietnam proved to be one of the most brooding and most solitary of his life.

Audie told McClure that one of the results of a war-torn nation was its suffering children. "There's always children. The children grow up and become soldiers. And somebody gets the soldiers together and declares a war. So the soldiers cripple and kill each other until one side hollers 'Uncle'. Then people ring bells, blow whistles, and talk about how great peace is for a while. But new children come along, new soldiers, new wars."

A more succinct prediction of Vietnam's future could not have been given by an American military advisor, or a Transcendental philosopher. Wanda Hendrix also recalled Audie wept once at a newsreel sequence at the movies when German orphan children were shown: "I may have killed their fathers," he told her.

Seeing the children, regarding dysfunctional families of every circumstance, Audie missed his own family. His recuperation was slow, and it kept his performance measured and cautious, which suited perfectly the deliberate nature of the nameless quiet American's attitude. Bruce Cabot recalled he didn't again see Audie Murphy smile until the day the company closed down its Saigon operation for the exodus to Rome to do the interiors. Spec McClure understood Audie always "had an intense need for solitude. Murphy spent hours in brooding silence."

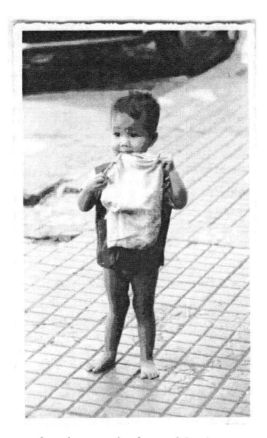

Willingham took a photograph of one of the dozens upon dozens of homeless children who wandered the streets of Saigon. This child was typical of what severely depressed and distressed Audie and caused his severe agoraphobic reaction. Photograph courtesy of Willard Willingham.

Long weeks away from home, and worse yet, being seriously ill in a foreign land, can cause tremendous stress and aggravation: it created in Audie a desire to mend his ways, according to a report in *Modern Screen* when he returned home. He realized how privileged he had been in life. Surviving a war, he earned rather effortlessly his film celebrity and had a family he had not seen since January. For most of his married life, owing to career responsibilities, he spent more than half his time away from home. He always called out, "Home at last!" whenever he returned from a protracted location shoot. He now realized he truly missed homelife, and told reporter Jean Frazier that he promised himself, "I will enjoy what there is of it."

The idea to give up gambling or wasting his money, which he confessed to movie reporters on his return, sounded unlike Audie, according to several associates. Don Graham, in his seminal biography *No Name on the Bullet*, also dismissed the reporting of Jean Frazier who interviewed Audie upon his return to the United States. Audie allegedly told the reporter about his fear of the possibility he might die so far from those he loved, without seeing them again, and it compounded his usual suffering and angst. As a consequence, he understood he might have trouble keeping promises in years to come, but for now he swore his oaths his good intention.

The nomadic children overpopulating this Third World reminded him that he, too, was separated from his family, deliberately by his own design. Audie said: "Children make a nicer person out of you. Anyway, it works that way for me." He told Spec McClure that the "only innocent things left on earth were children and horses."

Another odd allegation made by Jean Frazier was that Audie sought the comfort of a priest. Audie told her: "He listened to me, and after a while his face began to blend into a huge poster hanging on the wall behind him—a poster I'd seen all over the States, begging people to remember the poor children of this war-torn earth . . . by becoming a part of the foster-parents plan. And all of a sudden I knew that it didn't really make any difference if I was pulling in the paychecks because of talent or because of my war record—what mattered was that I had the money to spend. And—maybe now—that was how I could fight." She went on to reveal that he wrote a large check as a donation for nameless and faceless orphans. This kind of financial response had become standard with him, expressing his emotions through impetuous gifts of money. "Don't let me see any of them, or know any of their names," he reportedly told one of the orphanage officials, because he worried that, "I will start bawling again."

This curious account proved difficult for acquaintances to accept because, as Jesse Hibbs, Audie's director on *To Hell and Back*, reported, "He had sworn, after crying three days over the death of his mother, that he would never shed a tear again." Evidence of this conviction extended completely to his movie work; noticeable in emotional scenes, Audie's eyes welled up, but the dam of emotion never burst. "The tears were there, but would never spill over," stated Hibbs. Yet, his tearful episodes in Vietnam were divulged by Audie himself.

If such tabloid reports are correct, he tended to burst into tears easily at the sight of orphans, which indicated a sorely depressed state of mind. Friends and co-workers believed emotional outbursts like this simply were not in Audie's make-up. Whether the reporter fictionalized this account, or whether Audie gave a false report, cannot be determined. Often repeated stories of the star's sense of humor indicated Audie was not beyond pulling a reporter's leg. However, every biographer who has studied Murphy's life concluded something powerful, strange, or unusual, struck him in Vietnam. His experience on this picture remained unique in his career and life.

By his own admission in one upbeat account of his stay in Vietnam, Audie recalled that if he didn't have to work, he would remain in his hotel room at the Majestic. One day, he reported, "about three in the afternoon, a room clerk called to politely inquire when I was going out. I didn't plan to come down for dinner until about seven. He murmured something on the phone and hung up. When I did arrive in the lobby, there were several hundred people waiting there. I found out later they'd been there since three."

A stranger in a strange land, his character in the film had no friends, except a dog, which he walked along the dockside of Saigon and took on rides in his trishaw. True enough, Audie thought the world of dogs, but in real life in Saigon during that shoot, even the dog–a tan Boxer– was another actor. Audie was truly alone. The art of the film mirrored Audie's actual reality.

There were, to Giorgia Moll's recollection, two dogs in the role of Duke, the boxer. Giorgia had to do many scenes with the dog; fortunately, she loved boxers and had two of her own. "The problem with acting with dogs is that they only film your legs, below the knee, to have the animal in the shot." Beyond that, she liked the dog and he liked her, which made their scenes easier–but she had the disquieting suspicion that there was an interior boxer and an exterior boxer–or a boxer from Saigon and a boxer from Rome. Though movie magic, the movie intends there be only one dog in the picture. "And, he was a very sweet dog," laughed Giorgia Moll about the animals. Duke turned out to be the best friend of both Audie and Giorgia.

The cast liked to relax together after a day of work; they sat around playing cards, and exchanged anecdotes: Bruce Cabot, Claude Dauphin, and others, more affable than Audie or the imperious and cloistered Redgrave, swapped tales of the corrupt ways of Hollywood or gossip regarding their fellow actors. Since Audie loved to gamble and play poker, his aloofness certainly was out of character. On most movie sets, during the endless moments of waiting for set-ups, Audie would be the first to call out, "Hey, let's get a game going!"

Non-drinkers on the movie production gravitated to one another. Hornbeck, Mindlin, Audie, and Giorgia, avoided joining the nightly revelers who found comfort and solace in partying with heavy amounts of alcohol. Except for his coaching sessions with Giorgia Moll, Mankiewicz separated himself from his troupe nearly all the time, being seen only when he was needed on the set. According to Mindlin, the director enjoyed the solitary challenge of crossword puzzles and other word games. Mike reported, "Joe was kind of reclusive. In fact, he was not much of a presence, except for the times he was on location. As I recall, he spent most of his time alone in his hotel room." Mike was keeping mum about some things.

He was perfectly aware that Mankiewicz enjoyed the company of Noan's procured partners, and Redgrave had Fred Sadoff; Krasker had his boyfriend; Mindlin himself had come to Vietnam with "a lady friend–and I had a good time there." Whatever sexual activity Audie or Willard arranged for themselves wasn't apparent enough for gossip. According to his own words given to an interviewer, Audie claimed he "couldn't join in." He loathed more and more the eyes of the public on him whenever he went out of the hotel.

Movie companies on location invariably tend to be insular, and *The Quiet American* production was no different. When discussing such situations, Wanger warned the "tension of too close association" usually proved to be the real hazard of location shooting. Forced intimacy among the small group of sixty members of the Figaro troupe frayed personal relationships.

Not until a conversation with Claude Dauphin in Rome did Mike Mindlin learn not all privacy had been breached at the Saigon hotel. Though he had thought "there were no secrets among the Figaro people," he learned that Dauphin, during his entire stay in Vietnam, kept an extremely young girl in his hotel room. She had run away from home, taking refuge as a roommate of the French actor. No one guessed he had company every night. Dauphin reported to Mindlin that what amazed him most was the extreme passivity of Vietnamese women. "The girl would simply sit in the room, not knitting, not reading, not doing anything, except waiting for Claude to return every night."

More and more as the shoot progressed, Audie spent hours in the hotel, gazing at the street like some incarcerated victim, unable to enjoy the nightlife. Though his sidekick Willingham was available to help pass time, Audie wondered if his wife Pam should join him. He assured himself, "She shouldn't leave the children."

His own celebrity rendered Audie captive in Southeast Asia. Fans, panhandlers, street vendors, shoe shine boys, and whores didn't hesitate to impede walks he'd take in Saigon. Beside this, chance of attack or kidnap by terrorists was ever present. Though the city itself seemed emptier after midnight, there were always idlers milling near the docks–French or Europeans, Moroccans–a surprising number–and two or three shades of Asian. Harmless perhaps, they always remained vigilantly silent as a stranger passed. Furtive people on dark streets couldn't be trusted.

One photograph of Audie, taken at the apartment used for Michael Redgrave's digs in the movie showed Audie wearing a striped tie and dress shirt, in costume for his betrayal scene. From this balustrade Redgrave's character alerted the communist assassin that his victim would arrive shortly. In the photo, Audie moodily surveyed the street below crowded with the daily stream of pedestrians, oblivious to however steamy the weather remained. On his face was no smile of happiness, though with his health improving, he must have felt better than at any time in recent months. Instead, his vulnerability seemed all the more evident. A sadness permeated his expression. This quiet American was solitary and remote.

Responding to that forlorn appeal, Giorgia Moll recalled Audie with great affection. Despite his travails during the filming in Vietnam, she said he was "very gentle with a nice sense of humor." Throughout their scenes together, he put her at ease. It was nerve-wracking for her to be a green beginner in a major role among such experienced stars. "Oh, he was very warm then with me. He didn't seem like a war hero or soldier. He had a nice boyish face to go with his warm personality." She loved the wavy auburn hair and freckled face. That image is the intangible souvenir he gave her at the end of their working relationship on the picture. It was his memory she most cherished, for Giorgia was certain she had the best co-star imaginable: caring, kind, gentle, and sweet.

In the original script, the two attractive young actors had a sequence of scenes that built up their relationship. The filming recorded how they went from drinking milk shakes together to *The Quiet American* giving her English lessons. These served as prelude to a proposal of marriage and a prolonged courtship. Only a hint of all these scenes now exist in the final film version. At one point Redgrave as Fowler overheard a tape recording of Audie asking Giorgia to say, "prune," in order to have her pucker up for a kiss. The love scenes supplied the blossoming of a love affair, almost entirely to end up on the cutting room floor.

Numerous co-stars constantly have attested to the support and professionalism of Audie on the set. The word "comfortable" remained a constant in most discussions with how Audie treated fellow actors. "He was as responsive as any actor I ever worked with," said Ben Cooper. "We could do a long scene, a quiet scene, without any tension between us. That's why I enjoyed my pictures with Audie." Another co-star, Jan Merlin, reported, "If Audie liked you, it was as if you were working with an old friend. If he had no faith in you, he'd close off."

Giorgia too called his demeanor, "so comfortable he helped me to relax on the set."

Another actor reported Audie's appeal to women arose out of his gentle sense of humor. "He usually hid it behind a quiet little smile," which was quite attractive. "Women wondered what they could do to make him smile. I think that was his secret appeal." The evident shy quality was an inadvertent characteristic in Audie. He was so vulnerable he could not hide it, could not use it as an actor might, and never learned that his bereft state of mind contributed to his appeal as an actor and personality. "He was singularly unaware of what attracted his fans," commented another costar.

One of the few highlights for Audie in Saigon arose out of his friendship with hair stylist Ida Mills. A professional working in the business for over ten years, she and Audie found themselves kindred spirits. One of Mike Mindlin's favorite photographs in his collection shows a happy group on the steps of the most famous Saigon cathedral on Catinat Street, the Cathedral of Our Lady. Standing together were Audie, Ida Mills, Giorgia Moll, Bob Landry, and himself.

Perhaps a mother substitute for Audie, Ida Mills, British hair stylist on the film, became a lifelong friend of Murphy after their meeting in Saigon. He brought her to Hollywood where she worked with him for the rest of his film career. Photo courtesy of Vinh Noan.

Mindlin recalled an incident with Ida from those days: "Before I left for Saigon, Richard Avedon and his wife held a going-away party for me. One of the gifts I received was a safari jacket, which I did not particularly like. However, Ida Mills always expressed how much she loved the coat. So, on the way back to Europe, I made the safari jacket a gift to her."

Because of loyalty and fierce protectiveness of those he liked, Audie brought Miss Mills to California after the picture. He made sure she was hired for his films. Settling in the Hollywood Hills, she married, but remained close to the Murphy children. A true friend of the family, she was like an aunt to Audie's two sons thereafter and warmly received until she died many years later. A thin British woman with salt and pepper hair, she seemed to exude the maternal qualities one can see in the actress who played Audie's mother in *To Hell and Back*.

It seemed Ida had the same maternal interest in Audie. He appreciated the affection, and Ida likely fulfilled some platonic need in Audie's lonely time in Vietnam. She tended to him in his illness, bestowing tender loving care which Audie soaked up like a hothouse plant starved for water.

Award-winning feature photographer Bob Landry, whose classic *Look* covers of Hollywood notables remained as immortal depictions of the era, took numerous publicity pictures. However, the stillman of the movie was French photographer Raymond Voinquel. It was he who took photographs of Vinh Noan with all the principals of the Figaro cast and crew. Voinquel took all the lobby card stills and movie glossies. Again, because of their French connection, Vinh and Voinquel had a particular good friendship. Of the Voinquel pictures which Noan has in his scrapbook, Mankiewicz's pose typified warmth and support, being most demonstrative, his arm proudly and tightly around Noan's shoulder, like a father at graduation day with his son.

Audie seemed the stiffest of all the posers, going so far as to lift his chin up in order to appear taller than Noan in one of their pictures together. Yet, Vinh said: "We were exactly the same height, five feet seven inches." He concluded that Murphy's size undercut his credibility in scenes with Redgrave. "He looked like a little boy next to Redgrave," Noan lamented.

On the final day of shooting in Saigon, Vinh Noan helped to set up the pyrotechnics of the famous terrorist bombing scene. One worker was seriously injured during an explosion. Photo courtesy of Vinh Noan.

Mankiewicz had to wrap up his Asian location work on the scheduled date. There were no extensions of time. On Sunday and Monday, March 3rd and 4th, the final sequences had to be filmed; they concerned the movie's climactic scene of violence, the bombing of Place Grenier. The entire action never really occurred in the busy center of Vietnam. The initial blast knocking the Redgrave character out of his chair as he sat in a local bar and read his newspaper was an interior to be done in Rome.

When Redgrave hurried down to the site of the explosion, encountering smoke, a milling crowd, a few burning cars, and a handful of bodies on the ground, it was an outdoor sequence, shot in Saigon. Vinh helped set it up. He bought some used cars which they doused with gasoline and set ablaze, then arranged for the Fire Department to show up, after they set the cars on fire. Fire engines, police cars, and ambulances rushed into the scene; it was a brilliant innovation, making the moment seem larger and more graphic than the few seconds of screen time the script gave to the central incident of the novel and film. Hornbeck's editorial expertise put it together brilliantly.

In essence, the Vietnam experience ended with this spectacular segment in the canister. Whether it turned out as hoped or not, there could be retakes. Audie, Redgrave, Loo, Sadoff, and Dauphin, appeared prominently in that Saigon climax–but no amount of staging in Rome could replicate the same ambiance. The next day the crew dismantled their equipment, under the supervision of Bill Hornbeck.

After the principal actors left Vietnam, Joe Mankiewicz threw a cast party for the crew and local assistants. Vinh Noan holds the manniquin that doubled for Audie Murphy in the film's opening scene. Photo courtesy of Vinh Noan.

Though most previous stories suggested the filming in Vietnam continued for most of the month, the wrap party thrown by Mankiewicz for the crew was held on Friday, March 6th. He said good-bye to the local helpers, a group over 150 in number from the fledgling Vietnamese film industry which Production Associate Vinh Noan helped to create. None of the stars attended, but over a dozen military and security people were there. No longer needed for scenes, the lead performers in the cast made a hasty exodus from Vietnam. The local workers celebrated an end to their employment; the majority of the American company felt happy about completing this phase of the production. The twenty-five non-Asians at the party were the supervisory crew chiefs. The Vietnamese at the party, happy about the present, faced a more uncertain future.

Pipe in mouth, enthroned within the aggregate, Mankiewicz roosted amidst the crew, yet had a wide berth on all sides by his Asian helpers. The party thanked all the Vietnamese contributors to the film. With the stars already embarked for Rome, the representatives from Figaro were Mankiewicz, Johnny Johnston, Bill Hornbeck, and Vinh Noan who squatted in the front row, holding the mascot mannequin of the troupe, which also served as a stand-in for Audie Murphy in the opening shot when a body can be seen, face down on the riverbank.

The weekend was all Hornbeck and his crew needed to pack for the long trip to Rome. Having arrived by crossing the Pacific from the United States, they now flew in the opposite direction to reach Europe. On Monday, they took an Air France flight at 11:00 p.m., landing for short refueling stops at Bangkok, Karachi, Tehran, and Istanbul.

The journey from Vietnam to Italy took over twenty-eight hours. During one of the stopovers at Istanbul, Audie sent a telegram to his wife Pam. For the five or six weeks he was in Saigon, and when hospitalized with his appendectomy, he hadn't telephoned her. Audie's companion on the trip, Willard Willingham, communicated with his wife Mary who contacted Pam. They served as a double intermediary for the Murphys. Separated by distance and emotional turmoil, but it was unlikely that Audie had been too lonely in Vietnam.

Many of his cowpoke friends have spoken admiringly of his constancy with females associated with his movies. One co-star observed, "Audie did what most straight leads of films have always done in the industry. They inevitably have affairs with their leading ladies or ingenues or any other attractive woman found on the set whenever filming on locations. The longer the time away from home, the more certain it is to occur." Whether Audie followed this traditional practice in Vietnam is a well-kept secret.

9

THE SHOOTING SCHED-
ULE for Vietnam is clearly delineated in Hornbeck's diaries of the
location work: the Tet celebration, the Cao Dai Procession in Tayninh,
the Watch Tower sequence, the Dakow Bridge in Cholon, the garage in
Cholon, the Saigon marketplace, a Saigon temple, outside the Continental Palace restaurant, and the square in mid-Saigon. Over the entire
period in which the cast was slated for the shooting dates, Mankiewicz
filmed only fifteen days. Absent stars, airline strikes, broken equipment,
missing rushes, difficulty in choosing locations, the task of moving large,
heavy movie equipment, delays owing to Audie's ills, and so forth,
caused much of precious time to be lost. Mankiewicz spent sixty-four
days in Vietnam. Several cast members enjoyed the country for little
more than five weeks; some hated it completely during their weeks of
location.

Next stop was the studio at Cinecitta in Rome—prophetically enough
upon the Ides of March. It was preordained for Hornbeck to discover
they had won the race with equipment still in transit. Everyone in the
cast needed some rest anyhow, so Mankiewicz postponed shooting
until March 20th. For the unfortunate Hornbeck and Johnston, the day
off simply meant they must go out to Livorno to scout locations to
serve as stand-in for Vietnam. Hornbeck also learned about missing
supplies, which was another aggravation on his first day in Rome. Within
a day the supplies showed up, having been merely been misplaced. Yet,
his exasperation with the film project into which he had put full energy
and commitment grew larger. When he first left for Vietnam, months

earlier, it had been with assurances that principal photography would be completed by May fourth.

The cast and crew, housed at the elegant Grand Hotel and the Hotel Excelsior, were at Cinecitta in Rome explicitly for the interiors and botched exterior scenes which did not play well in rushes. At least now the Figaro company found itself housed in a real studio, the rushes were available to Mankiewicz promptly: a luxury he had not known for the entire month of February.

The arrival in Rome coincided with the production knowledge that the troupe had suffered extremely bad press while on location. *The Quiet American* rapidly developed a reputation, known around the world, as a quintessential ugly American. As a consequence, Mike Mindlin, responsible for publicity, found himself applying damage control and spinning a more favorable, flippant depiction of the Vietnam adventure.

In a piece for the *Sunday New York Times*, he tried to compare Rome and Saigon as comical backdrops for standard shenanigans involving the making of any picture. Among his lighter comments which masked the real dangers of Vietnam was a tally of the crashes of "Kamikaze chauffeurs" between the two capitals. He wrote: "At the moment Rome appears to be running slightly behind Saigon." In a cavalier manner he referred to the frequent and numerous automobile accidents befalling the cast and crew. It was obvious to everyone in the film industry that Figaro, Incorporated, had begun a salvage operation.

Vinh Noan thoroughly enjoyed Europe, having lived there as a student for several years. Upon arriving in Rome, he realized, like many hasty travelers, he had forgotten to pack socks in his luggage. So, one afternoon around lunchtime, he had a few minutes to leave his hotel room in Rome to find a store where he could buy socks. Along the way, he caught sight of a car dealership which had on its lot a beautiful, sporty Fiat convertible roadster. Since the daily commute to Cinecitta was fifteen miles outside of the Italian capital, Noan felt the overwhelming buyer's impulse. He went into the dealership, and purchased the car on the spot. The automobile made him quite popular with many of his Asian colleagues. Needless to say, he forgot to buy socks that day.

Of course, Giorgia Moll found it delightful to return to Rome. There, she had a reunion with her friends and mother. It continued to be a difficult picture; time away from shooting helped her keep her balance. She made the acquaintance of the two adolescent sons of the director, Tom and Chris Mankiewicz. Giorgia felt she had more in common with them and, not much beyond adolescence herself, she spent hours with them. They became "great friends and had much fun together."

On the other hand, Michael Redgrave enjoyed the production less and less, having an inkling the picture was in trouble. He felt furious with Audie when it took three hours to do their "Continental Hotel" scene. Redgrave's close-ups, filmed at the end of a long day, made him feel slighted by the director, who might have had the consideration to pick them up when his performance was still fresh. On top of this, Audie fed him off-screen lines in a completely lackadaisical and uninspired manner. Redgrave blamed him for not putting forth his best, to the detriment of the British star's performance. Mindlin recalled, especially in Rome, "Audie drove him crazy." In turn, Mankiewicz accused Redgrave of being "spongy," in his acting. Redgrave, exhausted and fed up with the movie by the Rome shoot, now intensely abhorred both Mankiewicz and Audie for their "tough guy" conduct.

Fred Sadoff played Dominguez, a Communist operative. In life he was Michael Redgrave's companion. Living openly as a gay couple, they stayed together for nearly twenty years. Photo courtesy of Vinh Noan.

In theory Redgrave understood the problem of repeated 'takes'. He stated in his book on acting, "After repeated takes, the actor has begun to 'set' his performance. As he begins to do this, consciously to polish these little moments which grew out of improvisation, he tends to lose that first impetus which gave life to the scene. He sometimes begins to forget the situation, or to anticipate the climax. This anticipation of a climax is one of the commonest traps of the actor, either on the stage or screen." Yet, he added that those who fell into the trap did not love acting with all their heart and soul.

According to his on-the-spot assessment of the production, Willard Willingham remained steadfast, keeping Audie in focus. Though he defined himself as Audie's "mentor," the stand-in stuntman transcended that characterization. He served as a ramrod to keep Audie in line, who was willing to desert the project on several occasions. If this issue arose, Audie met with firm resistance from Willard. The reason for such strong opinion from Audie's sidekick had been explained by another observer on the picture: the unnamed source maintained Willingham recognized that both he and Audie couldn't afford to pass up the salaries which Figaro paid. If Audie backed out of the project, Willard would be out of work too.

Willingham also insisted his professional expertise proved instrumental in preparing Audie for any difficulties in his performance. "Audie was ready in Rome," Willard announced. "I had coached him. We had gone over the lines many times. I explained to him what the motivations were. He clearly understood the scenes and what he had to do. I spent hours with him, preparing him. He was ready, and he was letter perfect when they filmed."

Another colleague disputed this assertion, maintaining Audie may have used Willard to feed him cues while memorizing his lines, but Audie was far too independent to put his trust into another individual. What Willard could never alter were the timbre of Audie's voice. Also, the residue of Audie's Texas drawl would be evident, unpopular among the aficionados of Greene's literature. His countertenor voice might sound too shrill next to the highly trained and modulated tones of a stage actor like Michael Redgrave.

In fact, Audie employed his usual manner of learning his role. It was for this reason that Willard Willingham became his travel partner for the journey to Saigon and Rome. Audie seldom "studied" scripts in a traditional sense of learning his part. He preferred to hear his lines read to him. Often, after one reading by Willingham or another assistant, Audie would have the dialogue committed perfectly to memory. Though he was never diagnosed dyslexic, this is a classic learning technique often adopted by those who suffer a learning impairment.

Redgrave himself admitted in his diaries how rattled he was by the power of Murphy's performance. Audie's unblinking harshness simply intimidated Sir Michael Redgrave. Another co-star found amusing that Audie also had a habit, while doing scenes, of pursing his lips. "I think he did it while concentrating. It showed he was concentrating on the scene." These were idiosyncrasies an actor like Redgrave found intolerable, and which built up over the shooting to an inevitable explosion of temper in Rome.

The notorious incident in which Redgrave complained about Audie's "acting" stands as the key indication of their problem. After a confrontation scene, Redgrave told Mankiewicz he must tell Audie "to blink." The dead-on stare unnerved the British thespian. What Redgrave failed to realize is how much this cold regard gave him to make the scene come alive. Another actor found Redgrave's attitude the true problem. When Audie provided such actions, "you have to use it and make something out of it." The glare of Audie bored into the Briton and indicated how much opposition Audie felt to Redgrave, as man and character. *The Quiet American* had silently poured his fury into the scene. As one colleague warned, "Audie could out-stare a cobra." Mankiewicz did not relay Redgrave's distress to Audie.

Willard Willingham, decidedly having a one-sided viewpoint, expressed that neither he, nor Audie, had any personal antagonism toward Redgrave. The aide-de-camp and sidekick of Murphy said he felt great sympathy for Redgrave because something was "seriously wrong with the man. I think, even then, he was gravely ill." Yet, as Willard saw it, of the two, it was Audie who was most inconvenienced by a bad and unprofessional performance. "You had to realize that Audie was up against one of the all-time great actors. For a man who played in small cowboy pictures, this motivated him to do his best work."

Willingham noticed, in 1957 at Rome, that Michael Redgrave showed the earliest symptoms of Parkinson's Disease, which later ravaged his mind and body. During his early middle years, Redgrave had moments when he and friends who witnessed the bizarre events admitted he went "dry." By this they meant he was unable to recall his lines, or sometimes which scene he acted, as well as become physically impaired. Past witnesses often mistook the condition for alcohol abuse. It may well be what Mankiewicz saw, Audie's double reported, for the first time, in the interview for this account.

Corin Redgrave related that he first noted his father's failing concentration as early as 1963. Without the medical techniques of brain scans, called MRIs, there was no proper diagnosis, which sparked rumors blaming the condition on everything from drinking to boredom and lack of intellectual acuity. According to Willingham who insisted his recollection of the matter was crystal: "Redgrave clearly was suffering from a serious memory problem at the time of *The Quiet American*."

Though Redgrave was fifty years old, the impairment of his concentration, his inability to retain new information, and other manifestations of short-term memory problems caused Olivier to remove his arch-rival from a National Theatre performance within four years. No other reports of a serious bout of the debilitating disease manifested itself for a decade or more, but there may well have been a precursor of the future illness in Saigon and Rome.

On March 20th, Redgrave's birthday, he felt the onset of a bad cold, felt irritable, and over-tired. No one associated with the film took notice of his natal day, and that may have prodded the sensitive man into a bad mood as well. Mankiewicz had scheduled the first day of Cinecitta shooting on Redgrave's birthday. As far as his overall health at this milestone of age of fifty years, no one understood what had befallen the British actor. Only in hindsight did Willingham have a medical cause to explain what he witnessed. "Redgrave would blow each scene. There were as many as thirty or forty takes for a few lines of dialogue. You cannot imagine how hard this was on Audie. He was doing what he had to do. It was Redgrave, the great actor, who kept muffing the lines."

Audie Murphy, by his own accounting, often said: "I've got a mean streak in me a mile long." He may well have become a kettle about to boil over when it came to Redgrave. Audie once said, "People think I brood about those Germans I killed. I don't. If my own brother had been on the other side, I would have tried to kill him too. If I had succeeded, he would have gambled and lost." Clearly, Redgrave cast himself in opposition to Murphy, and didn't understand the peril associated with crossing Audie. After thirty takes of a scene, Audie lost his edge and his mind began to wander.

McClure offered an insightful opinion of Audie's technique with Redgrave in his unpublished manuscript: "Usually in a movie and in the presence of people, Murphy wears a brooding, deadpan expression, which is completely misleading. He is in reality one of the most keen and comprehensive observers . . . His eyes are constantly darting slightly or he is using their corners to study his surroundings. His ears can follow several conversations at once, though he appears not to be listening at all. A glance is sufficient for him to take in a room filled with people. He sees life as caricature, and his judgment–which can by no means be classed as a snap–is practically instantaneous."

If Redgrave saw this, he understood little of Audie and dismissed the actor's style and performance. In all likelihood, Redgrave had no comprehension of his own failing faculties. Willingham insisted no one should be blamed for the problematic on-set troubles between the two actors. Audie was in agreement that the script was wordy and Redgrave's speeches too flowery. He explained those who talked too much caused "my mind to go seventeen miles from the conversation."

Infuriated by this attitude, the British actor was tempted to storm off the set, but instead used his petulance and irritation in the scene . . . exactly what Mankiewicz had intended. As a corollary, during filming of close-ups, it was not unusual for the lead or star actor to have someone else feed cue lines to their co-stars. Often these scenes may be done with actor addressing an empty chair. This common rudeness abounded in movie-making, and of which Redgrave was well aware. Instead of thanking Audie for remaining on the set late in the day to provide dialogue off camera for him, he berated Murphy.

As Redgrave pouted, it was "a miserable day. For it seems to me I'll never adjust to the problem of acting with someone like Murphy." He expressed disgust that a "great" director like Mankiewicz remained oblivious. "Perhaps for him it isn't a problem." However handled by the director and others, the maliciousness on set escalated. At the conclusion of another day's shooting, Joe Mankiewicz said innocently, "Take care of that cold," and something snapped in Redgrave. He petulantly dismissed the director with: "What do you think I'm going to do with it?"

Redgrave returned to his Rome hotel to meet with his daughter Vanessa after his outrage over the incident. He described to her how "intolerable and damaging" to the logic of stage acting a movie can be. In "a particular scene in the film of *The Quiet American* where (Michael) had thought he would approach it quietly and develop it into its emotional climax, Joseph Mankiewicz chose the opposite direction, wanting him to start the scene at the emotional climax and end it quietly." Vanessa Redgrave explicated in her autobiography how this will "go against, even invert" the normality of a scene. Above all, Michael Redgrave ruefully believed his techniques of building character were undermined by the cinematic styles of Mankiewicz and Murphy.

By March 25th, Redgrave's energy and interest ebbed for the rest of the shoot. Perhaps it was the physical wearing down brought on by the extensive travel and time changes which resulted in exhaustion, perhaps it came off the abruptness of climatic conditions, but like Murphy during his hospitalization, the actor whose professionalism was beyond reproach could barely act through three scenes. He brought the production to a shut-down until he was well again. Just when Mankiewicz most wished to speed up the process of filming, Redgrave could not go on.

On March 26th, Redgrave fell so ill with flu he missed that day's filming. According to Hornbeck, Redgrave's eyes, bloodshot and watery, were too obviously those of man with a severe head-cold. His illness, heightened by his increased contempt for Audie, worsened.

Murphy, he reported to a friend, " . . . was a natural–with a mass of experience, but no technique." Worse, Joseph Mankiewicz ignored Redgrave's constant critiques of Audie's performance. The British actor then openly accused Audie of being an acting "amateur."

Redgrave complained he could not "give a performance with one"– meaning an unprofessional. Rather than taking umbrage, Audie kept his temper in order to complete scenes quickly. Much in tune with Fowler, Redgrave ridiculed Audie's screen role for his "wide-screen" heroic attitude, or his Boy Scout good cheer to solve problems. Said one actor, preferring anonymity: "Redgrave had problems with Audie, but I suppose Freddie Sadoff kept Redgrave soothed after each day's work ended." As a consequence, in this way, Sadoff provided assistance to Mankiewicz by keeping the testy British star appeased, and Freddie more than earned his role in the picture by this "duty."

The genuine antipathy between Murphy and Redgrave leaked to the press in subtle ways. Once he was back in the United States, Audie gave interviews in which he regularly referred to his co-star as "Michael Rennie," another tall British actor whose noteworthy credits included *The Day The Earth Stood Still.* Another co-star warned not to assume he was being funny: "I don't think Audie was so cognizant of foreign actors that he would have been familiar with Redgrave's reputation. Audie may have been far more familiar with the Rennie name because of seeing that sci-fi film almost everyone went to see. My bet is he thought them the same person."

In all likelihood Redgrave heard the Murphy comment. In his manuscript of *Mask or Face,* he added the comment: " . . . my aversion to being referred to as 'the Film Star' amounts to nausea and I have resolutely refused to have my portrait in bold bad Technicolor on the stairways of local Odeons . . . as I have, politely I hope, declined to let anyone start a fan club for me. Nevertheless, I accept up to a point the proposition that no actor can be an entirely private person and I am amiable, within the bounds of decorum, towards fans, as occasionally happens, when they become uncivil, or accost me warmly by the wrong name . . . Mr. Rennie must, I am sure, share my feelings."

Whatever Audie's motive, a few unwitting press members simply copied down the name as given and printed it in their interviews and articles on the picture. In his own fashion of passive aggression and mischievous humor, Audie allowed the world to see his final digs at the great British actor. He couldn't tell one stage actor from another. It was a devastating piece of disrespect, whether intentional or not. He credited the aforesaid "Michael Rennie" with regaling the Figaro troupe while it stayed in Saigon with "his own crazy stories about London." Yee-haw, knee-slappers all! Since Audie and Redgrave seldom spent a moment in social conversation, this detail indicated the imp in Audie. Sir Michael Redgrave was not a man given to behaving in any way that could be called "crazy".

Overwhelmed by their long shoot since January, and feeling less than well, all contributed to Redgrave's curtness. He groaned, "I am so exhausted and stopped up with cold that I feel sort of a baleful dislike of (Mankiewicz) and the whole set-up." Good trouper that he was, Redgrave tried to "use" his emotions to improve the scenes on the interior recreation of Saigon's Continental Bar. The final version in the movie became a truncated scene; in the original, Bruce Cabot joined the party and served as a foil and counterpoint to Audie's heroic American. No other actor had more scenes clipped from the final version than Bruce Cabot.

In an opposite vein, the general tenor of the Figaro company changed for the better away from the set: partly this was due to the accessibility of Rome. For many, their wives and loved ones were able to be near. Vanessa Redgrave lived in Rome. Michael and Freddie seemed pleased to spend hours with her. She accepted her father's living arrangement in the Eternal City with the sophistication of a native. Mike Mindlin recollected how the obvious affair with Sadoff amazed him. "They were quite open about their relationship," which was brazen for the 1950s. "I thought it was, 'So English.' And, in Rome, Freddie and Michael kept an apartment. When Mrs. Redgrave, and the younger children came to visit, they stayed at a hotel—and would drop in to see Freddie and Michael. Yes, I just thought it was so English."

A clutch of wives descended upon the Figaro company in Rome. Mankiewicz reunited with his spouse, ever fond of dinner parties despite her psychological problems. Hornbeck's wife was with him; Rocky Cline's wife also arrived in Rome at the end of March. Audie, of course, had the company of Pam for their "second honeymoon," according to fan magazines. She arrived in Rome with Mary Willingham, the women joining their husbands after a six week separation while the men were in Vietnam and Hong Kong.

Audie found himself with free days when Redgrave fell ill. It was one of many times he was able to tour the area, quite a different place from that of his first visit to the Italian boot during the war. Always drawing crowds wherever he went, Audie created havoc with the Italian press and paparazzi by suggesting his gratitude to the Italians "for fighting on the side of the Germans during the war . . . figured it shortened the war by at least eight months." His sly wit had returned: he told friends that listening to Vatican bells ringing all day on Easter was making him "a bit punchy."

Audie's relationship with Mankiewicz and the Figaro people deteriorated because of the cost to him for his operation in Hong Kong: one of the operating surgeons sued him for medical treatment; reportedly $4500 which Figaro did not pay, and Audie remained bitter over a disputed expense he felt the studio should have covered. Whether this ill-will affected Mankiewicz seems fairly clear. Audie's own bad humor over the director's failure to keep his word script-wise probably led to some icy times between star and director. As if by design, Audie noticed his services on the picture translated into fewer and fewer pivotal scenes. His leading role was turning into little more than a supporting part.

Continuing the shoot in Rome created a somewhat unexpected problem. For the crowd scenes at Cinecitta, mimicking Saigon clubs and streets, the picture required a predominance of Eastern faces. It was hardly surprising there was an acute shortage of such nationalities in the local area. Consequently, rounding them up was assigned to Vinh Noan who was sent "to bring down a bunch of Asian extras from Paris," recalled Mindlin, to populate the various Saigon hang-outs and restaurants constructed for the movie scenes.

"There was a large group of Asians in Paris, and so I went up there," commented Noan. "I did not need people with film experience–

these were people who would fill up the nightclubs and restaurants in the backgrounds of the scenes." Given the task of bringing back thirty-five girls (some to play prostitutes) and about fifteen boys, Noan decided to put an advertisement in *Le Figaro* newspaper–an open call. To his utter amazement, five hundred Asians showed up at the hotel to be interviewed for the coveted film jobs.

"Joe had given me only one instruction: the girls for the Rendezvous Club had to be Asian, preferably Vietnamese, and I could accept a few half-Asian, half-Westerns girls too." Working hard at his task, Vinh brought back a group which Mankiewicz inspected upon arrival. The director noted one member of the group was pure French–against his wishes. "Well, he asked me why I brought back a French girl with so many Asians available back in France applying for the job. I simply told him she was the best fuck in Paris." The young French beauty appeared in the picture as one of the hostesses at the club.

Vinh Noan took one memorable gag picture on the set of Le Rendezvous Club at Cinecitta. The send-up dealt with the cast and the issues of the film. With all the club "girls" lined up around Audie, Giorgia Moll, in costume, sat on a stool listening without much patience as Audie gestured a sorry excuse for being a most popular young man. The girls pose, beaming at Audie with broad smiles–and the photo inferred that the escape from the perils of Vietnam clearly raised spirits and brought lighter moments to the making of the picture.

Audie Murphy and Giorgia Moll ham it up with the girls of the Rendez-vous Club duirng a break on the set in Rome's Cinecitta, March of 1957. Photo courtesy of Vinh Noan.

Off camera and off set, production people like Hornbeck continued to work on Saturdays. Now that they were in comfortable Rome, with all the scenes from Vietnam in the can, Hornbeck started to cut the opening minutes of the movie. From the revelry to the discovery of a body, the camera followed the head of a floating dragon head under the Dakow Bridge until it came to rest at the fingertips of Audie's dead character: the sequences were all outdoors and inclusive. So, on March 23rd, the first sustained minutes of the production reached a final form.

Never one to shy away from the social duties associated with his job, Hornbeck greeted Mankiewicz's highly concerned associate, Robert Lantz when he flew into Rome from the New York office on April 4th. The two had an informative dinner. A few days later Lantz previewed 4500 feet of cut film. In the meantime Hornbeck prepared sound loops needed for Richard Loo and Michael Redgrave. By Friday he was feeling poorly. He remained in bed as long as he could on Saturday, but finally rose to go to the studio to continue his work. The resulting physical collapse rendered him completely bedridden on Sunday. He told everyone he felt "lousy"–but Hornbeck understated how badly he really felt.

Like most workhorses, he continued to try to do his job. The sore throat was back again on Wednesday, and on Thursday the doctor's diagnosis declared it a case of strep. Though improved slightly on Friday, he continued to exert himself by working through the weekend. He ran rushes at night, met guests in the morning, and kept himself splashing in and out of the spring rain of Rome. On Wednesday his throat problems worsened, and he was unable to join Johnny Johnston on a location hunt to Livorno to arrange for the eventual move cast and crew of *The Quiet American,* to Leghorn–the central peninsula on the Italian western coast–for filming outdoor scenes that the film troupe hadn't completed in Vietnam. Mike Mindlin filled in, and the crush of so much work had him working at night.

First, however, the back lot had to become Tayninh. When the key processional scenes went before the cameras in early February, Audie had been in a Hong Kong hospital. So, now the courtyard scene in which Fowler witnesses *The Quiet American's* secretive dealings with the anti-Communist Third Force leader was prepared for the film canister. Utilizing carefully planned set design, camera angles, and skillful cutting to recreate the courtyard location, one could almost believe the moment took place in Vietnam, so shrewdly did Hornbeck cut in the actual footage done there.

During the last week of April, the crew left Cinecitta studio for the Leghorn. Since Mankiewicz was now overcompensating for the loss of the Vietnam location, his filming became excessive. There was much speculation about what would happen to the mass of footage the director accumulated. It couldn't be a black and white epic; that kind of movie seldom succeeded since silent days. Conversely, no one expected a ninety-minute spectacle, although it was, in its final state, a generic, talky Mankiewicz movie, intelligent, thought-provoking, and literate, in contrast to much of the studio drivel of the era.

At Rome Willard Willingham saved his strongest criticism for Giorgia Moll. He said she was "totally wrong for the role," and the intense and frequent scenes with Audie proved it beyond any convincing he needed. The stunt-double blamed her for all the failings in the scenes with Audie. As far as Willard was concerned, she was "too powerful," acting up a storm, overwhelming the low-key Murphy. Willard hinted too, this novice actress, with her histrionic background from Italian *commedia dell'arte*, overacted Audie off the screen in their intimate scenes. A practiced actor easily faked "chemistry" with his leading lady; Audie was ill at ease. Whatever his genuine affection for Giorgia off-screen, Audie wasn't able to generate what was expected of him for the camera.

Willingham persisted in claiming Giorgia's inclusion in the picture was "the reason the picture did not do well," as if the love scenes between Audie and Giorgia didn't include his friend's lack of expertise in depicting an interracial romance. Whatever occurred within their many love scenes, others–including Mankiewicz–became increasingly disappointed with the results. Though the director continued to film the couple's scripted sequences, there arose a general consensus that these moments would wind up on the cutting room floor.

According to Willingham, upon return to Rome, Mankiewicz had problems with Giorgia off screen, having to do with Moll's mother. When Giorgia went to Saigon, she traveled alone and made her own decisions. Once in Rome, Giorgia's mother appeared to act as her advisor and protector. What was a non-issue in Saigon became a point of contention at Cinecitta. Willingham recalled one brouhaha with the stage mother over the aesthetics of having Giorgia's underarms shaved. Neither Giorgia, nor her mother, accustomed to a traditional Italian custom, would agree to do what Mankiewicz wanted. The resolution had Giorgia wearing long sleeves in all her scenes. Willard summed up the entire experience with the Italian actress as "a real disaster."

Though the novel and film indicated *The Quiet American* is a moral man, the issue of love scenes indicated a show of skin. Mankiewicz expressed concern that with "some nudity or whatever he could get away with, he didn't want hairy close-ups." No matter what the director planned in this regard, an ardent Giorgia would still come across as sexually aggressive toward his reserved co-star. Audie never performed their intimate scenes with any kind of relish in front of the crew, though sequences of this nature traditionally draw the most attentive audiences. Moll didn't have the power to request a closed set and Audie was reluctant to do so. An insider suggested, after such scenes Willingham likely reassured Audie after such scenes, telling him how great he was, no matter how poor his performance.

Sequences in Saigon featured Audie and Giorgia building their love interest along some of the beautiful tourist spots. These moments contributed to making their motivations complex and passionate. However, the scenes ended up a thorn in the side of Mankiewicz. He did not remove, redact, or alter any the scenes from the script, but the dailies were indicative of an alarming problem. His two lovers were unbelievable, struggling to enliven dialogue meant to convey tempestuous love among two vibrant, sexual creatures.

Though Audie and Giorgia may well have been attractive to each other as well as the audience, they were at the mercy of Mankiewicz's interpretation of young love. Among the strongest scenes included a proposal by *The Quiet American*, under ironic supervision of Fowler, to Phuong in their Saigon apartment. The proposal scene, as done by Murphy and Redgrave and Moll, remains a droll piece of work; Giorgia has since proudly disclosed how French New Wave director Jean Luc Godard cited this scene as reason to cast her in one of his later films. Nevertheless, Miss Moll's future in motion pictures was restricted to on smaller European movies; her "big break" had come to naught.

Willingham also hurled blame for the failure of the scenes between Murphy and Moll on the director. Months after all the promises, Mankiewicz had not jettisoned much of his original concepts in the script. Where he intended to make changes, apparently, was in the editing room. As a result, the actors had to contend with "a long, dull, talky script." Willard insisted: "I never fully understood it, and the long philosophical scenes just ruined the picture." And, since he was interpreting the character and his motivations for Audie during their rehearsals and cue sessions, Willard derided the Mankiewicz dialogue. Willingham drew upon his own script-writing background to say, "You can make a bad picture with a good script, but you can never make a good picture with a bad script. Never." The upshot was, in

Willingham's critical judgment, that Mankiewicz was responsible for his own disaster.

In early May the production team returned to the Rome studio to finish interiors still needed: the Rendezvous Club, and several scenes in Fowler's Saigon apartment. For the first time, Mankiewicz recognized the deteriorating health of his lieutenant, Bill Hornbeck. The only way to force Hornbeck to rest was to cancel the rushes. Along with that, the director never went anywhere without his own personal pharmacy, having made a life-long study and collection of herbs, vitamins, miracle drugs, and other pharmaceuticals.

All during the Vietnam shoot, if he discovered someone ailing, he was the shaman with the medicine to make one better; it possibly was an outgrowth of his own odd version of hypochondria. However, he knew nothing in his medicine kit could help Hornbeck—except bedrest. Two days later the throat condition worsened. The film editor went to the hospital for X-rays, but when a movie was in production, Hornbeck never malingered. Within a single day, he was back at the studio, assembling a new projection machine for Mankiewicz.

By mid-May, Hornbeck spliced together enough of a rough cut that Michael Redgrave's narration, now on the sound track, added a polished dimension to the overall effect of the picture. The added voice-over was the connecting glue for the picture and brought Redgrave's performance to a new height and managed to cover up sequences already destined to be edited from the picture. With his dissipated, dulcet tones, his biting ironical shadings to lines Mankiewicz lifted from the Greene novel, Michael Redgrave's theatrical power brought synergy to the entire production, a most ironic result as his role was the epitome of ennui and hopelessness.

In his way, Audie too managed to put his brand on it. All the exteriors truly belonged to Audie. These active scenes were as much his as in any Western, while Redgrave dominated the static interior scenes; after all, he was the master of subtle Shakespearean dialog, and verbal jousting played to his strength. The outdoor sequences centered on one incident featuring quick, heroic action: the eerie night-time, Watch Tower scene amidst rice paddies.

This time, in close-ups, Audie and Redgrave were to do the work themselves. The setting had been carefully reproduced to match the original Vietnam site on a local rural road. Willard Willingham believes he enacted this scene for the final cut of the picture, but was only seen in one brief long shot helping the other double across the dark rice paddy on the real Ho Chi Minh Trail in Vietnam at the instant the tower in the background exploded in flames. Mankiewiciz knew the intimacy and power could only succeed if the two stars, Redgrave and Murphy, were shown doing physical action themselves to whatever extent possible.

The director wrote an exchange of dialogue to precede the scene of Murphy's character saving the life of Redgrave's Fowler. Fowler, who loathed all the Boy Scout goodness of the American, protested to be let alone, to be allowed to stay by the side of the road to die. *The Quiet American* will hear none of it and insisted he will carry the British journalist into the tall reeds for safety. To Fowler's resisting complaint, Audie snarled: "Write a letter to the *Times*," which threw the gauntlet down at Graham Greene who had spent many moments penning letters to the *London Times* editor, constantly griping about the making of *The Quiet American*. According to some observers, this proved how all directors relish the title "director" and use the opportunity "to do as they please, *a la* Huston, Kramer, and shits like that. Henry Hathaway was renowned for being a bastard. All directors try to live up to their publicized image from film to film, no matter what havoc it does to those around them."

The script called for the character of Fowler to be carried on the back of *The Quiet American* through the swamp and placed on the roadside. Not certain of the mud footing in this new location, Johnston and his team were told to test the waters "literally." Willingham, in costume and the exact height and weight of Murphy, was sent into the bog, up to his pectorals with the Redgrave double. "And he was forty pounds heavier than Redgrave," laughed Willingham. He put the man over his shoulders and carried him out of the miasma. As he took a step or two, he could not find firm groundwork. Though he might be able to stride through the bog normally, without a two-hundred thirty pound

205

weight on his back, Willard was sinking up to his knees deeper into the muck. He had no traction and found it nearly impossible to take steps.

Skilled carpenters were ordered to build a foot-wide platform that was placed under the water, along the route the actors waded to the roadside. Once submerged, the walkway had to be tested. And, of course, as required of a stunt double, Willard again entered the bog with the Redgrave Doppleganger. With a double on his shoulders, Willingham struggled with both the weight of the man and trying to keep his feet on the narrow pathway of slippery wood under the marsh. Once all the technical people were satisfied the lighting, and other conditions, were safe, the entire sequence was filmed with the doubles.

Mankiewicz then asked if his stars would to do the scene, and both agreed; Redgrave, despite barely recovered from influenza, wasn't to be outdone by the "amateur." Audie went further, by telling Mankiewicz he'd carry Redgrave over his shoulder, the distance, no doubles or faked long shots. Spec McClure's analysis about Audie's movie-making philosophy probably best explained the actor's comportment: "A man who can stand up to two hundred German soldiers and six tanks is not likely to be intimidated by a movie."

They rolled the cameras.

Climbing hastily out of the reconstructed watch tower, Audie and Redgrave hustled down the rickety ladder, Audie clearly being careful of himself. Following what had been shot previously in Vietnam with doubles, Redgrave simulated a fall and the injury to his leg. Audie dutifully assisted him as they ran toward the camera past their ditched car and into the rice paddy. They went thirty feet through the waist deep water to hide among tall reeds, reflected by flames form the burning tower off screen, then played the newly rewritten dialogue.

Redgrave was a little stiff, uncomfortable. Audie's hair was mussed, but just slightly. Nonetheless, after the long run both actors were breathless and sweating. It was a warm and damp evening. They were submerged in water up to their necks for long periods and had to duck beneath it a couple of times. Finally, the coast was clear. The gun-firing enemy had gone.

Hoisting Redgrave over his shoulders, Audie said: "We call this the fireman's lift." As he came to the end of the grueling carry, his knees buckled and the agony clearly carved itself into his baby face. Part of the trouble Audie encountered was keeping on the path of the narrow wooden walkway, as well as holding Redgrave balanced on his back, though he may have been tempted to dunk the British actor into the swamp along the way.

Had Audie been mistaken to put himself out with the physical stress to his body? Another film star claimed the brass of Figaro didn't give a fig about Audie doing the stunts himself. "He had his double with him. So, what were they to do? Applaud? It was his call. He had already held up the picture." In essence, the production company was only concerned with "getting the goddam thing in the can and stop spending money," as one insider commented, demanding anonymity. But, it was never smart to risk a star; that's what doubles were for.

In the grueling sequence of Fowler's rescue, Michael's face went from discomfort to the abject fear of death from a middle-aged man who professed to be carefree. Damp hair, plastered to his forehead, he grew ashen and anguished. On the other hand, with just a lock of hair displaced, Audie grew younger, stronger, resolute. In him one glimpsed the man-child in the ETO who killed hundreds of Nazis in a moment of fierce determination. Instead of tiring and wilting, Audie's face grew smooth, eyes set upon a goal. He shouldered Redgrave amid a fiery explosion, which rained debris in the background, and he shifted the semi-conscious victim onto his back for the final staggered steps out of the rice paddy. When they reached the burned car on the road's edge, the two men collapsed. Audie was panting hard, and Mankiewicz called cut.

Though Giorgia Moll was not involved in the night's shooting, she had eagerly attended to be with friends on the set. Once again, she marveled at the work of the set designers and the technical people who recreated the back roads of Vietnam on the outskirts of Rome. While watching the episode unfold, Giorgia Moll expressed amazement that many others voiced concerning Audie's physical efforts: "My God, I thought, how strong he is. I now can see the war hero." Vinh Noan had a similar thought upon viewing these scenes, "Audie was not an actor. He was a hero."

Next day, to the horror of Hornbeck, he discovered the roll used for the scene, the negative in the can, was "without any exposure." The bad news had to be delivered immediately in order for Mankiewicz to re-film the pivotal moment. For Redgrave, whose stage experience meant re-doing a role nightly for weeks on end, nothing could be easier than another try at it. Audie, of course, was another story; yet he showed up, ready as ever, the next night to re-do the pivotal moments not caught on film the first time. The shoot, including the plucky carry of Redgrave in two takes, was restaged; Audie carried his co-star the twenty feet once again.

Hornbeck visited MGM in Rome to see what they had in the way of stock sound footage for usage in *The Quiet American*, and Mankiewicz continued filming scenes between Dauphin and Redgrave, including the morgue section in which Fowler was "accidentally" locked in the room with the dead, extremely quiet, American's body. On May 23rd they filmed book-end scenes in Vigot's surete, or police office, which happened near the beginning and close to the end of the picture.

Ever conscious of the social obligations of film-making, Hornbeck continued to attend a series of "business" dinners while in Rome. Some-times these were strictly social, with a nostalgic twist, like his frequent dinners with Vincent Korda, from the old days. Sometimes he went to a party thrown by Joe Mankiewicz's secretary, Addie Wallace, or had lunch with Joe and his agent, Bert Allenberg, before screening the pic-ture once more for them. He dined with Johnny Johnston's brother (in from scouting in Pakistan). If, for some reason, he sidestepped a func-tion (like Bob Krasker's big Roman bash), he felt a trace of guilt for not representing the troupe. He dined too with Vinh Noan and his future wife, actress Mai Tram, in late May. A personal network always served in the movie world as stress relief and as a means of perpetuating one's professional standing.

With additional scenes yet to be filmed, Hornbeck informed Mankiewicz they had three hours and twenty-nine minutes of footage. The last scene to be re-done in Rome, parts shot in Saigon proving not up to par, was the Pavilion explosion scene. They had been unable to see rushes in Vietnam because, after two final days of shooting, they packed up and left the Asian country. Now, Mankiewicz, ever the perfectionist, wanted to re-stage moments for better quality. So, on Monday, June 3rd, additional footage of the disaster scene was made to replace what hadn't reached the standard the director demanded.

The conflicts between Vigot and Fowler became the director's focus. The detective cat and mouse game with Redgrave and Claude Dauphin in the concluding reel of the movie dealt with a crisis of feeling guilt by Michael Redgrave's character. Long after Audie's flashbacks in the movie had ended, the story continued as a struggle between the conscience of the police detective and the man who wanted to remain "uninvolved."

As the final day of filming occurred on June 5, Audie couldn't fail to notice the wrap-up of this picture coincided with the thirteenth anniversary of D-Day, when he had waded ashore at Anzio, a place where too many soldiers died needlessly. Earlier, Audie and Mike Mindlin had gone down to the battleground for a visit. Audie wanted to see it again. Mindlin felt it was a deeply moving and private moment for Audie. He spent a long time, ambling along the beach in complete introspection. "A very emotional experience for him," commented Mike.

Audie also went to Anzio with Willard. Though the war experience he loathed speaking about was an intense and private memory, Audie went to Anzio a half dozen times and reportedly shared this intimacy with a variety of people at Cinecitta; it seems doubtful that all the claimants experienced this personal time with Audie. But Audie did take his wife to the areas of his combat days and pointed out the changes in the area. The place was one of tranquil innocence. Life had gone on, and whatever horror happened there years ago, had moved on too.

A second, but more traditional, wrap party was held at the Cinecitta restaurant. On Thursday, June 6, 1958, six months to the day that Joe Mankiewicz landed on the tarmac in Saigon, the ordeal called *The Quiet American* celebrated the completion of its principal photography. The cast dispersed, probably never again to work with each other. Redgrave, like Murphy, continued to make films until the early 1970s.

Unlike Murphy's formula low-budget westerns, Redgrave performed in "status" films, but in increasingly smaller roles. Miss Moll went on to appear in an epic called *The White Warrior* and a few New Wave French films, like *Contempt*. Claude Dauphin played featured roles in dozens of movies, most forgettable. As for Mankiewicz, he made only five more movies during the next twenty years.

As filming in Rome wrapped, a disgruntled Audie found it peculiar that Redgrave and Mankiewicz actually thought this movie would bring a Renaissance to their artistic fortunes. As for the film, Audie considered Mankiewicz and Redgrave captive to delusions: "They will have a rude awakening when the damn mess is released." Mankiewicz and Redgrave never recovered from the experience; they were far more disappointed by the results of their efforts than Audie. Both often omitted *The Quiet American* from their list of film credits.

Once the Rome segments rolled for the cameras, Audie was greatly dismayed by the visible faults he saw in the viewing room. He grumbled the picture "had a chance until it was ruined in the cutting room." One might take this as insulting to the hard-working Hornbeck, but Audie knew the original footage was nearly double in length what the audiences in movie houses would see. From the start he sensed it could flop because the story as scripted was puzzling and inexplicable. Hornbeck was not the problem. How much of a dud the movie might prove to be was anyone's guess

Audie Murphy realized what he suspected from the start: that he had been mistaken to do this picture. He wondered if anyone would accept his attempt to stretch his range, using *The Quiet American* as his break-out vehicle. Common opinion reasoned Redgrave's Oscar caliber performance suffered because he lacked an actor of equal merit with whom to play his scenes. So far as the story's complexity went, Murphy epitomized the smug, firm, callow-looking, idealist—which he was supposed to express. He was affable and unaffected by the dominating narrative power of Redgrave's sarcastic and empty vessel of a journalist. Many Figaro people were startled at how strongly Murphy played against this veteran of English theater.

Mike Mindlin admitted movies remain an artistic process that postpone judgment until entirely put together. "Only then, when the final piece is in place, can you know what you have. Everything may seem fine until that moment. Then, you hear the screams." It would be in the hands of the publicity and press contingents of United Artists distributors to promote the film energetically.

Audie and his wife gave an interview later that year about their reunion in Rome. Audie related how he called his wife, on the flight out of Saigon, from an airport in Turkey, hoping to patch up his marriage, saying: "I can't go another week without seeing you. The kids will be fine for a little while. Darling, fly here!" In their sanitized version for the press, Pam came to Italy within two days to renew their marriage.

Audie spent most of the Rome portion of the production in the company of Pamela, always referring to it as a second honeymoon. Resigned to the grind of the shoot, he escaped by behaving like a tourist, escorting Pam around the countryside. He wrote McClure about seeing the Pope at the Vatican in a crush of audience numbering in the thousands. In Rome Audie's customary tart wit returned in full force, as exemplified by his correspondence with Spec McClure. After attending a large outdoor religious event, he wrote: " . . . wish I had the spaghetti concession!" Having Pam at his side tended to mellow him.

Audie started to reveal to people that he intended his next picture to be called *The Way Back*. It was based on a manuscript written in 1956 by Spec McClure, which remains unpublished and stored at the Baylor University archives. Audie responded to queries by explaining in his usual soft-spoken manner: "That's what I have found at last. A reason for living, and home . . . our home, the kids." He made some promises to sell his quarter horses, to avoid race tracks in the future, and to spend more time at his San Fernando Valley home. His wife, by his side, knew better than to comment.

Shortly after returning to California in late June, he granted an interview to the doyen of Hollywood, Hedda Hopper, who had always been his champion. De-briefed on his thirty-third birthday, Audie bluntly unburdened himself with Hedda, when he returned from his Vietnam experience, about the continuing pot-boiler westerns ahead of him: "The pictures I make there (Universal International) are cheapies–but that's the kind of thing I have to do until I finish my contract. I have eight more pictures to make under contract for them–and two of them can be done outside." He feared he would end up on television, in a dead-end series, with no hope of doing better films. And, he revealed an idea for remaking, for the fourth time, Hemingway's *To Have and Have Not* was among his plans.

Audie remained intransigent about some Hollywood activities. His first wife, Wanda Hendrix, had told him that knowing the right people, being seen in the right places, and proper publicity essentially made the career, not the film roles. Spec McClure stated: "He refused to associate with people whom he didn't like, to attend functions at which he felt uncomfortable, or stand for publicity that he believed to be ridiculous." Though the vehemence of his feeling abated somewhat as he grew older, he didn't participate in the publicity campaign for this latest picture after his return to the States.

In the meantime for the director and his staff, *The Quiet American* had not yet reached completion. Mankiewicz supervised to a limited extent the cutting of the film, but the main task fell to William Hornbeck. While Joe Mankiewicz dabbled in the theater (his Figaro company was producing a version of a Carson McCullers novel). Hornbeck remained with the picture on a daily basis for six more months.

Initially, there were over fifteen reels of film that Hornbeck tackled, trying to do at least three reels per day. The day after the wrap party, Hornbeck ran the picture for Mike Mindlin. That earliest version of the picture ran a whopping three hours and a half. Clearly, this was unacceptable to everyone, even Mankiewicz. The task of editing the morass of scenes and complexity of narrative belonged, of course, to Hornbeck whose major problem was in creating coherence and understanding of the plot, while trying to maintain the atmosphere and style of the direction.

As for all that edited footage, producer Eric Pleskow recently offered no hope that it might ever be retrieved. The nitrate film stock of the time would not survive forty years of storage, and he was of the mind that the Figaro "out-takes were destroyed" as a matter of routine policy, "unlike if the movie were done today." And, surely those missing love scenes between Audie and Giorgia were part of that destruction.

In mid-June Hornbeck moved all his equipment and projection machines over to Amata Studios in Italy. Despite the particularly hot Italian summer, he worked Saturdays and Sundays, and well into the night on every weekday. By Saturday, June 29, he ran the entire picture again, with his latest cuts: the length had been reduced to under three hours, but not by much. He and Mankiewicz joined up in early July and re-cut the first three reels, in complete agreement about keeping them in tact. During the summer hiatus from school, Tom and Chris Mankiewicz joined their parents in Rome for a preliminary showing of the film in mid-July. Continuing his grueling schedule of working each day on the fifteen other reels, Hornbeck produced by the end of July a movie that ran 13,630 feet—or two hours and thirty minutes.

Cuts centered on scenes that built the relationship of Phuong and *The Quiet American*. Now, their romance dashed abruptly across the screen, instead of delicately emerging with two reluctant lovers thrown together. The passion of the two stars, shown in complicated flashback, was reduced to the off-hand narrative comments of Fowler as he casually observed them in various locations around Saigon.

The film became somewhat incomprehensible, failing to depict a growth of attraction between the two young lead actors. Whatever screen characterizations Audie and Giorgia had tried to give, the audience would not see them, nor would anyone else but those who sat in the screening rooms of Rome during the summer of 1957 and turned thumbs down.

If the question arose as to why Mankiewicz cut only the scenes done by Moll and Murphy, the most careful and accurate answer came from Vinh Noan. With his own director's eye and producer's sympathy, he noted: "Joe was a director who was used to working with the best actors, like Bette Davis. So, he did not like to accept work that was not at its best." The upshot was that the love scenes, a series of romantic interludes with Audie and Giorgia, had been beyond them, were beyond Mankiewicz's tolerance, and were beyond the ability of Hornbeck to cure ineffectual acting through editing.

Murphy often complained he didn't like love scenes and felt embarrassed doing them. The two stars of the picture looked like teenagers and presented an adolescent image of passion on the screen. For the story to work as adult intrigue and betrayal, the director was left with a serious problem. The nature of the "Romeo and Juliet" character of Audie and Giorgia's love made Redgrave's furious revenge preposterous when acted out. Audiences would think of Redgrave as a lecherous old man, not someone competing with a peer for an adult temptress. Mankiewicz ordered the scenes taken out of the picture.

At the end of July Mankiewicz took a vacation, but Hornbeck carried on. Since dubbing, dupes, and loops, were at issue, he was joined for a week by sound engineer Basil Fenton-Smith, welcome company for the tedious stretch of work–though Hornbeck and his wife enjoyed one delightful getaway night when they attended the opera, *Aida*, at the Caracalla Baths. Such evenings were rare and would be restricted during a few additional months of film editing. The picture, however, took a shape that allowed it to be worth viewing outside the staff; when the dissolves arrived from lab processing, he quickly readied a print for showing to United Artists moguls–including Arthur Krim– for mid-August.

When Mankiewicz and his wife returned from vacation, Hornbeck had edited the picture to two hours and twelve minutes. However, equipment failures continued from overuse; Basil Fenton-Smith made repairs and the sound track was re-recorded in two days at Fona Roma. At this point, they were into September. Mario Nascimbene entered the process, supervising the music for weeks of work, but the tracks for music and effects were not fully completed until early October. When all was done and he viewed the completed film, Hornbeck himself shook his head and commented it was only "fair to good."

Italian composer Mario Nascimbene had little good to say about his work on *The Quiet American*. Though he had a delightful time with *The Barefoot Contessa*, which contained "scenes among my all-time personal favorites," he regarded Mankiewicz as the exponent of "great American cinema." However, on the Greene story, he found, "was frequently interrupted by too much dialogue that tried to explain too much. It brought the action to a halt, making it heavy and limiting it, and it left very little room for any kind of music." Nascimbene, did use some Vietnamese percussion instruments in the opening credits. Whether intentionally or not, the gong sound gave an exotic touch just as the cast names appear on screen.

Ready or not, Hornbeck traveled to New York in mid-October with his print. At the Century Screening Room on October 18th, he ran the picture for Robert Lantz and Walter Wanger. The finished product did not console Robby Lantz, having held reservations about the script since the onset of production. He told Mankiewicz of his doubts: "I expressed my opinion," he stated many decades later. But, of course, Mankiewicz was "willful." Regarding the disappointing picture's preview, Lantz jestingly said: "I have tried to blot it out." Wanger concurred in his estimation of the film. The two Figaro executives were to join forces on producing future productions of *I Want to Live* and *Suddenly Last Summer.*

Several days later Bill Hornbeck met with Mike Mindlin on the latest stage of the movie's business. The meeting examined the trailer or previews of the picture that would be released to theaters to increase interest in their picture. Because of the highly charged political situation in Vietnam, and giving credence to the notion that Mankiewicz had ties to the needs of national security within the federal government, Hornbeck went to Washington, D.C., on October 24. There the film was previewed for the Vietnam ambassador and a number of other concerned officials from the State Department.

The picture was trimmed to two hours and eleven minutes; the time to gauge public reaction now arrived. Hornbeck and Rosemary Matthews checked the location for the preview on October 29th. Stamford, Connecticut, was their choice for a special motion picture premiere at the Palace Theatre, no press allowed, on Halloween, 1957.

Figaro, Incorporated, posted several newspaper notices preceding the showing in Stamford to drum up curiosity. The local paper referred, as usual, to a "major Hollywood film" and how the city in Connecticut was being honored with a sneak preview. The tasteful advertisements, without giving out the film's title, hinted at a quality production. Figaro's choice of Stamford, so distant from Los Angeles probably had more to do with the fact that Mankiewicz had his offices in New York City, as did Lantz, Wanger, and other production executives.

The aggregation gathered in Manhattan the night before for the big Broadway debut of Robby Lantz's production of *The Square Root of Wonderful*, a highly anticipated play (her first) by Carson McCullers. Preliminary tryouts had indicated a bomb of the first order. And, though the play had been doctored by Tennessee Williams, as a favor to Lantz and McCullers, it wasn't likely to be well-received. Ever the wag, Mike Mindlin dubbed the fiasco, "The Square Root of Trouble."

The idea of an out-of-town preview for *The Quiet American* had its roots in the concept of keeping industry rivals from tainting audience reaction. It also meant shrewish Hollywood gossipmongers wouldn't be in attendance to bad mouth the film. As one frequent attendee of such showings stated: "Studio folk, often including director and stars and major craftsmen, will arrive at the theater, attempting to appear to look like the 'peasants' but are usually rather conspicuous by their huddled company and (back in the fifties) wearing their suits and ties."

On this night, however, the disappointed preview audience saw not a single star. Audie was in California, wrapping up work on his latest Universal-International western with Walter Matthau. Redgrave was in England, thrilled to be co-starring together on a play with his daughter Vanessa. Redgrave said shortly after his experience on *The Quiet American*, that: "I don't like to wear my stage personality all day. It should be something you look forward to assuming . . . there have been times when my parts affected me in my real life, but I discovered that it's bad for the part when that happens . . ." The statement reflected the bitterness about the work he'd done with Audie Murphy.

Giorgia Moll remained in Italy until she visited the United States for her national publicity tour in early 1958. The audience, without movie celebrities on hand, may well have been befuddled just as to what they were about to be subjected. As the audience entered the hall, they were handed opinion cards. They were expected to fill them out as they exited, their reactions highly prized. "The studio folk entered last, hovering at the rear of the auditorium in order to observe the overall reactions and be able to rush out immediately as the film ended so they could listen to the public's vocal comments as they loitered in the lobby while the theater emptied."

Audience delight with *The Quiet American* title credits conflicted immediately in that, as part of the music score, unfortunately, the stars' names appeared simultaneously with a foreboding gong. The audience had to be confused by an Oriental sound in context with the applauded name of Audie Murphy as it appeared on the screen. The sight of his dead body not long after the credits ended did not bode well either. Being shown the hero dead before the story was underway was far from a good old-fashioned Western. Worse yet, the bad guys got Audie! The opinion cards and vocal comments reflected the audience shock and anger without pulling punches.

Of course, the previous night everyone from Figaro, Incorporated, including Mankiewicz, Lantz, Hornbeck, Wanger, Johnston, and others, had suffered the disastrous opening night on Broadway of their company's first play. Suffice it to say, the news was not wonderful about the play that night—nor for this film shown in Connecticut the next night. Mankiewicz's movie received few kudos in Stamford, a more urban and sophisticated city than most. If Stamford didn't like the picture, it wouldn't play in Peoria either. One decision emerged immediately. Thinking it too windy, the picture was cut ten more minutes of length.

Hornbeck spent November re-cutting at the Pathe offices in New York. For general release, the picture would be two hours and one minute long. Whatever the fate of the picture and his labors on it, he knew any accolades—as well as the critical flak—would go to actors and director. Only those in the industry understood the sweat and dedication that the film editor put into the project.

As long as everyone busied himself with the complicated task of making a picture, high hopes for a good product dominated their thoughts. Yet, the simple fact was that Audie's illness in Vietnam caused him to miss weeks of shooting, and later prevented more action scenes from being filmed, and his love scenes ended up discarded. With this burden upon Mankiewicz, it tended to give the detrimental talky scenes more proportional screen-time; whatever balance of talk and action that the director planned had been undermined.

Nothing said by audiences in the previews could solve the problems. After tightening the picture and cutting down its length, the director had run out of options. Blame could be grounded in Greene's sour comments which injured the film's reputation. More finger-pointing could be made at Clift and Olivier for abandoning a project they never supported; some trouble could be traced to miscasting the Asian girl, or tied to Johnny Johnston's occasional errors in production. The heat of criticism could be attributed to slow-to-arrive dailies that left Mankiewicz hanging, or to airline strikes. In the end, Mankiewicz had to realize he couldn't make a great film without a great script and great actors. No one could.

The trouble with *The Quiet American* in its final form was that, like Humpty Dumpty, it fell off the wall at its inception—and no one was willing to desist from trying to put its pieces together again, no matter how they mismatched. It was just an inevitable, colossal, box-office failure.

Like two orphans in the storm, Audie and Giorgia suffered the cruelest barbs when the picture played to critics. When Giorgia started her two and a half month press junket, she was met at the airport in New York by Figaro publicist Mike Mindlin who welcomed her to America and had photos taken of her dressed in a conical straw hat—which she never wore in the picture. Barnstorming the United States, she remained astonished by the vehemence of attacks upon the picture and herself in local newspapers and through the mails.

In Beverly Hills at a public reception, a tipsy Louella Parsons caused her to flee the party in tears when the dowager Hollywood gossip made a verbal and physical assault on the young actress. She may have survived the dangers of Vietnam, but Giorgia couldn't stop the American predatory columnist from placing both hands on Giorgia's bosom and mortifying the girl during a well-attended press conference.

Still, Giorgia felt she and Audie shared similar feelings about their employment in the picture. "We were lucky to have done that movie," she observed. "We had a chance to work with a great director and a great actor, Mr. Redgrave. The experience made us both more mature about movies. It certainly gave me a chance to grow. Whenever a picture about Vietnam is made, I try to see it. The country and its people made a tremendous impact on me. Yes, I always think of Vietnam," she added wistfully.

10

THE FIRST AMERICAN casualty of Vietnam was truly Audie Murphy's movie image. Dismissing Audie as mere symbolism, a notorious book title of 1972 cruelly sneered about *How Audie Murphy Died in Vietnam*. Yet, the involvement of Audie in Vietnam occurred in Hollywood lore, as well as in American political jingoism. Audie Murphy went to Vietnam, and his appearance there proved a disaster personally, just as much as the nation's warfare proved politically.

The movie predated the American military venture into southeast Asia, yet foreshadowed it by depicting the first American casualty of the War. Indeed, the key to the plot hinged on the celebration of Tet, the Chinese New Year, filmed eleven years before the Tet Offensive during the Vietnam War, the defining military moment of the American involvement in 1968. Some contend Tet of 1968 marked the true occasion when the United States military received the shock of its history, and the war truly transformed into a lost cause.

"Wherever he walked—all hell broke loose!" . . . so stated the publicity banner for *The Quiet American*, as it played with the image and reality of its star actor, Audie Murphy. The disaster of the first American movie filmed in Vietnam in 1957 would be a harbinger of a later, greater disaster with thousands of "quiet Americans" in the role of the casualties. Forty years later, the wounds of the Vietnam War and its ramifications on the home-front are fading from memory and passion. Yet, the Mankiewicz film still remains a painful artifact.

Dismissed and lost in the haze of war protests of the 1960s with the desire of the public to forget a painful period in history, the movie seldom plays on television, even today. Still not released officially on video in the United States, its reputation hinges on misinformation, vendettas by long-deceased participants, and revisionist history of literature, echoing whenever a discussion of the movie begins. Many of those who were there still won't talk, and they often dissociate themselves from its failure.

The United Artists point man in those days, Eric Pleskow spoke with all the cynicism of a man who had been in the business for fifty years, who had seen the battles between movies and media, between truth and tabloid reportage. In his career he has focused on topical movies, thoughtful and meaningful. Responding with the standard reaction to box-office poison like *The Quiet American*, the Oscar-winning producer at first claimed the picture did not belong to United Artists. He asked, "Was it one of ours?" Pleskow echoed the endings of two other classic films: at the close of *Touch of Evil*, director and writer Orson Welles has Marlene Dietrich walk away into the dark, muttering: "What does it matter what you say about a man?"

Pleskow combined this perception with the viewpoint of John Ford who made the closing dialog in *The Man Who Shot Liberty Valance* that, when one must decide between the truth and the legend, "print the legend." Though that line originally applied to a John Wayne character in movies, Pleskow used it for Wayne's arch-rival, an Audie Murphy character, when he observed: "It doesn't really matter what you say or write about the making of *The Quiet American*.. After forty years, who will offer a challenge? No one."

A movie about Vietnam seemed a barometer for the attitude in the United States about a war in that faraway land a few years later. If he chose, Audie could trace the advent of his slide to this film. Trends in America passed Audie Murphy by in the 1960s: war protest, peace movements, and military in Vietnam. Men who wore uniforms in those days found themselves despised objects of derision. Army soldiers perpetrated massacres led by their officers who expressed a warped admiration for Audie and called him "idol." The association drove Audie to distraction. In Westerns, undergoing a similar metamorphosis, no man was clever or good any longer; the new bronc buster of cinematic rage rode the plains of the Spaghetti West. Clint Eastwood's version of the west made the hero just another dirty, amoral killer. In consequence, Audie's film career came to the end of the trail in the years of the Vietnam War, his whistle-clean image unacceptable to a new generation.

Vietnam had proved a debacle for Audie, Joe Mankiewicz, and the film. They trudged half-way around the world for a meager few background shots which might have been obtained easily by any second-unit director procuring a few cans of newsreel style footage. Only Redgrave, seen constantly pacing the streets of Saigon, existed in the real Vietnam. Other actors might well be standing in front of a projected image of the Asian country, for all their interaction with it.

Of the sum of two hours of released footage, the total screen time for Vietnam location added up to less than twenty minutes of the entire picture. Many frames of Redgrave motoring with Fred Sadoff were process shots, the car merely a prop placed before a silk-screen that showed Saigon streets in motion behind the actors. The scene was shot in Rome along with the rest of the interiors. Owing to Audie's ruptured appendix, his Saigon work was less taxing than the script originally required. He and Giorgia Moll walked briefly in the botanical gardens and drove down a Saigon street in his roadster. He sat in the trishaw on a Saigon street, waiting to be driven to his death in another sequence. Only the shooting schedule on the final two days, the Place Grenier bombing, included all the main actors on location (except Moll).

In late January a special showing in Washington, D.C., presented the picture as a benefit for the American Friends of Vietnam, which paralleled the putative group Audie's character represented in the film, called the Friends of Free Asia. Members of the group of American Friends included Arthur Schlesinger and then Senator John F. Kennedy, which enhanced Julian Smith's theory about the fates of Murphy and Kennedy having ties to Vietnam.

Julian Smith in his work on Hollywood's excursions into Vietnam drew one of the most intriguing parallels and theories about that southeastern Asia land: its two most important casualties were men who never fought there, John Kennedy and Audie Murphy. Smith hinted that conspiracy theorists who suggest Kennedy first enmeshed the country in Vietnam may be on to something, and perhaps one possible reason for his assassination could be traced back to this problem. According to Smith–Audie Murphy, having been a jingoist, was stripped of his patriotic credibility when the war created murderous soldiers like William Calley.

On one occasion Audie defended Lt. William Calley's actions in the My Lai massacre, incurring wide condemnation across America. Calley had testified he resented the fact that Vietnamese called Americans "cowboys," but explained that "we thought we would go to Vietnam and be Audie Murphys. Kick in the door. Run in the hooch, give it a good burst–kill. And get a big kill ratio in Vietnam." The winner of the most medals for combat in American history felt genuine confusion over this topsy-turvy world. When Audie said Calley merely made a military misjudgement, he found himself disdained by critics.

Audie's participation in a film centered on Americans in Vietnam made the future war ominous–considering Lieutenant Calley's role in the My Lai massacre, and the ultimate defeat of the United States in southeast Asia. In hindsight, the picture held a lesson for a public that never saw it, let alone found its message instructive.

Julian Smith observed, in flippant fashion, that John Kennedy and Audie Murphy represented the cross-spectrum of America which created the world of the Calley-style American. Murphy came from poverty; Kennedy from wealth. One developed from urban sophistication and Harvard; the other came from Ozark rural deprivation. One's life began in Texas, and the president's life ended there. Yet, each was a World War II hero who had a movie filmed about his exploits and wounds. Each now rests in Arlington National Cemetery, not far from the other. Exploring the ironies of their lives, Smith concluded the common thread is the fateful tie to America's policy on Vietnam.

When the movie premiered on Ground Hog Day weekend, 1958, only a few days were sufficient to show how wrong Audie had been to flirt with art. It was soundly panned by critics, as many knew it would be. It fell off the *Variety* gross charts in steep descent, like some precipice gaped at by bored tourists. It turned out to be a dismal failure, something to regret ever doing.

At the same time as Mankiewicz was in Rome, David O. Selznick worked on his epical *A Farewell to Arms* at one of the nearby lots in Cinecitta. Since the two directors, Mankiewicz and Selznick were friends, they invariably compared notes on whose film would be less successful; they agreed immediately on which film would gross a minuscule portion of the other.

The picture failed to be remunerative to its principals. In terms of salary, Redgrave made the equivalent of about $25,000 for his role in the picture–but 80 percent of it went to the tax people in England. Mankiewicz predicted the North American gross of *The Quiet American* would be equivalent to what a pot-boiling B-level picture, typical of Audie's work at Universal International, would make in California movie houses alone. Audie's salary, comparable to his co-star, did not cover his medical expenses, business and gambling debts, and personal cost. His foray into Vietnam proved expensive, ill-timed, unpopular; a hapless career move. He never achieved what he wanted: admiration of his peers. He continued to be assigned scripts suitable to his range–and none were deviations from what he hoped to escape.

McClure realized by this time, Audie was "thoroughly cynical. Murphy returned to the small-budget westerns strictly for money. His main ambition was to be able to make a living with no more acting. He realized that the final product of a player depended too much on incompetent people."

Audie did his best under extremely trying circumstances in Vietnam, but no matter how much one may admire him, his efforts were in vain. He should have been the ideal choice, but his lack of genuine acting craft was his obvious downfall. Being so guarded about himself, he lacked the ability to expose his own vulnerability, which could have rendered his performance masterful.

The public drew the line sharply on Audie when it came to this motion picture. Word of mouth destroyed attendance. No audience really cared about a talky detective story set in a confusion of politics–and Vietnam remained a place remote from America, not yet ensconced in living rooms night after night on television news shows. So, this ill-fated attempt called *The Quiet American* passed largely under-appreciated.

As for the luckless "man without a name," with its premiere set for early February of 1958, after the crisis, no one needed to remind Audie where he fell short. With his chronic gambling, his flagging popularity, his inability to create art out of minimal talent, he hazarded an adroit bid to become a better man, best symbolized by *The Quiet American*. Audie was the quintessential American idealist, simple and direct, honest and trusting, a man of honor, in a world that increasingly played a different game. Major stars end as a nova; the lesser just burn out.

In professional circles Audie's desire to elevate his career roles gave the impression he was impracticable. Though how he could be moreso than any of his pretentious colleagues, no one has ever explained. Michael Redgrave continued to accept all the second-rate movie roles rejected by Olivier to subsidize his stage career. His Parkinson's disease slowly ate away his career, then his health. When problems reached their worst stage, Freddie Sadoff left him. His last years were spent in a nursing home where he died in 1985. Nine years later Sadoff died of AIDS complications.

Bill Hornbeck did two more Mankiewicz films, but decided to finish his film editor career by working with his favorite director, the man whose philosophy of goodness mirrored itself on the screen: Frank Capra. Hornbeck's final film was sentimentally with Capra again–*Hole in the Head* in 1959. The mutual admiration with his beloved Capra continued. Years later, Frank Capra declared Bill Hornbeck was the greatest film editor "in the history of motion pictures." As Film Editor for all three Mankiewicz/Figaro movies, he had tied his reputation to those productions. After that, he switched completely into production where he ran Universal International pictures, finishing up with the box-office mover and shaker, *Earthquake.* His short, quiet retirement was notable for his decision to donate his personal papers to the university archive where Capra's had been sent. In the end, he chose Frank Capra over Joe.

Mankiewicz called *The Quiet American* "a bad movie made at a bad time in my life" in subsequent interviews. While in Rome, Mankiewicz had to have his wife committed to a clinic in Vienna. It was too little, too late. His wife's breakdown and subsequent suicide within the year added to his travails. Her belief that Joe Mankiewicz's behavior hinted at philandering–scarcely delusional–pushed the first Mrs. Mankiewicz over the edge. Worse, the great director lost all interest in movies in general. He oversaw the greatest catastrophe in movies up to the time: the over-budget and bloated *Cleopatra.* The asp bit Mank. He was fired on the final day of shooting. It sealed his doom as a Hollywood force. Five years after *The Quiet American,* Joe Mankiewicz married Rosemary Matthews, his assistant on the picture, finding a permanent happiness from the intermittent embroilments.

In 1990 two years before his death, Joe Mankiewicz greeted Giorgia Moll with a wistful kindness at the Venice Film Festival. Miss Moll and the director found themselves at an event where, with its gong start, *The Quiet American* filled the screen again. In one of her interviews for this book Giorgia Moll expressed great pleasure at Joe's solicitude and generosity during their final meeting. She felt again his genuine interest in her career, as she had years earlier during the filming. He had no regrets about selecting her. He said to his former leading actress: "It was never easy. I don't make my own productions any more. You know, I always found it so difficult to find money to make my pictures," and that, he explained to her, was why he was so inactive in the film industry for so many years.

Forty years after the making of the movie, Miss Giorgia Moll, living in semi-retirement, has graciously supplied a long list of comments on the film and her experience; the consummate *grande dame,* her memories of the picture remain sweet; she shares only pleasant and happy information about her director, co-stars, or her own forlorn attempt to break into American motion pictures.

Though she signed a five picture deal with Figaro, Incorporated, the failure of *The Quiet American* impacted on her future work. At the end of the filming, Figaro executives "lent me out to various Italian productions." She worked, again, on smaller comedies, with legendary Italian director Luigi Cominichi. Of course, she was back to where she had been before her "discovery" by Mankiewicz. Shortly thereafter

Figaro disbanded. Giorgia explained: "Then, since the picture was not a big success in America, and after three years, I was released from my contract."

Elaine Schreyeck continued to work with Joe Mankiewicz whenever and wherever possible. Together they completed movies as diverse as *Suddenly Last Summer* and *Sleuth*. On her own she moved into the new generation of successful films, working on James Bond pictures and with respected directors like John Boorman. She remembers her experience on *The Quiet American* as one of great enjoyment. Mankiewicz remains her idea of a premier director: " . . . first and foremost he was a good writer. The spoken word was so important to him." In the year before the director died, she sent him "my Christmas greetings . . . and I asked when he was going to direct another film— and he said: "When they can string more than two words together."

Vinh Noan's career as a director never reached the promise of 1955. Living in a country ravaged by war, witnessing over 50,000 dead American servicemen, Vinh never had the opportunity to make another picture on his terms. Instead, he ran the Saigon Film Center all during the 1960s, arranging for thousands of RCA black and white televisions to be strategically placed around the country for propaganda purposes. Transmissions were beamed to American airplanes that sent the pictures around all Southeast Asia. After he immigrated to the United States, Noan served as a special emissary to Vietnam for President George Bush and worked toward gaining the cooperation of the Communists to return the bodies of dead soldiers, to allow free travel within the country, and to improve the plight of Amerasian children so discriminated against by the rest of that nation.

Willard Willingham's career after *The Quiet American* continued with Audie. Moving beyond script doctor, Willingham and his wife penned a series of westerns for Audie . . . *Gunpoint, Bullet for a Badman,* and *Forty Guns to Apache Pass,* which Willingham believed presented the real Audie Murphy to audiences. Willard regarded it as the high point of both his and Audie's relationship. It also happened to be Audie's penultimate film appearance. After Audie's death, Willard's screenwriting career petered out. Living in retirement in the Hollywood Hills, he has remained staunchly respectful of Audie's memory. He was a man with the unbelievable good fortune to be of assistance to a movie god and cultural phenomenon.

Audie had set aside remorse over his "thespian" aspirations exactly one year after his incursion into Vietnam. In January of 1958, when he decided to do a remake of Ernest Hemingway's *To Have and Have Not* (released as *The Gun Runners*), he chose to remain closer to his home in California, indicating the main lesson Audie learned about distant "on location" movies. Before the year ended, his misfortunes continued to pile up; he suffered a bout of pneumonia during the holiday season. Wife Pamela kept visits with his two sons to a limited schedule in order to insure "proper rest." His workaholic attitude required careful monitoring, but he insisted on holding rehearsals for his next picture in his home.

Audie's fans continued to appreciate their enjoyment of him. Yet, in their fickleness, films like *The Quiet American* rendered him beyond their pathos. Movie-goers would just wait for the next oater. Still boyishly handsome in 1960, his life took on a last act patina. He almost drowned during the filming of the picture, *The Unforgiven*. It was his second film with John Huston who managed again to extract an amazing Murphy performance during this picture. The director told Spec McClure, "Audie is afraid of making a fool out of himself in front of the camera. So he tightens up. I assure him that I'll protect him. He believes me and gives his all."

In the 1960s, at a Hollywood studio to discuss a new movie, he stared at a group of executives at Universal-International. He was in a trance when someone asked him for his thoughts: "I was just thinking that, with one hand grenade, a person could get rid of all those no talent bastards at one stroke." It was merely Audie's way of putting off lunchtime visitors to his table at the Sun Room. He preferred to eat alone, and outrageous comments like those confirmed the opinion of many that Audie was a dangerous man.

All through the 1950s and 1960s, Saturday matinees at the movies meant seeing a grade B western. For Audie Murphy nearly every movie he made was an oater, tailor made for Saturday's young filmgoers.

Audie claimed, "I did not get a change in stories. I only got a change in horses." Expectations need not wander far in any direction because Audie always delivered a product his audience could count on. One seldom went to the movies to find Audie in a first-rate film, or one based on classic literature. If you did, you suspected that it was not Audie at his best.

The worst moment, and one of the great theatrical moments in the history of Hollywood, centered of the trial in which Audie was the defendant for attempting the murder of a dog trainer. His trial in March of 1970 was the media circus of its day, but had nothing on the O.J. Simpson murder trial of a generation later.

Had Audie's ordeal occurred years later, one can only imagine the intense press coverage it would have garnered. As it was, the basics of the case were garish: a beautiful woman with whom Audie has some connection, a pedigree German Shepherd named Rommel, a bully out of central casting, and a bantam good-guy who beat up the bully when he assaulted the lady. One spectator at the trial said, by just looking at him, you could tell Audie was "the stuff that gods are made of."

If Audie wished to encourage his image as a lonely man without a network of social support, this moment defined him. Where were his fans? the Veterans groups? those who would rise to his defense twenty years earlier? None took his side at this low-point of his life and in his most depressing of occasions. One problem with the arrest of Audie was that the weapon he brandished, allegedly a Magnum, had conveniently disappeared. He had given the gun to the President of Algeria as a Christmas present. Of course, the verdict of not guilty partially vindicated him, if only for lack of evidence. As one media person at the trial noted at Audie's appearance: "He really was *The Quiet American!*"

Don Siegel, the director of early Audie westerns, envisioned a new series of films about a psychopathic cop. The first film's title was *Dirty Harry,* and Siegel wanted Audie for the role of the villain. He signed up, but first had to go to Virginia on business. The small engine jet ride ended on a mountainside during a foggy rainstorm. The movie star died brutally. As he lay destroyed by the wreckage, a scavenger stole the wallet out of his pants pocket. It was merely another indignity done to a man who fought for a career of nobility—and lost nearly every time.

In June of 1965 Audie had added a codicil to his last will and testament that instructed his heirs that he did not want any ceremony at his graveside service. He did not want to be buried at Arlington National Cemetery and said to his family, "It is my express direction that no others shall be present at my burial, it being specifically intended to exclude any and all public officials and military personnel." He added he did not mean "to be disrespectful to anyone, but rather would prefer to have an unpretentious, unelaborate burial." He expected he had "imparted to my sons such strength and character that they will desire the solitude of their own thoughts at my graveside . . ." All of these instructions fell on deaf ears, and his service displayed all the pomp and circumstance he loathed.

When Errol Flynn's son arrived in Vietnam as a photo-journalist at the height of the war, he made a point of finding the apartment that served as Audie's Saigon residence in *The Quiet American*. The son of a Hollywood legend and aficionado of Audie's films, Sean Flynn during his seven year stint in Vietnam rented the second floor walk-up overlooking shops and restaurants in downtown Saigon, as his home. He felt kinship and karma tuned him into the wavelength of Audie Murphy by living in that special space. Sean unfortunately misunderstood the story. The apartment he rented during his Vietnam years was the residential setting for Michael Redgrave's dubious character, and the verandah he enjoyed was the spot from which Redgrave's character signaled the communist terrorists to arrange Audie's death in the movie.

In an ironic and horrible play on reality, Sean Flynn's "home" brought him as much bad luck as it had for Audie's film character. The ties between Errol Flynn's son and Audie Murphy remain haunting: Audie died in a plane crash at the end of May in 1971. Around the same time, in late May of 1971, Sean Flynn, still held hostage by Khmer Rouge terrorists for many months, suffered a fate like many quiet Americans; he disappeared forever into the Vietnamese jungles, reportedly executed by his captors by means of a blow to the back of the head with a hoe. Each man died, never ever knowing the terrible fate of the other.

Not long after the American pull-out from Vietnam, and only a few years after Audie's death, the capital city of Saigon, with its canals linking it all over southeast Asia, a creation of the French occupation, found itself baptized Ho Chi Minh City. The Communists had beaten and dispatched the interfering Americans, and now the Mekong Delta was theirs. At long last Graham Greene's Saigon disappeared, to be found now only in the flickering images of a movie called *The Quiet American*.

After seeing the picture, Spec McClure had an interesting assessment of his friend: "Off screen Audie was one of the finest actors I have ever seen. He knew exactly how to play upon peoples' emotions. The qualities could have been transferred to motion pictures if he had only been given the opportunity. But who thinks a war hero can act? That was the attitude of Hollywood—an attitude which cost the movie industry a great star."

Before the Vietnam experience, Audie explained himself to Spec with disarming directness: "I have a deadly hatred of fear. It has me by the throat, and I have it by the throat. We have been struggling for many years. And, I still don't know which will win the battle. But that very hatred of fear has driven me to do a lot of things which I have never bothered to explain and which nobody understands. Fear is a blot on the thinking processes, crippling the individual's ability to act. I am not brave. I simply perform first and think later."

Audie concluded he was as simple as that.

ACKNOWLEDGMENTS

THE MAN I most wish to thank is Jan Merlin, a friend to Audie, and now to me. His generous assistance with the making of this book remains a most wonderful gesture I will never forget and always appreciate. I have learned much from this grand actor, award-winning author, and kind-hearted man. At my age I never thought I would find a mentor and a wizard, but this Merlin is both for me.

Another extraordinary man is Willard Willingham. Perhaps closer to Audie Murphy than anyone else, he shared the trip to Vietnam where he worked as Audie's stunt-double and stand-in. His erudite manner and wit proved a delight as he provided me with details he has never before expressed about his experience on *The Quiet American*. In addition, he has graciously opened his personal collection of photos from the production to share with posterity.

Of course, the major contributors to this tale are its participants: a man who has long since passed from our ranks, but whose foresight in keeping a daily diary of the events in Vietnam has made so much of the story comprehensible: William Hornbeck, Film Editor for this and so many other legendary Mankiewicz productions, gave his papers to posterity, and for me he has provided a treasure trove of insight. As a personal assistant to Joe Mankiewicz, his vision of the events is the closest and most rare.

Two academic libraries provided me with a passport their excellent collections, and without the dedication of research institutions, the past would be truly lost. Wesleyan University Film Archives provided a pleasant ambiance to read and to learn. While there and in subsequent correspondence, Mr. Leith Johnson, curator, was of great assistance to me in this project. Baylor University, through the technological services of online research, gave me access to materials far away, but as close as my PC. From Baylor came the extensive and often forgotten papers and manuscripts of David McClure, to whom I owe much for his care to document so much during his life with Audie.

Miss Giorgia Moll, now living in Rome, responded with all the courtesy, graciousness, and diplomacy, one would expect from a great actress and a great woman. Her generous cooperation gave this account of the movie a deeper resonance. As a sidekick to Audie Murphy, and one of his Vietnam professional advisers, Frank Vinh Noan–a director in his own right–gave me considerable information about the shoot, the conditions in Vietnam, and especially about the most heroic man there, Audie Murphy. His long discussions and generous opening of his personal collection of memorabilia touched me. He too gave permission for his never-before-published photographs to be used in this volume.

Also, several key Figaro executives opened their doors to me. First, Robert Lantz, agent emeritus of the literary world, friend to Mankiewicz, a charming and delightful man, gave of himself to the benefit of this story's telling. As well, Mike Mindlin, formerly vice president of publicity and advertising for Figaro, and present every step of the way on their adventure, provided me with his insights and perspective in a series of illuminating interviews, graciously and generously sharing tidbits from his own autobiography which should prove a fascinating story.

The founder of Orion Pictures and thirteen-time Oscar-winning producer, Eric Pleskow, provided me with the sharp and tangy views of a major Hollywood producer, a treat in itself. France Nuyen shared her recollections too! Miss E.C. Schreyeck offered her time and insights. As continuity person and script supervisor for Joseph Mankiewicz, she saw it all up close. Without her, this story would not be as perceptive and real for readers of posterity. With a glorious career in movies, she is one of those who have given so much to film but do not receive enough credit. One of the great character actors in the history of movies, Marc Lawrence, provided his, insights willingly and happily.

At the Audie Murphy Research Foundation, two people need

recognition; first is Terry Murphy, the son of actor and hero Audie, a man now dedicated to the preservation of his father's legacy, and Larryann Willis, Executive Director of the Foundation, an energetic spirit who has tenacity and vivacity to give to the Murphy memory. Ted James of Celebrity Collectables gave of his expertise and added another dimension to this study.

One of the best friends of Audie was Ben Cooper, whom I shall now count as one of my friends too. His insights into the Industry and the film world of the 1950s is so deeply appreciated. Starring in two movies with Audie, he is exactly the kind of man I'd expect Audie to respect. My long time friend, the late Jim Kirkwood, author of *A Chorus Line*, met everyone during his career in show business. It was his conversation to me about meeting *The Quiet American* himself, Audie Murphy, that sparked my first thoughts about this book.

Colleague Prof. Nicholas J. Krach of Curry College in Milton, Massachusetts, always served willingly as a sounding-board and offered his perceptions of the film's photography and technical issues, giving of his time and professional expertise.

My deepest appreciation goes to Nancy Kelly, Secretary of the College of Hampshire College in Amherst, Massachusetts.

Others who should share my gratitude are Jose Diaz, Nancy Fedele, Dr. Bob Keighton, Judy Kennedy, Priscilla Pope, and so many others to whom I am indebted.

RUSS

SELECTED BIBLIOGRAPHY

Arnold, Maxine. "His Love Wears Wings," *Photoplay,* May, 1951.

Audie Murphy. Fleetway Library Biography. 1960.

Berg, A. Scott. *Goldwyn.* 1989.

Bosworth, Patricia. *Montgomery Clift.* 1979.

Brooks, Tim. *Complete Directory to Prime Time Network TV Stars.* 1987.

Chronicle of the Movies. 1990.

Clarke, Clive. *The Prince, the Showgirl, and Me.* 1994

Cooper, Ben. Interview with author.

Crist, Judith. *The Private Eye, The Cowboy, and the Very Naked Girl.* 1970. Curtis, Tony. *Autobiography.* 1995.

DeVitis, A.A. *Graham Greene.* 1964.

Douglas, Kirk. *Ragman's Son.* 1993.

Edwards, Ralph. "This is Your Life, Audie Murphy," *Photoplay,* June, 1954.

Elam, Jack. Interview with AMRF, Summer/Fall, 1998.

Ellsworth, Robert. "Beauty and the Beasts," *Genre,* November, 1998.

Findlater, Richard. *At the Royal Court.* 1981.

Frazier, Jean. "Thank God I'm Home," *Modern Screen,* September 1957, pp. 48, 71-72.

Geist, Kenneth. *Pictures Will Talk.* 1978.

Gossett, Sue. *Films and Career of Audie Murphy: America's Real Hero.* 1996.

Gould, Helen. "Deep in the Heart of Hollywood,"*Photoplay,* August, 1953, pp. 64, 78-79.

Graham, Don. *No Name on the Bullet.* 1989.

"Graham Greene," *Current Biography.*

Greene, Graham. *The Quiet American.* 1955.

Halliwell, Leslie. *Filmgoer's Companion,* 12th Edition. 1996.

Harris, Radie. *Radie's World.* 1975.

Hendrix, Wanda. "Hero's Wife." *Photoplay,* December, 1949.

Herr, Michael. *Dispatches.* 1969.

Heston, Charlton. *An Actor's Life.* 1986.

Higham, Charles. *Errol Flynn: the Untold Story.* 1978.

Hornbeck, William. Papers at Wesleyan University Cinema Archives

Huston, John. *A Book.* 1983.

James, Ted. Celebrity Collectables. "Will of Audie Murphy."

|Research Information on Fred Sadoff.

Kael, Pauline. *Kiss Kiss Bang Bang.* "Quiet American," 1968, pp.422-23.

Kirkwood, James. Interviews and correspondence with author.

LaGuardia, Robert. *Monty: a Biography of Montgomery Clift.* 1978.

Lantz, Robert. Interview, correspondence, and discussion with author.

Lenihan, John H. "Kid from Texas: the Movie Heroism of Audie Murphy." *New Mexico Historical Review,* O86.

"Life Story of Audie Murphy," *Picture Show.* June 30, 1951.

Magers, Boyd. *Western Clippings,* Sept./Oct., 1999, #31.

McAvoy, Layne. *How Audie Murphy Died in Vietnam.* 1972.

McClure, David C. *The Way Back* and other unpublished manuscripts at Baylor University, Texas Collection.

Merlin, Jan. Correspondence and interview with author.

Miller, Cynthia. "Rage in Heaven," *Modern Screen.* December, 1949.

Mindlin, Mike. "No Rest for *The Quiet American,*" *New*

York Times, April 28, 1957.

Mindlin, Mike. Interviews and discussion with author

Moll, Giorgia. Interviews and discussions with author.

Morgan, Thomas. "The War Hero," *Esquire,* Dec., 1963.

Murphy, Audie. "The Perfect Passport," *Film Show Annual,* 1957.

Murphy, Pamela. "I'm Not the Type," *Movieland,* Feb. 1953.

Murphy, Terry. Correspondence with author.

Nascimbene, Mario. *Autobiography.*

Nolan, William. *King Rebel.* 1965.

Nuyen, France. Correspondence with author.

Page, Tim. *Danger on the Edge of Town.* 1989.

Page, Tim. *Page After Page.* 1987.

Parkinson, David. *Graham Greene Film Reader.* 1996.

Phillips, Eugene, SJ. *Graham Greene: The Films of His Fiction.* 1974.

Pleskow, Eric. Interview with author

Pratley, Gerald. *Cinema of John Huston.* 1965.

Quiet American. Pressbook, United Artists, 1957.

"Quiet American," *Encyclopedia of Novels into Film.* 1998.

"Quiet for a Quiet American," *Screen Album,* May-July, 1958.

Randall, Tony and Mike Mindlin. *Which Reminds Me.* 1989.

Redgrave, Corin. *Michael Redgrave, My Father.* 1996.

Redgrave, Michael. *In My Mind's I.* 1982.

Redgrave, Michael. *Mask or Face.* 1958.

Redgrave, Vanessa. *Vanessa.* 1991.

Riese, Randall. *The Unabridged James Dean.* 1991.

Rimoldi, Oscar. "What Price Glory? Audie Murphy." *Films on Review.*

Ross, Lillian. *Picture.* 1952.

Ross, Lillian. "Michael Redgrave Speaks," in *The Player.* 1965.

"Same Old Dream," *Movie Life.* November, 1947.

Sarris, Andrew. "Mankiewicz of Films," *Show,* March, 1970.

Schary, Dore. *Heyday,* 1979.

Schreyeck, E.C. Correspondence with author.

Smith, Julian. *Looking Back: Hollywood and Vietnam.* 1975.

Spoto, Donald. *Laurence Olivier.* 1993.

Thomason, David. *A Biographical Dictionary of Films.* 1972.

Tozzi, Romano. *John Huston: Hollywood's Magic People.* 1976.

Vinh, Frank Noan. Interviews, correspondence, and discussions with author.

Walker, Helen Louise. "I'm not the Type," *Movieland,* February, 1953.

Wanger, Walter and Joe Hyams. *My Life with Cleopatra,* 1963.

Westmoreland, Gen. William C. *A Soldier Reports.* 1976

Whiting, Charles. *Hero: Story of Audie Murphy.* 1989

Wickam, Andy. "Return of *The Quiet American.*" 1983.

Wilkie, Jane. "Memoirs of a Small Texan," *Modern Screen.* July, 1955.

Willingham, Willard. Interviews, correspondence and discussions with author.

Zeitlan, Ida. "Lonely Joe," *Photoplay.* January, 1951.

INDEX

BVG